Business
CASE STUDIES

AS and A Level

Ian Marcousé
and
David Lines

Longman

Third Edition

Pearson Education Limited
Edinburgh Gate
Harlow
Essex
CM20 2JE
England and Associated Companies throughout the World

ISBN 0582 406366

First published 1990
Second edition 1994
Third edition 2002
Third impression 2004

Printed in Malaysia, (VVP)

The Publisher's policy is to use paper manufactured from sustainable forests.

We are grateful to the various companies whose annual reports we refer to in this book for permission to reproduce their copyright material, and to the following for permission to reproduce copyright material and information:

Coca-Cola of Great Britain and Ireland for information in Case Study 6; Findlay Publications Ltd for an extract based on an article in the journal *Machinery and Production Engineering* 17.2.89 in Case Study 46; Haagen-Dazs UK for information in Case Study 2 and Case Study 12; information reproduced with the permission of Matalan plc in Case Study 30; McDonald's Restaurants Ltd for extracts based on information from McDonald's *Behind the Arches* by John F. Love in Case Study 3; information reproduced with the kind permission of The Body Shop International plc in Case Study 85; information reprinted from *The Grocer* in Case Study 1; Times Newspapers Ltd for an extract from *The Times* 5.2.82 in Case Study 103; Whitbread Group plc for information in Case Study 73.

We are grateful to the following for permission to reproduce photographs and other copyright material:

The Advertising Archives pages 18, 19, 20, 38; Camera Press pages 37(Stewart Mark), 301, 316; John Frost Historical Newspapers page 317 (photo: Trevor Clifford); McDonalds Restaurants Ltd page 7; OKI (UK) Ltd page 130; Pictor International page 167; Popperfoto page 228; Rex Features page 244; Topham Picturepoint pages 232, 313; photo John Walmsley page 1.

Artwork by ODI
Cartoons by Martin Shovel

CONTENTS

Operations Management
AS

A2

People in Organisations
AS

A2

External Influences, Objectives and Strategy
AS

A2

ACKNOWLEDGEMENTS TO THE THIRD EDITION

Business Case Studies began thanks to the promptings of a delightful student – Leda Barrett – and the quick response of Brian Willan at Longman.

Now, 12 years later, the third edition of Business Case Studies owes a considerable debt to the 50 Heads of Department who were kind enough to return a questionnaire that asked about people's favourite cases. These have been preserved – though some needed updating – and 30 new ones added.

As before, thanks are due primarily to London's City Business Library and Guildhall Library.

The work involved in producing a book is easy to underestimate, but Jill and Maureen know all about it, so our thanks, love and apologies to them.

Ian Marcousé and David Lines

HOW TO USE THIS BOOK

To the student reader

Business Case Studies third edition provides five ways to help you succeed in your exams:

1 There are 25 studies of actual, 'classic' business case histories, such as Nokia and Sony Playstation. Not only can these provide you with practice in exam technique, but they can also enrich your essay writing. The study of the collapse of Rolls Royce, for example, shows the importance of careful cash flow management and the problems of being over-reliant upon a single, new technology product. The material in these studies can be quoted in exam essays as the basis for analysing the question set. The 'classic cases' are listed on page xv.

2 Many of the other case studies are written in such a way as to help explain, or reinforce, difficult topics such as working capital or business ethics. So even if you do not produce written answers, reading the texts should be helpful.

3 On page ix, Ian Marcousé, Chief Examiner for AQA Business Studies and a former Chief Examiner for OCR, provides an account of the thinking behind the setting and marking of exam case studies. He has also edited all the cases and questions to ensure that the 100 + cases are similar to the style of case study exam papers.

4 Most A level courses include a coursework component. This book can help you to identify possible topics for an assignment. Some of the case studies are based upon actual students' projects, including "Fat Sam's Franchise," "The Survival Game" and "Good Management Practice in Retailing".

5 When revising for exams, you will need not only to learn the definitions of terms such as business strategy but also be able to put these concepts into context. The "Key to Main Concepts" enables you to look up a term such as 'Ansoff's Matrix', then identify the three cases that use this theory. A quick read through one or two of these cases will do a great deal to fix the term in your mind.

To teachers and lecturers

Business Case Studies has always attempted to offer a surfeit of cases, to enable you to choose ones that fit your syllabus requirements and the needs of your students. Some are aimed at single topics – usually harder ones such as cost centres or decision trees. Others give broad coverage within a syllabus section, such as Finance or People. These broader studies should help prepare candidates for modular examinations. In addition the Awarding Bodies see case studies as a means of promoting integration, so many of the studies follow that philosophy.

Within each section of the book, the cases are placed in approximate order of difficulty. Each is clearly labelled AS or A2, together with any concepts that need to be taught prior to the case being tackled. As with the previous editions, the cases are deliberately made quite challenging. This is partly because of the likelihood that the text and questions will be discussed in class before being tackled in writing. It is also because *Business Case Studies* has always sought to bridge the gap between text-book exercises that rely too much on testing comprehension and the – quite demanding – nature of most case study exam questions. Students brought up on these case studies will have little to fear from AS or A2 exams.

The timings provided are viewed as appropriate for exam/test conditions. When students are working collaboratively they will need extra discussion time.

Twenty-five of the cases are 'classic' business stories. They have been researched with care to provide students with accurate background material to enrich homework essays and exam answers. They also provide stimulus to class discussion. It is recommended that students should cover all of these. Of the new ones, the most obviously attractive for classroom use are Sunny Delight, Nokia, Playstation and Railtrack. You should also have a careful look at the Superjumbo, Whitbread and "Hard Cash From Software" cases.

Pages xvi–xviii provide a tabular display of the concepts contained within each of the studies. So if you have just covered Ansoff's Matrix, you can see which exercises examine that topic. In addition to this display, each study has a number of 'key concepts' listed beneath the title. These are topics central to the study but not explained in the text. So students may need to have covered them previously before tackling the study. This display acts as a warning to help you avoid setting impossible tasks for your students.

One other point to check before giving students a case is the level of numerical difficulty. An approximate categorisation of each study is provided on pages xiii–xiv. The cases are divided into four categories:

- N = No maths required
- I = Interpretation of data only
- E = Easy calculations
- D = Demanding calculations (pitched at the standard to be expected in A level exams)

Answers to the questions are supplied in the accompanying *Business Case Studies Answer Guide* (ISBN: 0582 406374). Numerical answers are set out in detail and possible answers to the written questions are also given.

Note to the Third Edition

Business Case Studies has been expanded to over 100 cases: 30 newly written plus 73 from the second edition.

The 30 new cases have been written with four main factors in mind:

1 the need for a number of new cases that fit into the AS mould. Typically, these have a relatively accessible question style and – of course – topics that the main examination boards have categorised as AS specification content

2 the requirements of the QCA subject core

3 the need to keep abreast of the developments in Business Studies theory

4 the motivational value of providing students with material they can identify with, e.g. the Nokia story.

For teachers coming to this book for the first time, it is important to appreciate that many of the cases are timeless. Please do not regard Laker Airways or De Lorean Cars as *too* old. Students still find these stories extraordinary and highly instructive. The only problem with them is that student answers are so full and interesting that they take an age to mark!

THE EXAMINER'S VIEW

Writing an AS or A level exam case study is little different from producing one for this book. The writer must have in mind a series of issues that need to be examined and then find a story line that is sufficiently detailed, interesting and/or plausible to help the student through the process. Naturally, students assume that examiners are keen to identify their weakest aspect and then fail them. This ignores the fact that we are teachers ourselves and have our exam papers scrutinised by other teachers who are quick to point out if a question seems confusing or too difficult.

So what qualities are required for an A grade case study?

As with all exams, the foundations are built on good understanding of the language of the subject. No one would object to a 15 mark exam question that asks candidates to discuss the value of scientific decision making to a small firm. Yet if you do not know what scientific decision making means, you may waste 15 minutes waffling in the hope of generating some marks. The ideal answer starts by defining key terms. This puts the examiner on your side. Teachers love correct definitions, so take care to learn the main ones, and use them in your answers.

Having defined the terms, make sure that you develop your answer both by the use of classroom/textbook theory, and by application to the scenario, i.e. the business case. For example, case study 86 on Chessington World of Adventures gives huge scope for discussing the problems of operating a highly seasonal business with a temporary workforce offering a non-essential product. In exams, many students ignore even the most obvious of contexts, limiting themselves to the occasional mention of the name of the company or its key staff. When asked a question about stock control, budgeting, sales forecasting or staff scheduling, the unpredictable nature of demand at Chessington can lead a good student to develop an interesting answer.

The other vital issue is writing a conclusion. The skill of evaluation counts for between 25 and 40% of the marks in exam case studies, and this is a skill you are most likely to show when drawing conclusions to your own answer. Many candidates put off writing a conclusion until the last minute. This results in superficial, sketchy sentences that do little more than summarise (i.e. repeat) the argument. What examiners want is a quite lengthy, thoughtful reflection on the question in relation to the circumstances of the business. So when answering questions from this book, always write a conclusion if there are more than 6 marks at stake. This will get you in practice for the real thing.

The Examination Board Requirements

The two largest examination boards for Business Studies are AQA and OCR. Each has a heavy focus upon case studies as a form of assessment. For AQA, 55% of the A level marks are from case study exams; for OCR the figure rises to 85%. Cases are used in business studies because they test theoretical knowledge in an unfamiliar context. This is an excellent way to discover what a candidate really knows about the subject. It also gives candidates the scope to develop full, quite complex answers that fuse business theory with business practice.

Current requirements for each of the main Awarding Bodies are detailed overleaf. When looking at the details for the specification you are taking, you may notice references to 'pre-seen' and 'unseen' case studies. A pre-seen case is one in which the text is issued prior to the examination, so that candidates can look at it and discuss it with staff before the exam. The questions are issued on the day of the exam in normal conditions of silence and secrecy. An unseen case is one that is seen by candidates only when the exam starts. Most of the Awarding Bodies offer a mixture of pre-seen and unseen papers. The largest of the Boards, AQA, uses only unseen cases. (At the time of publication it was becoming likely that this policy might change for AS examinations.)

Skills Tested by Case Studies

Whether the text has been seen beforehand or not, all case studies test skills that are less apparent in other forms of examination. So, when using the cases in this book, practise the skills outlined below, because they are the ones the examiners are looking for and which attract the highest marks.

Application skills

Textbook theories are all very fine, but knowing when and when not to apply them is a special skill which case studies assess well. For instance, the textbooks may say that people are better motivated by a democratic leader. On a jumbo jet, however, the safety of all those on board rests on the knowledge that orders can be given and obeyed immediately. A 'democratic' debate in such an environment could be highly dangerous.

A case study sets out a particular business context, and it is very important to take it into account when answering questions. Theories exist to be applied, but their application must be made carefully and with due consideration to the circumstances. Nevertheless it is vital to avoid the trap of writing 'common sense' answers rather than ones that are rooted firmly in theoretical knowledge.

Analytic skills

Analysis is shown in case study answers in three main ways:

- focusing your answer tightly on the precise terms of the question
- building up arguments through a sequence of logic that forms reasonably long paragraphs (rather than a series of one-line bullet points)
- using theory relevantly to build up your arguments.

Yet case studies give you even more opportunities to show analytic skills. Often the featured business faces problems or opportunities that are a complex mix of financial, marketing and operational factors. Your ability to assess the reasons for the problems or the consequences of their continuation is an analytic process in itself. Therefore careful thought about the immediate and underlying problems of the business is likely to bear fruit.

Evaluative skills

Evaluation is judgement. This can be shown in the way you weight your arguments (many candidates are too quick to say: 'If that happens it'll be a disaster and they'll go bust') and in the wisdom and maturity you show. Most commonly, evaluation is a skill shown in the conclusions drawn to the arguments the candidate has put forward. If a candidate has put forward three arguments for and two (stronger) arguments against, s/he may impress the examiner by explaining why the two outweigh the three. Longer case study questions invite evaluation through terms such as 'discuss', 'consider', 'evaluate' and 'to what extent'. When you see these triggers, respond by leaving time for a full paragraph of judgemental conclusions.

Creative skills

As in real-life business, it is not always the obvious or conventional path that leads to success. Although exam answers to case studies require a firm base of academic theory, candidates do not have to be restricted to that alone. Often someone who really thinks about what the facts *imply* will earn more marks. A level mark schemes do not prescribe a specific line of answer; a candidate with an interesting or original (yet relevant) answer can score highly.

Communication skills

Business depends on the ability of one person to be understood by another. The ability to write accurately and fluently is therefore a significant influence on case study marks. The cases in this book can help you practise writing in-depth answers to chunky – often difficult – questions. This will help enormously in boosting your marks towards top grades.

Using diagrams within your answers can also be helpful, though it is important to keep them quick and simple, or else they may take longer than is justified by the number of marks available.

Skills of numeracy

Nothing divides students more obviously than their reaction to numerical questions. It is usually a matter of love or hate. *Business Case Studies* offers many numerical questions because they appear in almost every exam case and they usually spread out candidates' marks more sharply than written questions. A 10 mark question on marketing is likely to produce a mark range of between 4 and 7 for almost every candidate. A 10 mark numerical question will produce every mark between 0 and 10. A hard-working student who gets a number of 6/10s on written questions may lose everything by a 0/10 on the numbers. So even if you dislike the numerical side of the subject, you must try your hardest to grasp the concepts and methods well enough to get some marks from numbers. It may help you to remember, here, that a reasonable attempt may generate 6 or 7 out of 10, even though you do not manage to get the answer (or even provide a final answer at all). Examiners give credit for every part of your workings.

A summary of what is needed

In order to succeed in case studies, you must:

- know the basic theory
- be able to apply the theory to the business circumstances of the case
- construct arguments in answer to the questions; never rely on bullet-point lists
- use your intelligence to identify underlying issues and problems faced by the firm
- be creative and entrepreneurial in the solutions you suggest to the problems the firm faces.

Exam Board	AQA	OCR	Edexcel	CCEA	Scottish Higher
AS Unit 1	Marketing & Finance Data response 75 mins	Business Objectives & Environment **Unseen case study** 75 mins	Objectives & External Data response 75 mins	Business Objectives & Environment Data response 100 mins	Business Management **Unseen case study** 150 mins
AS Unit 2	People & Operations Data response 75 mins	Business Decisions Data response 75 mins	Marketing & Production **Unseen case study** 90 mins	Finance & People Data response 80 mins	
AS Unit 3	External Influences & Objectives & Strategy **Unseen case study** 90 mins	Business Behaviour **Pre-seen case study** 90 mins	Finance Data response 75 mins	Marketing & Operations Data response 80 mins	
A2 Unit 4	Marketing, Finance, People & Operations **Unseen case study** 90 mins	One from Finance, Ops, Marketing & People **Unseen case study** 75 mins	Analysis & Decision Making Data response 75 mins	All A2 subject content Data response 100 mins	
A2 Unit 5	Any A2 module Numerical report & essay 90 mins	Thematic enquiry **Unseen case study** 75 mins	Business Planning **Unseen case study** 90 mins	Synoptic **Unseen case study** 100 mins	
A2 Unit 6	External Influences & Objectives & Strategy **Unseen case study** 90 mins	Business Strategy **Pre-seen case study** 90 mins	Corporate Strategy **Pre-seen case study** 90 mins	All A2 subject content **Pre-seen case study** 100 mins	
Case study proportion of total marks	AS: 40% A2: 70% A level: 55%	AS: 70% A2: 100% A level: 85%	AS: 40% A2: 70% A level: 55%	AS: 0% A2: 70% A level: 35%	50%

NUMERICAL DIFFICULTY

CLASSIC CASES

These 25 cases have been researched with care to enable them to be quoted directly as evidence to support arguments within essays or other written answers. Each provides a useful example of major issues, strategies or problems. Some are quite old, but the classic status of stories such as Ford's Model T or Laker Airways means that age is no barrier.

KEY TO MAIN CONCEPTS

CONCEPT	CASE STUDY NUMBER
Objectives and Strategy	
Ansoff's Matrix	73, 92, 95
Business organisations	65, 74, 85
Company aims & objectives	10, 43, 48, 62, 66, 68, 76, 83, 88, 92, 95, 99, 100, 103
Corporate strategy	64, 65, 73, 76, 88, 92, 95, 97, 99, 100, 102, 103
Decision trees & decision making	72, 73, 93, 94
Ethics	3, 65, 67, 69, 77, 85, 100
Growth (effects & problems)	41, 55, 62, 74, 90, 94
Identifying an opportunity	2, 4, 8, 18, 17, 21, 24, 35, 66, 78, 81, 98
Internal & external constraints	43, 54, 62, 86, 96, 100, 103
Mission & culture	6, 34, 42, 45, 47, 49, 51, 59, 71, 77, 85, 86
Problems of start-ups	16, 27, 35, 62, 66, 78, 81, 82, 83, 87, 98
Retrenchment & rationalisation	74, 76, 99, 101
Social responsibility	45, 58, 66, 68, 69, 71, 77, 85, 86, 88
Stakeholders	34, 40, 45, 66, 67, 68, 71, 77, 101
Takeovers & mergers	11, 29, 74, 73, 91, 101
Marketing	
Adding value	1, 4, 95
Advertising & branding	1, 3, 6, 12, 30, 78, 91
Asset v market-led	4, 7, 10, 92

CONCEPT	CASE STUDY NUMBER
Distribution	2, 4, 6, 7, 12, 16, 41, 97, 101
Elasticity of demand	8, 15, 63, 88, 97, 100
Extrapolation & correlation	9, 12, 89
Market analysis	7, 8, 10, 14, 95
Market research	1, 4, 6, 8, 9, 10, 11, 12, 16, 20, 24, 83
Market segmentation & niches	2, 4, 21, 30, 39, 63, 85, 86, 93, 100
Marketing budgets	1, 7, 14
Marketing Model & decision making	5, 10, 31, 87, 89
Marketing ethics	1, 3, 12
Marketing mix	1, 2, 4, 82
Marketing objectives	4, 5, 8, 13
Marketing strategy	3, 5, 6, 8, 11, 13, 14, 30, 41, 85, 88, 89, 98, 101, 103
New product development	1, 4, 9, 12, 13, 38, 69, 74, 75, 102
Pricing	9, 12, 13, 31, 88, 100, 101, 103
Product life cycle & portfolio	1, 2, 3, 5, 6, 7, 13, 38, 78, 102
Sales forecasting	4, 16, 24, 78, 86, 89
Finance	
Break-even analysis	9, 11, 16, 18, 39, 40, 78, 84, 87
Budgeting & cost control	21, 22, 86, 98
Cash flow	8, 16, 17, 18, 19, 20, 24, 32, 70, 78, 96, 97, 98, 102, 103
Contribution	11, 40, 93
Cost & profit centres	21

People in Organisations

Operations management

External influences

MARKETING SUNNY DELIGHT

AS MARKETING

CONCEPTS NEEDED:

Product life cycle, Marketing mix, Test marketing, Ethics

In early April 1998 a new sales phenomenon burst upon UK grocery retailing. The launch of Sunny Delight was one of the most successful ever. By July the *Sunday Telegraph* was announcing that: 'The bubble has burst for Coca-Cola: it has been overtaken as Britain's best selling soft drink for more than 50 years ... Forecasters say it could notch up sales of more than £400m this year.' This proved a wild exaggeration, but there was no doubting the scale of the success.

The story began in 1995, when Procter & Gamble (a huge American multinational with brands ranging from Ariel to Pringles) decided to move into the rapidly growing market for fruit drinks. The company came up with two possibilities: a fruit juice drink named Punica or a more artificially created 'vitamin enriched chilled juice' named Sunny Delight. In the spring of 1996 both were test marketed: Punica fruit juice in Grimsby and Sunny Delight in Carlisle.

By the autumn of 1997 – after extensive testing over an 18 month period – Procter and Gamble (P&G) dropped Punica and invested

£12 million in factory capacity for producing Sunny Delight. The company decided to position the brand squarely against fruit

juices, appealing to parents' desire for children to drink healthier products than Coca-Cola, and to children's desire for a sweeter taste and more street cred than pure fruit juice. Sunny Delight was packaged in a bottle shape and size similar to fresh orange juice and priced well above its real competitor, Coca-Cola. At 89p, it would be expensive as a regular part of a packed lunch, but P&G's Carlisle experience gave it the confidence to be this ambitious. Cleverly, the company also decided to invest in its own chilled cabinets, which were given to supermarkets and independent grocers. This would differentiate the product and ensure that it appeared to be fresh juice. In actual fact its ingredients made chilling unnecessary (contents list: water, sucrose/sugar 10%, fruit juice 5%, citric acid, vegetable oil, emulsifier, thickener, potassium sorbate and dimethyl dicarbonate). With P&G's huge marketing strength, obtaining distribution and prime display positioning proved no problem.

London advertising agency Saatchi & Saatchi spent the £5 million launch budget on a TV campaign based on the slogan 'The great stuff kids go for'. The commercials showed kids having fun with healthy outdoor activities such as roller skating, then coming home and reaching in the fridge for the fresh looking bottle of Sunny Delight. As one commentator put it: 'Children like the taste of Sunny Delight and mums think: at least it ain't Coke.' Another pointed out the clever 'prominent use of *vitamin enriched* on the label ... you overlook the fact that there is not very much fruit juice.'

The marketing mix proved hugely effective. In Britain's playgrounds 'Sunny D' became the must-have drink. P&G struggled to keep up with the demand as the new product outsold Coke in June 1998. Perhaps it was too

successful, as it attracted press coverage and the concern of food campaigners. The Food Commission pointed out the deceptive presentation of a product that looked like fruit juice, yet its contents were only 5% juice. *The Guardian* pointed out that a 500ml bottle contained the equivalent of nine spoons of sugar (comparable with six to seven spoons in a 330ml can of Coke), but sales kept bounding ahead. Even if mums were starting to doubt the product, 'pester-power' was keeping sales high. *Marketing* magazine was later to herald Sunny Delight as 'the most successful grocery brand launch of the 1990s'. Its first year sales level of over £80 million compares with Red Bull's first year sales level of £2 million. Del Monte had taken 20 years to build fruit juice sales to £30 million per year. Sunny Delight was outselling it, yet charging a higher price for a product that was very much cheaper to produce.

In May 1999 the trade magazine *The Grocer* reflected on the lessons Sunny Delight offered to all manufacturers:

- innovation can achieve a breakthrough, even in a mature market
- the value and power of painstaking initial research and test marketing
- how to prevent 'me-toos', as the unique pack, heavy advertising and very prominent shop displays meant that no one had yet tried to imitate Sunny Delight.

In the same month *Marketing Week* magazine pointed out that Sunny Delight's success was all the more impressive given that latest research showed that 'the new product development success rate has slipped from 1 in 6 three years ago to 1 in 7 today'.

Yet at the height of its success the Sunny Delight story turned sour. Despite the many

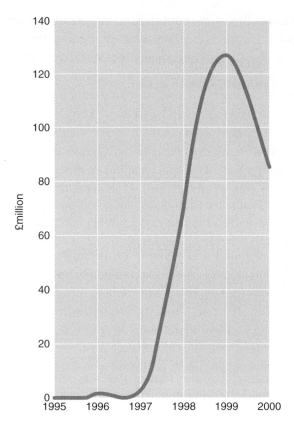

Sunny Delight product life cycle, 1996–2000

criticisms of the brand on health and ethical grounds, it took a freak incident to make consumers stop and think seriously about that extraordinary ingredients list. On one of the lightest news days of the year, 27 December 1999, every British paper headlined the story: 'Girl Turned Orange By Sunny Delight'. A doctor reported that a five year old girl's face and hands had turned orange as a result of drinking 1.5 litres of Sunny Delight a day. Although this was an exceptionally high quantity for a five year old to be drinking, it made people question what they had assumed to be a relatively natural, healthy drink.

During 2000 P&G ran an increasing number of special price offers through supermarkets to keep sales up; they also launched Sunny Delight Light, with 30% less sugar. But the magic had worn off and sales started to slip by volume and – especially – by value. During 2000, value sales fell by more than 33%. Despite this setback, P&G and the grocery trade remained confident that Sunny Delight would remain a major force in the soft drinks business. Even in the disappointing year 2000 it outsold Pepsi and Pepsi Max combined. Not bad for a product launched in 1998.

Sources: The Grocer; The Observer

Appendix A: Sales of selected drinks in retail outlets 1998–2000

	1998	1999	2000
Sunny Delight	£72.3 million	£136.3 million	£85.6 million
Del Monte fruit juices	£31.1 million	£33.2 million	£33.9 million
Coca-Cola	£157.5 million	£185.6 million	£165.7 million

Source: Information Resources, quoted in *The Grocer* magazine

Questions
(60 marks; 70 minutes)

1 Outline two benefits P&G may have gained from test marketing Sunny Delight. **(6 marks)**

2 Evaluate the factors that may have led to the success rate of new product development slipping 'from 1 in 6 three years ago to 1 in 7 today'. **(10 marks)**

3 **a** What would the theory of the product life cycle imply about the future of Sunny Delight after 2000? **(4 marks)**
   b Outline two extension strategies P&G might undertake to extend the profitable life of Sunny Delight. **(8 marks)**

4 Some marketing analysts believed that Saatchi & Saatchi's advertising was the most important aspect of Sunny Delight's marketing mix. To what extent do you agree with that view? **(12 marks)**

5 Analyse how the marketing of Sunny Delight today compares with P&G's approach in 1998–2000. **(8 marks)**

6 Health and nutrition experts hated what they saw as P&G's cynically deceptive presentation of its new brand. P&G believed the brand was a legitimate attempt to increase sales of fruit-based drinks. Discuss whether P&G's marketing of Sunny Delight was ethical. **(12 marks)**

HÄAGEN-DAZS - DEDICATED TO PERFECTION

AS MARKETING

CONCEPTS NEEDED:

Product life cycle, Marketing mix, Niche marketing

In the 1950s a New York manufacturer of an ice cream brand called Ciro's decided to extend its distribution from ice cream parlours to supermarkets. Reuben Mattus had spotted that rising affluence plus freezer ownership encouraged consumers to buy ice cream all year round. Not surprisingly, this distribution strategy was soon imitated by larger rivals. They were able to offer incentive deals to the retailers that Mattus could not match, so sales of Ciro's slipped back.

Thwarted by his competitors, Mattus tried a different approach. Using fresh cream, all natural ingredients and less air blown into the mix, he produced an ice cream with a finer flavour and texture. To distinguish it from other ice creams, he gave his new product a Scandinavian sounding name and packed it into pint pots instead of 2 litre packs. In 1961 the first Häagen-Dazs ice cream was sold in New York delicatessens.

With its high ingredients cost and small scale production, the price of Häagen-Dazs had to be high to be profitable. This was off-putting to shopkeepers, who feared that customers would refuse to buy it. So Mattus visited shops personally, giving staff a taste of the product and promising to buy back any product that did not sell. By removing the shops' financial risk, gaining distribution became more possible. Steadily Häagen-Dazs spread to New York grocers, then to supermarkets and national store chains.

Without the desire or the finance to promote the product through advertising, Mattus relied upon word of mouth to generate customer demand. Fortunately, Häagen-Dazs customers loved talking about the product. By the mid-1970s the ice cream's popularity was such that remaining Ciro ice cream products were phased out to turn the production capacity over to Häagen-Dazs. Mattus developed the theme 'Dedicated To Perfection' as a focus of staff training, materials purchasing and production control. He was determined that growth would not be at the expense of product quality.

At the same time Mattus's daughter came up with the idea of creating a 'dipping store' in which vanilla ice cream bars were hand-dipped in melted chocolate to create a hand-made choc ice. From this 250 Häagen-Dazs stores were developed in America, each offering an opportunity for people to sample the products.

By the early 1980s Häagen-Dazs had become established as *the* super-premium ice cream throughout America. In 1983 the company was sold to the Pillsbury Company, on condition that the company's quality standards always be maintained. Pillsbury, the multinational owners of Burger King, aimed to develop Häagen-Dazs inter-nationally. By 1984, Häagen-Dazs had become Japan's best selling super-premium ice cream.

Three years later, with sales levelling off in America, Pillsbury started to look seriously at the European market. Little progress had been made by 1989, however, when Pillsbury was bought by the British company Grand Metropolitan. The American firm with the Scandinavian sounding name was now British owned, and was soon to launch its product in Britain.

Meanwhile, by 1992 American sales were slipping under pressure from a strong competitor. Ben and Jerry's produced high quality ice cream at high prices, but with bigger chunks of chocolate, almonds or toffee. It also established an image as the quirky, environmentally conscious small business battling the might of a multinational.

Häagen-Dazs responded by producing a new range of flavours called Exträas. But this me-too approach flopped. Fortunately for Häagen-Dazs, its reputation for luxury ice cream was sufficient to keep it as the number one super-premium brand. The company had been slow to see the consumer requirement for more varied, exciting taste experiences. Yet the foundations built by Reuben Mattus were strong enough to keep Häagen-Dazs at the top.

Sources: Financial Times; Häagen-Dazs UK Ltd

Questions
(50 marks; 60 minutes)

1 Outline the incentive deals a firm might offer in order to achieve retail distribution for its products. **(8 marks)**

2 Evaluate the marketing mix used by Häagen-Dazs. **(12 marks)**

3 **a** Sketch a fully labelled product life cycle diagram to show the stages in the development of Häagen-Dazs in America, using the dates provided. **(9 marks)**

 b What may have prevented the product from growing more rapidly in America? **(6 marks)**

4 Use the example of Häagen-Dazs to discuss the business benefits and limitations of niche marketing. **(15 marks)**

McDONALD'S
– MARKETING
HAMBURGERS

AS
MARKETING

CONCEPTS NEEDED:

Marketing mix, Market research

In 1954, a salesman of milkshake machines paid a call on a customer in Southern California. It was a small drive-in restaurant that sold a limited range of products at unusually low prices. The salesman (Ray Kroc) was impressed with its assembly line production method, and even more by the queues of customers. Although the hamburgers sold for just 15 cents each, this one outlet had annual sales over $300,000.

Kroc saw the potential of the business, and offered the owners an arrangement which

would give him sole rights to franchise their name, production method and logo throughout the United States. The owners (Richard and Maurice McDonald) would receive a quarter of all Kroc's franchise income, which was to be 1.9% of all the franchisees' sales revenue. The golden arches which formed part of the original restaurant design structure were turned into the familiar 'M' trademark.

During this period, customer demand stemmed from McDonald's low prices, rapid service, and dedication to service and cleanliness. Its appeal was to families at a time when rival drive-ins attracted the smaller teenage market. Growth proved rapid, and by 1960 the 225 McDonald's franchises provided annual sales of almost $50 million. In 1961, Kroc bought the McDonald brothers out for $2.7 million. Had they held on to their 0.4% royalty they would have earned over $1,000 million by the late 1990s.

Following the buyout, the McDonald's Corporation profits flourished due to increasing numbers of outlets, and new contracts that took a much higher percentage of the franchise operator's income. However, annual sales per store were static at around $200,000 so the individual franchises needed ways to boost their own revenues. Some focused on the limited menu (and were responsible for creating the Big Mac in 1968 and the Egg McMuffin in 1973), while others concentrated on publicity.

In Washington, a clown character was being used with success on local television: renamed Ronald McDonald he became used nationally from 1965. Franchise operators found the TV advertising caused immediate sales increases, and that it helped overcome the traditional takeaway sales slump during the harsh northern American winter. So they agreed to contribute 1% of McDonald's $260 million sales in 1966 to a national advertising fund. This helped sales per store to jump to $275,000 from around $200,000 in the early 1960s.

It was at the local level, too, that sales promotions originated. Some became enormous successes nationally, including a mint-green Shamrock Shake sold on St Patrick's Day, and scratch cards yielding instant prizes of Big Macs. Better promotions were capable of boosting short term sales by 6%, and adding some novelty to the customers' visit.

Throughout this period of local initiative the McDonald's Corporation made surprisingly little contribution to the marketing effort. Only in 1968, at a time when rivals such as Burger King were closing the gap on McDonald's, did it form a marketing department. Its head decided to base his objectives on Ray Kroc's view that 'We're not in the hamburger business, we're in show business.'

Advertising agencies were invited to compete for the account by answering 10 questions, including whether McDonald's possessed a 'unique selling proposition'. One agency replied no, McDonald's had only a unique sales personality, for its proposition differed 'depending on whether we're talking to moms, dads, or kids'. The agency recommended building up the personality into one of warmth, fun, relaxation – and won the account.

The new campaign focused on the emotional pleasures of eating out: family togetherness, fun, and a sense of reward. Prolific use of television advertising was seen as the key to doubling revenues per store to $620,000 by 1973.

Although other factors were involved, the importance of advertising was also evident in Britain. The first British outlet to open (in Woolwich, London in 1974) started poorly. In its first year its revenue of $300,000 was too small to prevent losses of $150,000. The second outlet proved no better. Yet when profitable West End stores justified television advertising, the situation turned into one of runaway success.

By 2000 McDonald's had a 78% share of the £1,700 million UK burger market. Its media advertising spending of £52 million was more than all other restaurants and fast food outlets put together.

During the 1980s and 1990s McDonald's swept round the world. More than 10,000 restaurants were opened outside the USA, including Russia, China and France. Well over half 1999's worldwide turnover came from outside America. The company had become the world's largest property owner and one of the world's richest businesses.

This brought some problems, such as the wave of public sympathy in France when, in the summer of 2000, a farmer was jailed for three months for attacking a half-built McDonald's outlet. His protest was against the 'McDomination of the world'. In the autumn of that year, a Scottish nutritionist called for a 'fat tax' on hamburgers. He pointed out that a typical burger meal contains up to 60% fat. With a doubling of obesity rates in the past 15 years, why shouldn't burgers be taxed like cigarettes and alcohol? In addition to criticism on ethical grounds, McDonald's also faced questioning from financial analysts about why there had been 'no significant new product since the Chicken McNugget in 1982'. It could be argued, though, that this merely emphasises the strength of the McDonald's marketing strategy. What other business in the world could be as successful despite an 18 year gap since its last new product success? Ray Kroc died in 1984, but the empire he built is as successful as ever.

Sources: McDonald's: Behind The Arches, J. F. Love (Bantam, 1995); *The Guardian*

Appendix A: Extracts from McDonald's accounts 1986–1999

	1986	1990	1993	1996	1999
US sales ($m)	9,534	12,252	14,186	16,370	17,237
Rest of the world sales ($m)	2,898	6,507	9,401	15,442	21,254
Total sales ($m)	12,432	18,759	23,587	31,812	38,491
Pre-tax profit ($m)	848	1,246	1,676	2,251	2,884
Capital employed ($m)	4,827	8,974	9,987	14,241	16,892

Questions
(60 marks; 70 minutes)

1 a Outline the evidence of the importance of advertising in
McDonald's sales story. **(8 marks)**
b Why may advertising have been so important? **(8 marks)**

2 Judging by the McDonald's advertisements you have seen
recently, discuss how far the firm's advertising strategy has
moved away from its 1968 guidelines. **(12 marks)**

3 Calculate the percentage increase in McDonald's US dollar
sales
a between 1966 and 1986. **(3 marks)**
b between 1986 and 1999. **(3 marks)**

4 During the 1990s McDonald's reached sales maturity in
America and therefore switched its focus to the rest of the
world.
a Analyse the sales data in the table to see how
effective this strategy proved. **(8 marks)**
b Outline two reasons why people outside America might be
concerned about 'the McDomination of the world'. **(8 marks)**

5 To what extent do you agree with the statement that the
absence of a new product success since 1982 'merely
emphasises the strength of the McDonald's marketing strategy'. **(10 marks)**

REAL SUCCESS

AS MARKETING

CONCEPTS NEEDED:

Market research, Added value, Marketing mix, Product differentiation

Looking back it was obvious. Yet when Julia first mentioned it there were sneering comments from several on the Product Development Group (PDG). Now, with an 11% (and rising) share of the small family car sector, motoring journalists were talking about the car's revolutionary effect on thinking within the motor industry worldwide.

The project can be dated back to Julia's appointment as the first woman Chief Executive of a major car producer. Vauxton Motors was the British arm of an American motor giant – profitable, but only just. Julia was appointed from outside the car industry. Her background was as Marketing Director, then Managing Director, of a major confectionery company. Her switch to the car industry was a journalists' dream. She quickly became quite a celebrity.

In her first week in the job she went to the monthly PDG meeting. In itself this was an event, as the previous Chief Executive had never attended. Julia found it an eye-opener. As she explained afterwards to her assistant: 'The PDG is dominated by engineers. They're great on horsepower per litre and drag factors, but rarely allow consumer needs or taste into the equation. So their plans are all about

making cars faster, quieter and more fuel efficient, but without knowing customer priorities.' Julia decided to embark on a major programme of market research, both qualitative and quantitative.

Past research had tended to focus upon men, but Julia insisted on a completely open approach to the qualitative research. When the psychologist presented the results from the group discussions, the responses from the women proved especially interesting. In response to the invitation to talk about 'favourite and least favourite car journeys in the last month', the group of married women outdid each other with horror stories about their kids on long car journeys. From this and other evidence came a completely new idea for a car development project: a family car designed to make journeys more fun.

Further research refined the concept. The family car buyer's ideal would be a car designed to keep the kids happy in the back, so that the adults in the front could enjoy a less stressful journey. Specifically, the new car should have the following:

• individual seat-back TV screens

- headphones stored in a console in the rear doors, offering a choice of radio or TV

- mobile phone recharging points

- insulated storage for keeping drinks and snacks cool

- a secure waste paper basket

- individual fresh air vents for the rear passengers.

Just as Virgin Atlantic had stolen a march on British Airways in the 1990s by making personal entertainment and comfort a key part of flying, so Vauxton would do the same in the car market.

Despite a cool response from the PDG, the project development leader was able to identify a core staff of enthusiasts. A key issue was how much of a price premium car buyers would be willing to pay for the extras. A quantitative survey established that the majority of the target market would pay no more than a 10% price premium, so the team had to find a way to keep the extra costs down to well below £1,000. Despite the difficulty of finding suppliers able and willing to meet Vauxton's demanding requirements, the new car was up and ready within 16 months.

With one month to go until the launch date, the marketing director presented his launch strategy to Julia. The car was to be branded the Vauxton *Real*. The objective was to achieve an 8% share of the UK small family car market within one year. This target was based on the findings of a specially commissioned quantitative survey. Instead of aiming at a small niche of upmarket families (easily able to pay a price premium), the plan was to mass market the product with the copy line 'The world's first *real* family car'. This USP would be pushed by a £7.5 million TV advertising campaign, supported by a huge programme of celebrity test drives designed to get masses of articles written about the wonders of the new car. It was Julia's idea to go one step further, and offer Tesco an exclusive six month deal to be the only grocery chain to stock the product. Tesco agreed to give the car a huge amount of display coverage in over 400 stores.

The launch went superbly. Julia found herself on a series of breakfast and daytime TV programmes as the media lapped up the story about the car's origins in what families really want and need. Demand boomed, through Tesco outlets, Tesco Online and Vauxton's own car dealers. Unfortunately the factories proved unable to boost production in line with demand, so waiting lists grew and delivery lead times lengthened. Julia regretted her meanness in restricting the sample size to 200 on the survey that estimated potential demand for the new car.

Nevertheless, at the end of the first year, with UK market share well above the planned level, *Real* was about ready for launch into the other main European Union car markets of France, Italy and Germany. As *Real*'s popularity in Britain meant that no price discounting had been needed to sell the cars, the new product was already making profitable returns on the £800 million invested by Vauxton. The big profits would be made, however, if the car could be a success throughout Europe. That remained to be seen.

Questions
(60 marks; 70 minutes)

1 Use examples from the case to explain the differences between qualitative and quantitative research. **(8 marks)**

2 Explain why Julia 'regretted her meanness in restricting the sample size to 200'. **(8 marks)**

3 Julia's marketing background encouraged her to focus the business on satisfying customer needs and wants. To what extent was this the crucial factor in the success of the *Real* car? **(12 marks)**

4 Explain how the company added value to the *Real*. **(6 marks)**

5 Discuss the advantages and disadvantages to Vauxton of competing in the mass car market through product differentiation, instead of targeting a smaller, wealthier niche. **(14 marks)**

6 To what extent was distribution the key element in the marketing mix used in the *Real* launch? **(12 marks)**

STRATEGIC MARKETING IN ACTION

AS
MARKETING

CONCEPTS NEEDED:

Marketing Strategy, Boston Matrix

It started when a big envelope flopped into Terry Carter's in-tray. He opened it, read the two page proposal, then started to look through the accompanying pages of text. It was the original manuscript for what was to prove a huge best seller: *Biology*, by S.T. McCauliffe. It was to become the standard text for 50,000 AS and A level students and many others such as nurses and first year medical students. Within five years of being published it had sold over 350,000 copies at £20 each: a whopping £7 million of sales turnover. The publisher, Garfield & Ruddock, went from a 9% share of the market for Biology books to a stunning 54%. Within AS/A level alone, 'McCauliffe' held a share of over 80%.

As soon as the book started to sell strongly, Terry developed a series of stories about its success. In a presentation to Garfield & Ruddock's sales staff he explained how he discovered S.T. McCauliffe, encouraged him to write and then nurtured the book through redrafts and rewrites. Terry ensured that all the staff and senior management at the

publisher saw the book's success as his personal triumph. Terry was promoted from Publisher to Senior Publisher and then to Publishing Director in just three years.

Therefore, when Sophie – the new, young Science Publisher – told Terry of an exciting new Biology proposal, he was interested. Biology was the most profitable part of his profit centre (Science Education), and it was his power base. Sophie explained enthusiastically that a young Biology teacher had come up with a radically new approach. Instead of following the syllabus with page after page of text, the book was lively, more based upon diagrams and fun exercises, yet still built up to high level analysis and scientific knowledge.

Sophie was stunned when Terry reacted to the new material with a rather blank expression. He eventually said: 'Just leave it with me.' His instinct was to bury it, but he forced himself to think it through. The new proposal was aimed squarely at the AS/A level market. It would be a big book, selling for perhaps £25. It therefore would only be bought by the same schools and colleges who currently were buying McCauliffe. 'Cannibalisation' thought Terry. Then he considered a cut-down version of the book, aiming it at student self-purchase; perhaps pricing it at £10.99. This would enable Garfield & Ruddock to expand the market (and their share of it) instead of splitting sales between two text books. As he explained it to Sophie: 'We'd be mad to dent the sales of McCauliffe, which is a phenomenal cash cow. Let's do it my way.'

Unfortunately the author did not agree. Her intention was to change Biology teaching: 'to bring it into the 21st century'. She *wanted* to hit sales of conventional text books such as McCauliffe. With the author unwilling to play ball, Terry made himself sound enthusiastic while in fact he stalled on the proposal. After four months, the author started to ring round other publishers. Most were too daunted by the market power of the McCauliffe book. They knew that most teachers saw it as their 'bible' and doubted the ability of any book to break the consumer loyalty that underpinned the best seller. They also knew that the last rival to McCauliffe was hit hard by a vigorous marketing campaign by Garfield & Ruddock, which included special price offers, a barrage of sales leaflets and a heavy approach to any independent bookshops that stocked the newcomer.

One small publisher bit on the bait, however. Large textbooks take a long time to produce, but within 15 months *Biology in Action* was ready for launch. The publisher decided to avoid a head-on fight with Garfield & Ruddock, and therefore kept the launch low key. Instead of a direct mail blitz and advertisements in the *Biology Review*, a slower approach was taken. The publisher and author went to regional teacher conferences and found 'champions' of the book – people who liked its radical approach and were keen to use it and to talk about it to others. Garfield & Ruddock ran a '25% off!' promotion for three months, but once it was over, sales of *Biology in Action* started to push ahead. Sophie couldn't resist showing Terry Carter the latest figures.

Questions
(70 marks; 80 minutes)

1 Outline the business significance for Garfield & Ruddock of:
  a 'cannibalisation' **(6 marks)**
  b consumer loyalty **(6 marks)**

2 **a** S.T. McCauliffe's contract gave royalty payments as follows: 8% of the sales value for the first 20,000 copies, 10% for the next 30,000 and 12% thereafter. How much did he earn from the book in its first five years? **(6 marks)**
  b Given this, how might he have reacted if Garfield & Ruddock had published a rival Biology text? **(7 marks)**

3 A critical part of the case is Terry's approach to Sophie's new book proposal.
  a Discuss what objectives seem to underpin Terry's decision making. **(10 marks)**
  b Evaluate whether his strategy may prove mistaken in the long term for Garfield & Ruddock. **(12 marks)**

4 Analyse the situation facing Garfield & Ruddock within the Biology market, using the Boston Matrix. **(9 marks)**

5 Discuss the issues of marketing strategy and tactics involved in the rival publisher's launch of *Biology in Action*, and Terry's response. **(14 marks)**

THE COCA-COLA STORY

AS MARKETING

CONCEPTS NEEDED:

Marketing strategy, Market research, Product life cycle

Coca-Cola was first sold on 8 May 1886 by a pharmacist called John Pemberton. He had devised the syrup as a headache remedy, but found that it mixed well with soda water. The first advertisement for the drink appeared in the *Atlanta Journal*: 'containing ... the wonderful Coca plant and Cola nuts'. The name proved memorable but Pemberton wanted a stylish trademark. He found it when his bookkeeper wrote the brand name with a flourish in an accounts ledger. That script was registered as a trademark in 1893 and has been used ever since.

Yet it was not Pemberton who created the Coca-Cola business empire. In 1886 only nine drinks were sold per day at just 5 cents per glass. So he sold the name, the formula and the manufacturing equipment to a wealthy trader, Asa Candler, for $2,300. In 1892 Candler founded The Coca-Cola Company, and his capital plus his understanding of distribution ensured that the drink spread rapidly. Candler's marketing strategy was to sell the drink through soda fountains rather than through shops. So the syrup was transported in (red) barrels from Atlanta, and mixed with soda in a glass at the point of sale. By 1899 sales had progressed to 281,055 gallons.

Then came the real revolution. Two young lawyers saw the opportunity for Coca-Cola to be made more widely available by selling it in bottles. In 1899 they arranged to meet Candler and asked him for a bottling contract for the whole of the United States. To their surprise he agreed – and set a price of 1 dollar on the contract. This established the franchise structure that has operated throughout the world ever since. The Coca-Cola Company supplies a concentrated essence to bottling firms that turn it into syrup, add carbonated water, then bottle and distribute it. So the Atlanta head office is responsible only for producing and delivering the concentrate, and for marketing the brand. The new approach generated sales growth to 6,767,822 gallons by 1913.

The original 1899 bottle had no special shape or design. By 1913 the success of Coca-Cola encouraged many imitators to offer 'Cola

6,000,000 drinks a day

Sola' or 'Pepsi Cola' in similar bottles. So the owners of the Coca-Cola bottling franchises contacted various glass manufacturers to hold a competition to design a distinctive new bottle. In 1916 the characteristic glass Coca-Cola bottle – still used today – was patented and launched. Sales pushed ahead still further, to 18.7 million gallons by 1919.

That year two other important events occurred. The Candler family sold the company for $25 million to a group led by Ernest Woodruff, whose son Bob became Coca-Cola's chief executive for the next 40 years. He was responsible for turning this soft drink into a worldwide symbol of the 'American Dream'. Helping him finance that was the other event of 1919 – the onset of Prohibition in the United States. For although the period is remembered mainly for the illegal production and sale of alcohol, the law abiding majority of Americans turned to soft drinks. Coca-Cola sales grew ever faster, and its distinctive name and bottle made it

increasingly possible to sell it at a price premium.

Bob Woodruff's approach to leadership was to set standards and strategies, and to ensure that everyone knew they were being followed as firmly at the top as elsewhere in the organisation. He viewed the company as a force for good, not just a force for profit. For example he insisted that Coca-Cola delivery drivers 'must always set a good example in the way they drive'. He tried to give a sense of purpose, of mission, to all his employees, as can be seen in his three short 'commandments':

1 Absolute loyalty to the product and the company.

2 All partners must earn a good salary.

3 Simplicity of the product (one drink, one bottle, one price).

That third statement was stuck to until the 1950s. So for over 40 years Coca-Cola meant just one product. This narrow focus may have been important in the company's success, because the drive to diversify often attracts a firm's most talented executives, and much of its investment capital. Only when Pepsi gained market share during the 1950s as a result of the launch of a larger pack size did Coke allow itself to break its rule. From then on, The Coca-Cola Company redefined itself as a soft drinks company, which encouraged it to launch Fanta in 1960 and Sprite in 1961.

The 1960s might have seen the end of the apparently unstoppable rise of Coke. Not only was it a 70 year old product at a time when youth and experimentation were fashionable, but also the product had developed a rather staid, middle-aged image. The following advertising slogans show how this had come about:

'The friendliest club in the world'	1946
'For home and hospitality'	1951
'Refreshment through the years'	1951
'Sign of good taste'	1957
'Happy pause for the youth of all ages'	1958

At the end of the 1950s Coca-Cola appointed a new, younger advertising agency. During the 1960s the marketing strategy became increasingly youth orientated. This not only meant new catchphrases such as 'Things go better with Coke', but also visual imagery became focused on young people having fun together.

By 1984 worldwide sales of The Coca-Cola Company were worth $7.4 billion (representing about 283 million cans per day). It was the biggest soft drinks producer in the world by a considerable margin. Yet its market share

Thirst stops here

The road maps of the world are dotted with happy places to pause. And ice-cold Coca-Cola is there to make a pause *the pause that refreshes.* Familiar red coolers everywhere signal you to refresh yourself and be off to a fresh start.

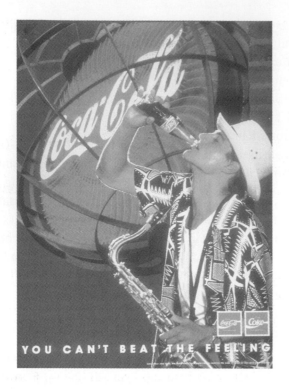

YOU CAN'T BEAT THE FEELING

sweeter and less fizzy – 'like a Pepsi left open'. The outcry forced the company to backtrack, so on 10 July it announced that the old Coke would be reintroduced as Coca-Cola Classic.

Pepsi had gloated over Coke's original decision, as it appeared to confirm its long standing claim that in the 'Pepsi Taste Challenge' its product was preferred to Coke. Yet the whole episode proved more beneficial to Coke than to Pepsi. The wave of nostalgia for 'the real thing' plus the publicity about the sweetness of both new Coke and Pepsi strengthened Coca-Cola's traditional image. By the end of 1985 Coke's share of the United States cola market had grown by four percentage points. Ever since then it has rarely been challenged.

From 1886 to 2000 Coke's sales progress was almost uninterrupted. Health trends were met by low calorie or caffeine-free versions and changing consumer habits by family-sized bottles, multipacks, or automatic vending machines. The key to the firm's success has always been in the magic of its image, as captured in the two slogans: 'The real thing' and 'Coke is it!' For just as Levi's are not just **a** pair of jeans, Coke is not just **a** cola. The brand name, the logo, its status as the original, and its distinctive bottle have all been woven into a definite marketing advantage. An advantage that not only enables Coke to outsell other colas decisively, but also enables the Atlanta firm to charge a price premium. For profitability, Coke is it.

had slipped from 22.5% to 21.8%, while that of Pepsi had increased by 0.1%. Coke's new Chairman considered this a threat, especially as research showed that younger people were particularly prone to favour Pepsi. His worry was that he was presiding over the classic break within a product's life cycle between growth and decline. So a new formula drink was concocted, and then tested in great secrecy among a staggering 190,000 sample. The taste of the new Coke appeared to beat the old by 61% to 39%, so its launch was prepared.

In April 1985 it was announced to a horrified public that, after 99 years, Coke was to be relaunched with a 'Great new taste!' An immediate rush to try the new formula was followed by a barrage of criticism. Within a few days *USA Today* published an opinion poll that showed 59% of consumers preferred the old Coca-Cola, 25% Pepsi, and only 13% the new Coke. The new was derided for being

Sources: The Chronicle of Coca-Cola Since 1886 (The Coca-Cola Company, 1993); *Financial Times*; *Coca-Cola Superstar*, F.S. Palazzini (Barrons Educational, 1988); *Coke: Designing a World Brand*, S. Bayley (Conran Foundation, 1986)

'Coca-Cola' and 'Coke' are registered trade marks which identify the same product of The Coca-Cola Company.

Questions
(50 marks; 80 minutes)

1 How did Coca-Cola marketing strategy change over time and what were its consistent themes? **(12 marks)**

2 Discuss the pros and cons of Woodruff's three 'commandments'. **(10 marks)**

3 **a** By 1984, what was the approximate value of the world market for soft drinks? **(4 marks)**

    b Do you think the company was right to be so concerned about its slippage in market share? Explain your reasoning. **(10 marks)**

4 Coca-Cola researched its 1980s Pepsi problem in an apparently scientific manner, yet consumer reactions were a complete surprise:

    a Why may this have been so? **(8 marks)**

    b What further market research might have helped prevent this? **(6 marks)**

THE PRODUCT PORTFOLIO PROBLEM

AS
MARKETING

Concepts Needed:

Market share, Distribution, Boston Matrix

Streamer plc has dominated the British cider market for over 50 years. Its Sparrowhawk and Target brands have been national best sellers for decades. The company benefited from customer loyalty, plus the inertia of the pubs, clubs and off-licences that kept on buying Streamer brands because they always had done. Up until last year Streamer plc held over 50% of the cider market.

The big change began two years ago, when the Chancellor of the Exchequer reduced the tax rate for cider in the Budget. With beer tax levels held constant, customers started to switch to cider. Streamer passed the tax reduction on to customers by cutting its prices, in order to boost sales volumes. A smaller rival used a different strategy, however. Devon Cider Ltd chose to develop extra strength ciders with a distinctive image, priced at the same level as equivalent beers. The extra profit margin (from the lower tax rates) was used to pay for extensive advertising. So 'Silver Light' and 'Red Streak' became household names through a blaze of television commercials. With gross profit margins four times higher than Streamer's brands, Devon Cider became a highly profitable company.

Streamer's first response had been to dismiss Devon's new brands as a minor irrelevance. However, both products appealed to the young women who had always been the main consumers of Sparrowhawk, so Streamer had to act. To the surprise of outsiders, the company's first action was to dismiss its Marketing Director. The successor immediately set to work developing a distinctive bottled cider called Clear Rain and also a more modern product to launch on draught in pubs and clubs. The latter would make the most of Streamer's distribution strengths.

Launched six months later, the draught Scrumpy Star proved a great success. Its

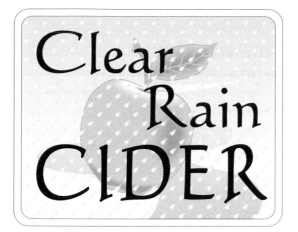

stylish advertising and fresh taste made it fashionable, and its higher price made it more profitable than Streamer's older products.

Sales of the bottled product started equally well, but faltered after a large amount of product trial failed to be converted into repeat purchase. Streamer put more advertising money behind it, to try to strengthen its image, but once the campaign stopped sales fell back disappointingly.

This problem was becoming increasingly evident just as the time was looming for Streamer's annual marketing strategy review. This year, the Board decided to trim the marketing budget to £3.8 million. This would not be enough to support each of the four brands adequately, so the strategy team would have to decide how best to split up the money.

Appendix A: Quarterly figures for average cider sales per month (thousand barrels, seasonally adjusted)

| Period | Streamer's Brands | | | | Devon Cider Total | Total Cider Market |
	Sparrowhawk	Target	Scrumpy Star	Clear Rain		
1st Quarter 2 years ago	120	170	–	–	130	560
2nd Quarter 2 years ago	126	175	–	–	130	574
3rd Quarter 2 years ago	135	183	–	–	131	596
4th Quarter 2 years ago	137	186	–	–	138	613
1st Quarter 1 year ago	131	188	–	–	154	640
2nd Quarter 1 year ago	129	189	–	8	168	655
3rd Quarter 1 year ago	124	189	–	17	168	661
4th Quarter 1 year ago	110	182	22	24	171	670
1st Quarter this year	106	180	38	19	177	686

Questions
(50 marks; 70 minutes)

1   Identify the use made by the cider companies of each of the
    following marketing concepts:
    a product differentiation
    b value added   **(10 marks)**

2   Analyse the importance to a business such as Streamer plc of
    making 'the most of' its 'distribution strengths'.   **(10 marks)**

3   Calculate the percentage market share for each of the
    Streamer brands plus the Devon Cider company for the
    1st quarter two years ago, 1st quarter one year ago and
    1st quarter this year. Construct a diagram on graph paper to
    show the main trends involved.   **(15 marks)**

4   Use the Boston Matrix to analyse Streamer's product
    portfolio in order to make recommendations about how the
    budget should be divided.   **(15 marks)**

FROM BEACH TO BOARDROOM

AS
MARKETING AND
FINANCE

CONCEPTS NEEDED:

Marketing objectives, Market analysis, Price elasticity, Cash flow

Tim sipped his strawberry daiquiri thoughtfully, then said, 'What if it's true about global warming?' Shirley could understand the thought process. The beach was very hot today. But it wasn't like Tim to think about anything very much when sunbathing. She grunted 'What?' but that was the end of the conversation.

In the evening, though, at the Greek taverna, Tim returned to his theme: 'If global warming means more dramatic weather – floods especially – there'll be an increasing need for air freight. Firms using JIT systems need reliable deliveries. In a crisis, when lorries can't get through, surely they'd pay big money to get guaranteed supplies.' This was not idle talk. Shirley and Tim ran a small business based upon helicopter rides for tourists. From Southampton a £45 ride took tourists over and round the Isle of Wight in 30 minutes. This was pretty good business in the summer, but for much of the year they struggled to generate the income to keep them in daiquiris.

On returning to Britain, Tim got the season up and running, while Shirley looked further into the new idea. She started with friends who worked locally at IBM in Portsmouth and Ford in Southampton. An old school friend put her in touch with IBM's Purchasing Controller. How big an issue was continuity of supply and how much would IBM be prepared to pay for peace of mind? There was no doubting the importance of the issue. Shirley learned that a project team had been set up to consider supply continuity. It worked on a matrix basis, drawing members from many different functional areas within the business. When she left, Shirley felt optimistic that they were on to something. The key statement made by the IBM Controller was: 'We carry only one hour's stock of many materials and components, and every hour of lost production costs the business £30,000.'

At Ford, Shirley found a similar story. This time, though, she had thought of a new line of questioning. Would clients be willing to pay a regular fee to guarantee service priority in the case of road or rail disruption? She had come to realise that this was crucial. Otherwise there would be months, perhaps years, of zero income, followed by the occasional bonanza at a time of crisis.

Helped by her discussions, Shirley decided to conduct some proper quantitative research. She wrote a questionnaire then mailed it to 500 manufacturing companies selected from the *Yellow Pages* website. All she had hoped for was a response rate of 1 in 5, so it was pleasing to end up with 160 completed questionnaires.

The answers showed a great deal of interest in the idea of helicopter back-up for flying in emergency supplies, but less agreement over an appropriate pricing structure (see graph).

When Tim saw the research results he was rather despondent: 'Over 70% are saying no or no monthly fees. I don't see how it can work.' Shirley remained more upbeat. She had received phone calls from four companies asking when the service was starting, so she knew that some were very interested. She could see that if they could sign up just

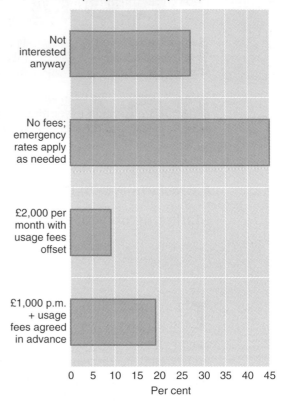

Which pricing structure best meets your needs?
(Sample: 160 companies)

Analysis from Shirley's survey

50 clients their annual cash flow position would be transformed.

The next step was to investigate the cost implications of the new service. If floods hit, there would clearly be a dramatic rise in the demand. If 50 clients were signed up, how many helicopters would be needed to meet clients' needs? Clearly it could not be cost effective to buy or hire helicopters on a permanent basis, to sit around on an airfield until needed. So Shirley decided to sign up tourist helicopter pilots from around the country, offering them £1,000 as a one-off fee, plus a guaranteed £120 per flying hour. For that, the pilots signed a contract promising to give Shirley priority over all other work, as long as they were given eight hours' notice.

Shirley signed up 100 helicopter pilots throughout Britain just in time for an interesting test case. Sabotage of the Suez Canal led to fears of an oil shortage which in turn caused panic buying of petrol and diesel. As freight haulage lorries started to run out of fuel, the phone started ringing as several of the surveyed companies inquired whether the service had started yet. Cleverly, Shirley not only rushed out a direct mail leaflet that was sent to 50,000 firms, but also succeeded in getting herself featured on the BBC South TV News programme.

Within four weeks 30 companies had signed up on the basis of a £1,000 per month fee. Three months later Shirley had pushed the figure to 50. As the fears of a fuel crisis fizzled out, the monthly income could be enjoyed as pure cash flow. One year on from Tim's daiquiri moment, they were back on the beach. But this time it was the Caribbean, not Greece; and the drink was champagne.

Questions
(60 marks; 70 minutes)

1 Outline the marketing objectives and strategy adopted by Shirley and Tim after returning from holiday.　　**(10 marks)**

2 Explain the impact upon a business such as Tim's of low capacity utilisation outside the tourist season.　　**(8 marks)**

3 **a** As the graph in the text shows, doubling the monthly fee to £2,000 cut responses from 19% to 9%. Calculate the price elasticity implied by this.　　**(6 marks)**

　b In the future, how might Shirley and Tim attempt to lower the price elasticity of their new service?　　**(8 marks)**

4 To what extent was the success of the new venture a result of the market analysis undertaken by Shirley?　　**(12 marks)**

5 **a** Draw a graph to show the approximate impact upon Shirley and Tim's cash flow of starting their new service. The graph should plot the cumulative cash position for a 12 month period, with cash starting at zero.　　**(8 marks)**

　b Briefly explain the implications of the graph for the amount and type of capital that the business should have raised before starting the new service.　　**(8 marks)**

THE RUSSIAN LAGER

CONCEPTS NEEDED:

Market research, Pricing, Revenue, Break-even analysis

Project Steps was the codename for Allied Ales' new lager brand. Many in the marketing department thought it their most promising prospect for years. The idea had emerged from a series of group discussions among young, frequent lager drinkers. They had sounded tired of the usual pub offering of German, American or Australian beers, and when one suggested a Russian lager ('like ice'), others reacted well.

Since then the product had been tested quantitatively among a quota sample of 300 people. They had been shown a test advertisement and a variety of possible pack designs. Separate research had tested brand names on a random sample of 200 men. These surveys had given encouraging findings, convincing most in the company that the correct name and advertising slogan was:

'Petersburg from Russia. Like Ice.**'**

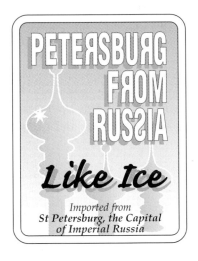

Next came the pricing research, which was designed to show what price premium, if any, drinkers were prepared to pay for the distinction of a lager imported from 'St Petersburg, the Capital of Imperial Russia'. A bitter argument broke out among the five members of the development team. Some were convinced that a 6p premium was right, while others advocated a 20p difference.

The results showed the following:

Price per pint (in relation to main rivals)	Projected sales per year (50 pint barrels)
+20p	1,300,000
+12p	1,600,000
+ 6p	2,000,000
+ 2p	2,400,000
same	2,600,000

Another issue that remained to be resolved was how large an advertising budget to set. Most felt that £6 million would provide a sufficiently heavyweight TV campaign. Two of the team worried that this would take too large a chunk out of the £160 million sales anticipated (at pricing of +12p). Certainly it was true that there were a lot of costs to cover, with fixed production overheads of £20 million and variable costs of £70 per barrel. Decisions would have to be made in the near future.

Questions
(50 marks; 60 minutes)

1 Outline the factors that would affect a firm's choice of whether to use qualitative or quantitative research. **(6 marks)**

2 **a** Distinguish between random and quota samples. **(4 marks)**
b What problems do market research firms face in obtaining accurate random samples? **(6 marks)**

3 **a** Use the projected sales value of £160 million to calculate the selling price per pint of beer. **(8 marks)**
b Calculate whether a 6p price premium or a 20p premium would generate the higher revenue. **(4 marks)**

4 Calculate the break-even output and safety margin at a 6p price premium. **(6 marks)**

5 How might a firm make sales projections based on quantitative research findings? **(6 marks)**

6 Consider what other information the marketing team should examine before deciding what price to set. **(10 marks)**

EVEN LEVI CAN MAKE MISTAKES

A2
MARKETING

CONCEPTS NEEDED:

Market research, Marketing model

During the 1980s, Levi's US division was looking at ways of diversifying away from its heavy dependence on a jeans market that appeared to be saturated. It had already introduced Levi's shoes, shirts and socks, which sold quite well among people who were already buying Levi jeans. Now it wanted to move into the market for higher priced clothes, in order to attract a new type of customer to the Levi Strauss brand. As menswear had always been its biggest seller, it decided to concentrate on the male market first.

To decide how to meet this objective, a market research company was commissioned to investigate men's purchasing habits and attitudes to clothes (a Usage and Attitudes study). A large quantitative survey was conducted among a quota sample of 2,000 men who had recently spent at least $50 on clothing. When analysed, the survey revealed that the entire menswear market could be segmented into five types of buyer:

- Type 1 **Traditionalist** (probably over 45; department store shopper; buys polyester suits and slacks; shops with wife)

- Type 2 **Classic Independent** ('a real clothes horse'; 21% of market, yet buying 46% of wool blend suits; buys at independent stores; expensive tastes)

- Type 3 **Utilitarian** (wears jeans for work and play; 26% of the market; Levi loyalist)

- Type 4 **Trendy Casual** (buying 'designer', high fashion clothes; might buy 501s, but usually considers Levi too mass-market; 19% of the market)

- Type 5 **Price Shopper** (buys whatever and wherever the lowest prices are found; no potential for Levi; 14% of market)

As the Type 2 Classic Independent men fitted in with Levi's objective, the research company was asked to computer analyse the findings so that the behaviour and attitudes of this specific group could be split out from the rest of the sample. The large total number of

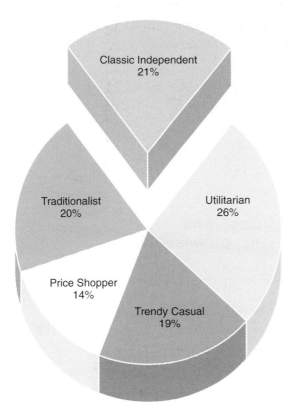

Classic Independent 21%

Utilitarian 26%

Traditionalist 20%

Price Shopper 14%

Trendy Casual 19%

Menswear market segmentation

interviews made it possible to have confidence in the reliability of the data from this sub-sample. It emerged that Type 2 men wanted traditionally styled, perhaps pinstriped, suits; that they liked to buy through independent clothes shops or tailors, rather than at department stores; and that they liked to shop alone, whereas others liked having their wife/girlfriend with them.

To tackle this segment of the market, Levi decided to introduce 'Tailored Classics', a range of high quality wool suits, trousers and jackets. The research showed that these buyers valued quality and fit rather than low prices, so Levi decided to price the range 10% above that of the competition. To avoid direct product comparisons – and to ensure

that not too large a salesforce was needed – Levi chose to distribute through department store chains.

Having decided on this strategy, its acceptability to the target market was tested via a series of group discussions. These were conducted by a psychologist who was to look for the real motivations behind respondents' opinions or behaviour. The psychologist reported that the Type 2 men had two misgivings: first, they were concerned that the garments would be in standard fittings, and so would not provide the tailoring they wanted; second, although they could believe that Levi could make a good suit, they still felt uncomfortable about the Levi name. One said:

'**W**hen I think Levi I think jeans. If they're making suits I have to be convinced.'

Another felt that:

'**I**f I went to work and someone said: "Hey, that's a good suit, Joe, who's it by?" I wouldn't feel comfortable saying Levi.'

The company's marketing executives responded to this by deciding to concentrate on the separate jackets and trousers in the launch advertising, and let suits 'slipstream'. The Director of Consumer Marketing felt certain that:

'**T**he thing that's going to overcome Levi's image for casualness as no other thing can, is a suit that's made by Levi that doesn't look like all the other things we've made. Once that gets on the racks people will put an asterisk on the image that says: "Oh, and they can also make a good suit when they put their mind to it."'

Soon after this decision, salesmen started

contacting retail buyers. After four months of selling to the trade, it was clear that the range's sales targets would not be met. Even a price cut did little to redeem the situation, and Tailored Classics achieved only 65% of its modest sales targets.

Levi could find consolation only if it could learn why it went so badly wrong.

Sources: Channel 4: *Commercial Breaks*; *Financial Times*

Questions
(60 marks; 80 minutes)

1 Distinguish between quantitative and qualitative research. **(6 marks)**

2 Analyse the messages within the research findings that Levi's management appeared to ignore or underestimate. **(10 marks)**

3 **a** For what reasons may Levi have used a quota rather than a random sample? **(6 marks)**
  b What factors might influence the size of sample you choose for a quantitative survey? **(6 marks)**

4 **a** In constructing the pie chart shown, how many degrees within the circle should be given to the Type 2 segment? **(4 marks)**
  b The US menswear market was then worth $4,000 million. If Levi had achieved a 10% share of the Type 2 segment, what sales value would this have represented? Show workings. **(6 marks)**

5 Discuss the decision making process Levi used in terms of the marketing model. How well did it use it? **(10 marks)**

6 Market research could be thought to be like an insurance policy; you pay a premium in advance to eliminate your risk of making a heavy loss. Consider the value of this statement. **(12 marks)**

LET THE BUYER BEWARE

CONCEPTS NEEDED:

Break even, Market research, Marketing strategy, Contribution

It had all happened by chance. Melanie had been moaning to a friend about the problems of running her small design company. The friend knew of another woman (Cathy) who was thinking of selling a business. So they arranged to meet.

Cathy started the firm seven years ago, by finding a manufacturer who could mass-produce her design of baby and toddler footwear. In her first year the turnover was only £7,342 but retailers seemed to like her products, so she kept going. Two thousand pounds was spent on display stands at the Junior Fashion Fair at Olympia in the following two years, and orders began to pour in. Stockists soon included shops such as Bentalls, Children's World, and many independent babywear outlets.

By the fourth year, the Babyboots range of products had expanded to four size bands (0–6 months; 6–12 months; 12–18 months; and 18–24 months), and within each band were eight different colours, four different linings, and four different fabrics. The range has not really altered since. That year, sales were £78,780 and Cathy was making a £13,000 profit even after paying herself a small salary. Given that she did little more than take orders, pack them, carry them to the Post Office, and then phone the factory for new supplies, this was good money. Her office was (and is) a small room at the back of her house, and the stockroom the house's basement.

Early in the fifth year, though, Cathy had a baby and began to find it hard to find the time and energy to keep the business going. 'I realise now that I should have sold it then,' she told Melanie.

Over the two years since the baby, Cathy has done nothing active to market her products. She has relied on existing customers, plus three agents who sell her goods on commission. Two operate in the south-east footwear trade on a 5% commission, but provide very little business.

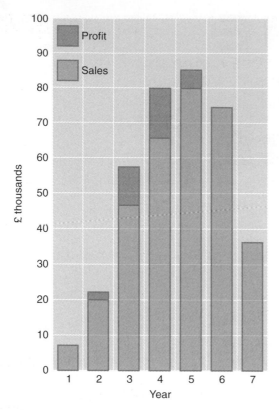

Babyboots sales and profit record

Now Melanie is trying to decide if she should make an offer for the Babyboots business, and if so, for how much? In making up her mind, she has to decide what she would do to revitalise it. For 'the books' reveal that sales slumped from £74,000 to £35,900 in the latest year. Cathy maintains that this is a temporary result of her neglect, but could it be due to factors that would have longer term implications?

Melanie's questioning reveals that Babyboots has competition not only from a British firm (Padders), but also from Korean suppliers who sell at half the price charged by the two British rivals.

The attempt to find out more financial details is hampered by the fact that no full accounts have been prepared for this year or last. Nevertheless, the information below gives a lot of useful data – all provided willingly by Cathy. She also explains that she buys from her manufacturer at £1.55, spends three pence per display bag, and charges her customers for postage. The list price of Babyboots is £2.05, though half her customers are paying an average price of £1.95 (this includes the agents' commission).

The third is in Scotland, and sells to chemist shops for an 8% commission. This man sold £10,000 of Babyboots last year – more than the six Bentalls department stores.

Babyboots sales and profit history

	Latest Year	Year 6	Year 5	Year 4	Year 3	Year 2	Year 1
Sales £000	36	74	85	79	57	22	7
Contribution £000	–	–	20	23	17	6.5	2
Gross profit margin %	–	–	23.7	29.3	29.6	29.4	29.0
Overheads £000	–	–	15	9.3	6.4	4.4	2.4
Profit £000	–	–	5	13.7	10.6	2.1	−0.4

Questions
(60 marks; 70 minutes)

1 List three further questions you would want to ask Cathy, if it was your money at stake. Explain the reason for each one. **(9 marks)**

2 Outline three pieces of research you might carry out independently of Cathy in order to help to decide the potential for Babyboots (remember we are talking about your money, so don't consider massive, expensive surveys). **(9 marks)**

3 **a** Melanie estimates that she would keep Babyboots' overheads down to £8,000 per year. Using this and the other information provided, draw a break-even chart for Melanie's first year. **(12 marks)**

   b Use it to estimate the likely profit or loss in her first year, if she manages to halt the decline in sales, and to let her know the sales revenue she will need to break even. **(5 marks)**

4 **a** Outline two marketing strategies that might boost profit in the coming year. **(8 marks)**

   b Explain which you favour and why. **(7 marks)**

5 If the asking price was £12,000, would you buy the business? Outline your reasons. **(10 marks)**

HÄAGEN-DAZS UK – A CLASSIC PRODUCT LAUNCH

A2
MARKETING

CONCEPTS NEEDED:

Market research, Distribution, Pricing strategy, Advertising ethics

In 1989, in a strategic decision to move into the fast food business, the British firm Grand Metropolitan bought up Pillsbury, the American owner of Burger King and other food brands. It is said that Grand Metropolitan only 'discovered' Häagen-Dazs after the purchase. No time was lost, however, in developing its potential in the British market.

As a catalyst to consumer awareness of the brand, a lavishly appointed Häagen-Dazs outlet was established in London's Leicester Square in mid 1989. Long queues quickly became the norm, despite price levels 50% higher than other ice cream parlours. This was testimony to the quality of the product and proved that a gap existed in the market for a super-premium brand. Yet might it only be a market for lavish treats when out for the

evening, or was there a wider, retail market opportunity? And if so, how could it best be exploited? These were questions for an advertising agency to answer.

After talking to several different agencies, Häagen-Dazs UK decided upon Bartle, Bogle and Hegarty (BBH), best known for the Levi 501s advertising. The agency's brief was to help Häagen-Dazs create a new 'gold standard' and become the ultimate ice cream in the market. At the time a premium sector existed in which Loseley and New England were the most prestigious and expensive brands. Häagen-Dazs UK decided to open up a new super-premium sector, with ice cream priced at £2.99 per half litre. This was three to four times the price of standard dairy ice cream and 50% higher than its two closest competitors.

The first task was to provide the background research upon which long term, strategic decisions could be based. A large scale survey showed that the target market for premium ice cream sold through retail outlets was 25–44 year olds with high disposable income but without children. These became the criteria for selecting the sample for the group discussions that followed.

Groups of six to eight men and women were prompted into discussion by each being given a half-litre tub of Häagen-Dazs Vanilla to eat as they talked. They were asked when and where they could imagine consuming the product. Usually the answer was eating it alone, as a reward or as a 'dream-like' compensation for a bad day or date. The big step forward came, however, as the group leader asked when they might share their Häagen-Dazs. Interviewees talked of sharing a spoon with their partner, feeding each other, and of 'mellowing out' together in front of their favourite video. Häagen-Dazs now had a unique way of advertising a food product: as a sensual pleasure to be shared.

The research provided the material for BBH's account planner to write the creative brief. From this the creative department would be able to consider how best to advertise the product. It was decided that the brief should be met by the use of press media rather than television. For not only is television an expensive way of reaching affluent adults, it also lacks the subtlety of mood that BBH wanted. So the agency's media department was asked to plan a campaign aimed at affluent adults in their moments of relaxation. This led to spaces being bought in the weekend colour supplements and women's consumer press.

Meanwhile, a parallel survey had been researching the suitability of the American pack design for the British market. In a large scale quantitative survey consumers found the pack significantly different to other ice cream brands. Group discussions showed that once people tried the ice cream they could identify the package with authentic high quality. So the company decided to leave the imported packs unchanged.

On Sunday 21 July 1991 the first advertisement appeared – one of four black and white photographs that juxtaposed product messages with sensual imagery, with the slogan 'dedicated to pleasure'. The launch advertising burst lasted eight weeks and cost a

cream through sexy images. Did it exploit women? Did it meet the Advertising Standards Authority yardstick of 'Legal, Decent, Honest and Truthful'? Whatever the answers, sales kept rising.

The financial impact of the advertising was dramatic, with sales doubling between July and August 1991. In 1991 as a whole, sales were five times their 1990 level. Häagen-Dazs went from a 2% share of the £50 million premium ice cream market in October 1990 to 22% by October 1991.

little over £300,000. A further three-week campaign before Christmas took the year's spending to £450,000.

From the start, editorial coverage of the launch was considerable. Much of it represented marvellous free publicity. Some of it focused upon the ethics of advertising ice

The diagram below relates the launch advertising to Häagen-Dazs sales to retailers.

This achievement relied not only upon the advertising, but also on offering millions of product samples. Also crucial was the distribution drive by the Häagen-Dazs sales

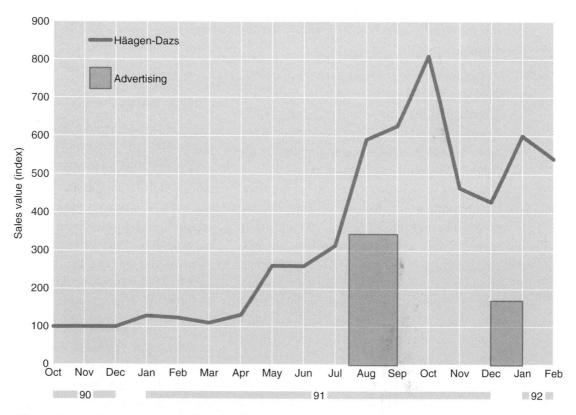

Häagen-Dazs sales growth compared with advertising

team. In April 1991 Häagen-Dazs was stocked in shops selling less then 20% of London's ice cream; by July this distribution level was over 40%.

An innovative feature of the distribution strategy came from the earlier group discussions. Mentions of sharing Häagen-Dazs in front of a favourite film encouraged the sales team to supply refrigerated cabinets to Blockbuster Video. This proved so successful that, during one week, Häagen-Dazs was second only to *Terminator 1* as Blockbuster's biggest money-spinner. During the sales drive, some supermarket chains had turned Häagen-Dazs down, refusing to believe that their customers would buy such an expensive product. Once the advertising campaign had started, however, the same stores phoned up asking for the product. Clearly the distribution growth was both a cause and an effect of the rising demand.

Most important of all, in judging the effectiveness of the launch marketing strategy, was that sales and distribution not only went up but stayed up. Many products are highly sensitive to changes in marketing spending, with sales jumping up but then falling back once the advertising campaign or special offer has ended. The marketing triumph of Häagen-Dazs was that customer loyalty built up so quickly. In America it had taken 20 years to achieve what Häagen-Dazs UK managed in two.

Sources: Biss Lancaster; Häagen-Dazs Report by Nick Kendall at BBH; Häagen-Dazs UK

Questions
(60 marks; 90 minutes)

1 Discuss the importance of the role of market research in the success of Häagen-Dazs. **(12 marks)**

2 Assess the strengths and weaknesses of the price level decided on by Häagen-Dazs UK. **(10 marks)**

3 a Interpret the information provided by the graph within the text. **(8 marks)**

  b The graph compares sales with advertising. Explain what other factors should be taken into account before drawing conclusions about the effect of the advertising upon sales. **(8 marks)**

4 a What might be the key factors determining the level of brand loyalty enjoyed by a product? **(6 marks)**

  b What benefits could Häagen-Dazs derive from high brand loyalty? **(6 marks)**

5 Discuss whether it is ethical to promote an ice cream through sexy advertising. **(10 marks)**

MARKETING MYOPIA

A2
MARKETING

CONCEPTS NEEDED:

Marketing objectives/strategy

'**I**t was rather obvious, really.'

These five words infuriated Michelle more than any others; <u>not</u> a smart move by James on their first date. She had just gone through a short explanation of the triumph that had given her the promotion to Marketing Controller by the unusually young age of 27. Uniprocter plc was famous for many things, but young stars was not one of them.

Michelle's triumph came as brand manager of Clinadent toothpaste. The brand's key consumer proposition was 'Fight plaque with Clinadent', which had earned it an 8% share of the £1.5 billion European market for toothpaste. She had managed the brand well, but her breakthrough came after reading the classic article by Theodore Levitt on 'Marketing Myopia'. It made her think hard about her job.

Maybe she wasn't really in the toothpaste business at all. Perhaps she was in the oral care business. In which case, how else could Clinadent's anti-plaque proposition be carried to the consumer? Toothbrushes had already been tried, but what about chewing gum? An anti-plaque chewing gum. It would bring Uniprocter head-to-head with Wrigley's,

and its famous 90% share of the chewing gum market. A quick check revealed that the European market for chewing gum was a thumping £2 billion per year. Surely this was worth fighting for.

Michelle's bosses were hard to persuade, but after qualitative research and detailed product development, the project looked encouraging. Yet how could distribution be achieved? Uniprocter's sales muscle was focused upon grocery, supermarket and department stores. Chewing gum sales were primarily impulse sales through outlets such as sweetshops (UK), bars (France and Italy) plus garages, cinemas and a series of other localised markets. Michelle's solution was to contact a multinational rival that was already selling into these impulse outlets, but had no chewing gum product. For a commission worth 20% of the wholesale price, it would distribute the Uniprocter gum.

Six months of hard work were still needed before Clinex Protex chewing gum was launched into the Italian market, with immediate success. Michelle had budgeted for a 3% share of the £250 million Italian chewing gum market after three months, but the actual achievement was 5%. And there was no cannibalisation of existing sales; in fact, the new gum was bought by younger consumers who then tended to switch to Clinadent toothpaste. Launch advertising spending of £3 million left a big hole in the first year profits, but the exceptionally high gross margins of 80% allowed Clinex Protex to break even within nine months.

The roll-out of Clinex Protex to Germany and France was equally successful. Michelle's progress up the Uniprocter career ladder was assured. Yet there was still a problem for Michelle; too many people underestimated her achievement because they thought it was 'so obvious' a diversification. She was determined to break the Uniprocter glass ceiling by becoming its first female Marketing Director. But that would need a more radical success.

She should not have been so indiscreet, but she started to blurt out her new idea to James. She visualised a whole range of Clinadent confectionery, starting with mints, then moving to a chewy fruit, then to boiled sweets and perhaps even to chocolate. These would be great-tasting, sugar-free sweets that cleaned your teeth! She envisaged launching Clinex Protex into the vast American market for chewing gum, then following up with the confectionery range. Markets worth over $12 billion beckoned.

Fortunately for Michelle, James was gentleman enough to appreciate the need for secrecy. Indeed his thoughts on possible consumer resistance proved valuable, as he had lived in New York for five years. His local business knowledge also enabled him to warn Michelle of the ferocious competitive battle she would have to expect from US confectionery manufacturers. Not that this put Michelle off; Uniprocter was too big a business to be frightened by competition – as long as the consumer proposition was strong enough.

Appendix A: Actual data on Clinex Protex chewing gum

Market	Market share after three months	Local market size (per annum)	Local retail margins (retail profit as a % of retail selling price)
Italy	5.0%	£250 million	50%
France	4.5%	£290 million	60%
Germany	5.8%	£380 million	50%
UK (forecast)	5.0%	£220 million	40%

Questions
(60 marks; 75 minutes)

1 Examine two marketing problems Uniprocter is likely to face
when competing with Wrigley's 90% market share. **(10 marks)**

2 a Use Appendix A to calculate the value to Uniprocter of
Clinex Protex annual sales in Italy. **(6 marks)**

b Use the data in the text to calculate the net profits from
these sales, after taking into account the gross profit
margins and the cost of advertising. **(6 marks)**

3 Discuss the advantages and disadvantages of Michelle's
market strategy of diversification. **(12 marks)**

4 a If Uniprocter could achieve a 4% share of the US market for
gum and confectionery, at net profit margins of 10%, how
much profit would that represent per annum? **(6 marks)**

b Given the low market share, the product range might still
be regarded as a 'problem child'. What does this imply in
terms of the marketing approach that should be taken
towards the range? **(8 marks)**

5 Michelle has decided on a cost-plus pricing policy for the new
confectionery range. To what extent may this put at risk the
success of the new range? **(12 marks)**

14 THE MARKETING PLAN

A2
MARKETING

CONCEPTS NEEDED:

Marketing budget, Marketing plan, Market penetration

The launch of the low interest rate Visa card had been a great success. Rarely had a new financial product from a small bank caused such a stir. All the newspapers covered the story and it even received a mention on BBC TV News. The media story was simple: if Brooklyn Bank could offer a credit card charging an annual interest rate of 10%, why were the big banks charging 20%? Many suspected that it was a case of **market**

penetration by the Brooklyn Bank and that the interest rate would rise later on. The company assured its customers that this was not so.

Three months after the launch, with the £120,000 advertising campaign completed, Bill Stein – the UK Banking Director – conducted a review. His sales target had been for 100,000 customers, a modest share of the 16 million credit cardholders in Britain. In the event 320,000 people contacted Brooklyn for an application form; half were converted into customers. Their rate of usage of the card enabled him to estimate a gross profit of £20 per customer per year.

One week before, he had commissioned a report from his data processing section to analyse all the customer application forms. This provided a full demographic breakdown – valuable material to help construct a marketing plan for the next two years.

Bill's first task was to clarify his objectives. Brooklyn had started up in the UK with one branch to service American customers in the

Extracts from breakdown of customer demographics

Age breakdown		Social class (occupation)	
Category	**%**	**Category**	**%**
18–24	3	AB	40
25–34	23	C1	38
35–44	38	C2	18
45–54	24	DE	4
55+	12		

City of London. The successful launch of the Visa card provided a foothold among ordinary British consumers. This enabled him to consider two types of goal:

1 customer targets for the Visa card, such as 250,000 within two years;

2 targets for developing new products for the customer list built up by the Visa card, such as selling pension plans.

After discussion with his marketing manager and advertising agency, a decision was made to concentrate on the Visa card for the coming year, then develop new products the year after. This would prevent his limited staff resources being spread too thinly, and should ensure continuation of the successful start made by the credit card. He was able, therefore, to produce this brief statement of Brooklyn's marketing objective for the coming year:

'**T**o gain 5,000 new customers per month, with minimal losses of existing customers, in order to achieve an average of 190,000 customers during the coming year.'

Having identified the objective, Bill next worked out the marketing budget. His American parent company's rule of thumb was that marketing expenditure should be set at 10% of the expected annual gross profit. A quick calculation persuaded him that he could not afford television advertising, so he decided to focus upon upmarket (broadsheet) newspapers.

Before further planning, Bill had to tackle a classic problem of advertising strategy: should he focus upon coverage or repetition? With a limited budget, if he used all the broadsheet dailies and Sundays he could afford no more than one advertisement every two months. By advertising only in the *Daily Telegraph* he could cover some 42% of the target market once a week for a whole year. After much thought, he decided that his product's **unique selling point** (USP) was so strong as to make repetition less important than coverage.

Bill's final major decision concerned distribution. Should he be relying solely on advertising plus word of mouth to bring in new customers, or would it be wise to get a distribution outlet such as Independent

Financial Advisers (IFAs) and accountants, or building societies too small to have their own credit card? He spent a week taking IFAs and building society bosses out to lunch. This convinced him of the enthusiasm of these potential distributors, but also made it clear that their commissions would take half the gross profit margin on the cards they sold. In addition, they would expect Brooklyn to provide the brochures and **point-of-sale** display materials to encourage consumer interest.

Questions
(50 marks; 70 minutes)

1 Explain the meaning of the following terms (in bold print in the text):
market penetration
unique selling point
point-of-sale   (**9 marks**)

2 Outline the importance to a business of obtaining a full demographic breakdown of its customers.   (**7 marks**)

3 What should be Brooklyn Bank UK's marketing budget for the coming year? State your assumptions.   (**10 marks**)

4 Prepare a sales and marketing plan for the Brooklyn Visa card for the coming six months, based on the evidence in the case. You will need to explain your decisions about how to proceed in the footnotes to your plan. The plan should show your sales targets, distribution plans, advertising bursts and below-the-line activity.   (**24 marks**)

PRICE ELASTICITY AND PROFITS

A2
MARKETING

CONCEPTS NEEDED:

Price elasticity, Fixed costs per unit, Contribution, Profit

The success of the low calorie chocolate sector amazed everyone in the industry. It had started so weakly, with a 100 calorie bar with whipped nougat filling, topped with crispy rice and covered in milk chocolate. Produced by a small firm from Finland, it received good distribution from a curious retail trade, but achieved less than a 0.5% **market share**. When one of the biscuit companies managed a successful launch, however, the three dominant chocolate firms (Mars, Cadbury's, and Rowntree/Nestlé) felt they had to protect their 90% market share.

In the first year after the three major firms launched their low calorie chocolate bars, supply shortages kept prices high. Then, a series of new product launches made the marketplace increasingly competitive. One firm found that whereas a 2 pence price increase from 40 pence in the first year had cut demand by only 1%, 18 months later a similar price rise on a 40 pence brand called

Lo led to a sales reduction from 50,000 units a week to 45,000. Given that its variable costs were 10 pence per unit, and fixed costs were £13,000 per week, this had quite a serious impact on the brand's profits.

In this new phase, the producers realised they had to look to improve their profitability by cutting costs rather than increasing prices. With low enough costs, they might even be able to increase profits by cutting their prices. Because **contribution** was already so high, most producers started by looking at ways of cutting their fixed and **semi-variable costs**. Only one decided to tackle variable costs first, on the grounds that:

'**A**s fixed costs don't change, it must make sense to look for cuts from the variables.'

The Finnish originator of the market sector found that its sales slipped back sharply.

Its new Managing Director was alarmed to find that average total cost per unit was now 4 pence higher than its average selling price, leading to a £4,000 loss per week on its sales of 100,000 units. When a Marketing Manager came with a proposal to double sales by improving distribution, he spluttered:

'**D**on't be ridiculous; that'll just double our losses!'

Questions
(50 marks; 60 minutes)

1 Explain the meaning of the following terms (in bold print in the text):
   a market share
   b contribution
   c semi-variable costs   **(9 marks)**

2 Explain two actions that could be taken to reduce fixed costs in such a way that sales are not affected.   **(8 marks)**

3 Outline three factors that could lead to an increase in the average price elasticity of products within a particular market sector.   **(9 marks)**

4 a Calculate the price elasticity of the chocolate in the first year and compare it with that of the brand called Lo.   **(7 marks)**
   b Work out precisely the serious impact on Lo's profits.   **(7 marks)**

5 Analyse the comments made by the producer and the Finnish Managing Director.   **(10 marks)**

A SMALL BUSINESS START-UP

AS
FINANCE

CONCEPTS NEEDED:

Distribution, Market research, Cash flow forecast, Break even

'He'll never give it to us,' said Michael glumly. Jane agreed that 17 year olds could hardly expect to get a £1,000 bank loan, but she was determined to try. They sat nervously in the bank manager's waiting room, avoiding looking at each other.

Since leaving school, they had both put so much work into their business plan that it was impossible to believe they might have to abandon it. Both had worked to save £750 in a year, so £1,000 from the bank would give them the £2,500 they needed as start-up capital.

From their homes in Surbiton they planned on serving the wealthy homes of Weybridge and Esher with a Dewfresh Flower Delivery door-to-door service. Mike knew the routines of the New Covent Garden wholesale market, and realised that he could buy boxes of Grade One daffodils for £20 per 100 bunches, which could be sold to customers for 90 pence per bunch.

They had worked out their fixed costs at £1,000 per month, and had conducted a survey of 100 adults in Esher and Weybridge. From this they estimated that they would get 2,000 orders per month, with an average value of £5 per order. As the variable costs should amount to only £2 per order, this seemed promising.

As part of their preparations for their visit to the bank, Jane had worked out a cash flow forecast. This showed that they would have used up all the £2,500 by month two, but profits should bring money in after that. Jane's main worry was that customers would want to receive some credit.

Then a door opened and they were ushered in ...

Questions
(50 marks; 60 minutes)

1 Develop two reasons why Mike and Jane might be better off obtaining supplies from a wholesale market, instead of directly from the flower producers. **(6 marks)**

2 Explain three reasons why their market research survey might prove inaccurate. **(9 marks)**

3 Why was Jane worried about customers wanting to receive credit? **(4 marks)**

4 Draw a break-even chart based on the figures given. Assume that the highest number of orders they could cope with is 2,500 per month. Plot fixed costs, total costs, and total revenue. **(9 marks)**

5 Assuming orders do start at a rate of 2,000 per month, outline three reasons why they may decline in following months. **(9 marks)**

6 If disappointing sales cause only 1,000 orders per month, what profit or loss will they make? Show your workings. **(5 marks)**

7 Discuss how they might promote their new service, to ensure that people in their target market get to hear about it. **(8 marks)**

BOMBAY PIZZA

AS
FINANCE

CONCEPTS NEEDED:

Cash flow forecasts

I t was when Sunil Tanna's daughter went out with a group of Indian friends for a pizza that it struck him. In his business trips to Bombay he had never seen a pizza outlet there. If Indian teenagers liked pizza in Birmingham, why not in Bombay?

Three weeks later, while making a January visit to India for his air conditioning company, he stayed on for an extra couple of days' 'holiday'. He quickly confirmed that there was no pizza outlet in the Bombay telephone directory and spent the rest of his time researching the prices of comparable fast foods, wage rates, locations and the availability of ingredients. Sunil considered the £400 it cost as money well spent.

The following month he identified a British supplier of pizza dough making machines and conveyor-belt ovens (which cook the pizza in three minutes and ensure that the pizza cannot burn). In total this capital equipment would cost £12,800 on delivery in Bombay, though transport charges plus Indian import tariffs would push this up to £18,000. His month's expenses were £200.

In March Sunil paid a professional chef £2,400 to devise eight pizza recipes suitable for Bombay (four vegetarian). In each case the chef drew up cards that set out precisely the method of preparation and cooking. Sunil would have to hire a good manager to run the first outlet, but he did not want to have to find (or fly out) an experienced pizza cook.

Luck did not provide a further business trip to India, so he had to pay for his own flight to Bombay to acquire a site in a busy, middle class area of the city. His strategy was to pitch his pizza prices at around Western levels, making the decor Chicago/Italian-American, using the brand name Al Capone's Pizza. This would cash in on Indian awareness of Hollywood gangster films. The site he chose required an initial payment amounting to £800, plus £200 a month rent starting immediately. All in, Sunil's April travel expenses came to £1,600.

While in Bombay in April, Sunil arranged for the design and refitting of the site to turn it into a Chicago pizza restaurant. This was completed during May at a cost of £8,000. He also hired a manager whose salary of £600 per annum commenced at the start of June. The manager immediately hired staff at the following monthly rates:

cook : £25*
2 waitresses : £15 each
delivery driver : £10
cleaner : £5

Once a delivery motorbike had been bought for £200 in early June, everything was in place for the start of the staff training programme. Unfortunately a combination of supplier and Customs delays meant that the pizza machinery turned up only in July. It was installed, tested, and did not work. It emerged that it needed a power adaptor which was ordered from England. That added £400 to the cost of the machinery, which was now due to be paid.

At last, in August, everything was ready and with £500 spent on local advertising, Al Capone's Pizza opened to a large, curious crowd. The average customer spend proved to be £5 at a cost of sales of £2. This would need to cover the monthly overheads of £680 plus the rent and wages of £320 per month.

Monthly customer figures	
August	1,600
September	1,200
October	1,100
November	900
December	800
January	900
February	1,000
March	1,200
April and onwards, a monthly average of	1,200

*Although the wage rates in this case seem incredibly low, they are exactly as researched by the real Mr Tanna.

Questions
(45 marks; 70 minutes)

1 Construct a cash flow forecast for the first 12 months of the business, that is from January–December. State any assumptions you consider necessary. **(15 marks)**

2 Discuss how a business such as Mr Tanna's might benefit from constructing a cash flow forecast before starting on a new project. **(12 marks)**

3 **a** How do you think that Mr Tanna developed his business next? **(8 marks)**
  b Evaluate the problems he may face in the near future. **(10 marks)**

RACE AGAINST TIME

AS
FINANCE

CONCEPTS NEEDED:

Break even, Raising capital, Cash flow

Both his parents had been shocked at the thought, but Doug had no doubts. He wanted to start up his own manufacturing business, making gearboxes. They argued about the long term decline of British manufacturing, the problems of the motor industry and the fluctuating foreign exchange value of the pound, but Doug would not be deflected. As he said, it was not as if he was going to make just *any* gearboxes. Rover Cars might struggle, but Formula 1 was booming.

Through the friend of a friend, Doug had been lucky enough to get a job straight from school as a track assistant for the Benetton Ford motor racing team. Over the years, through his love of the sport and some hard work at evening classes, he had become a qualified engineer. He specialised in maintenance and repair of gearboxes for Formula 1 cars.

Three years ago he was poached by Eddie Jordan to become the Head of Maintenance Engineering on the Jordan racing team. The experience had been fantastic, but now he yearned to start up on his own. Fortunately he had been able to talk it over with Eddie Jordan, whose entrepreneurial instincts made him sympathetic. The Jordan team had been suffering from some supply problems with gearboxes, so it seemed sensible to consider starting up as the world's one and only specialised gearbox manufacturer for racing cars. A friend worked at Companies House and checked for Doug that the company name D.B. Racing Gear Ltd was available.

Doug spent six weeks putting together a carefully costed plan. To be successful, his business would need to have state-of-the-art computer controlled machinery, a complete Computer Aided Design suite plus some very highly skilled staff. The most expensive machine (£760,000) could be leased for £16,000 per month, but £360,000 of equipment would need to be paid for up front. In addition, the factory unit Doug had in mind would cost £60,000 to convert, plus monthly rent and rates of £9,000. In the long run, the biggest cost by far would be staff. Doug felt he had to allow a monthly salary bill of £25,000 for a staff of 15.

With a sport as rich as the multi-billion pound Formula 1, start-up venture capital proved quite easy to find. Doug had £120,000 and he found three other investors willing to invest the same, in exchange for a 16% stake each. Even NatWest proved helpful, offering a £100,000 loan and an overdraft facility of £80,000 – both backed by the security of the £360,000 of brand new machinery. If Doug's business failed, the bank would seize these assets, leaving the ordinary shareholders with very few assets to back their investment. Doug wondered whether to press the bank for a larger loan, but decided against.

The key to success would be sales income and therefore cash inflow. He knew that Jordan and two Formula 3 teams were keen to give him orders. They knew the gearboxes would take four months to produce and were prepared to pay instalments of 10% in each of the four months, with the remaining 60% coming in month six. This delayed payment would give them time to make sure of the quality of the workmanship. The total value of the three orders was £600,000, making it possible for the first six months of Doug's business to run at a profit (see Appendix A).

Having completed his calculations, Doug met the three potential investors, to persuade them to turn their promises into cheques. When shown the cash flow table, one of the investors was concerned: 'Doug, we start out with £580,000 but end the period with only £245,000. How can we be making a profit?' Fortunately one of the other investors was an accountant, who could explain the difference between cash flow and profit.

Convinced, the three plus Doug wrote out cheques totalling £480,000 to D.B. Racing Gear Ltd, then shared a bottle of ice cold champagne. A frantic month spent recruiting staff and organising deliveries ensured that the business was ready for start of work on the first Monday of month 1. Now the race was on to complete the first orders within the contracted, four month production period.

Appendix A: Forecast revenue, costs and profit for months 1–6

Revenue £600,000	Materials	£40,000
	Fixed overhead costs:	
	Labour	£150,000
	Machinery and property	£150,000
	Depreciation on assets bought	£36,000
	Interest	£5,000
	Other overhead costs	£120,000
	Total costs	£501,000

Appendix B: Cash flow forecast (not yet complete)

	0	1	2	3	4	5	6
Start-up finance	£580,000						
Cash in from customers		£60,000					
Start-up outlays:							
Machinery purchases	£360,000						
Other start-up costs	£60,000						
Monthly cash outflows:							
Variable material costs*	£8,000	£8,000					
Labour costs	£25,000	£25,000					
Machinery lease	£16,000	£16,000					
Property rent & rates	£9,000	£9,000					
Interest							
Other monthly outlays:		£20,000					
TOTAL CASH OUT	£478,000	£78,000					
NET CASH FLOW	(£478,000)	(£18,000)					
Balance b/down**	£102,000	£84,000					£245,000

*Bought for cash in the month before production

**This is the accumulated cash flow, i.e. the forecast bank account total (or overdraft) for the end of the month

Questions
(60 marks; 70 minutes)

1 Doug raised £580,000 of start-up capital: £480,000 in share capital and £100,000 as loan capital.

  a Why may Doug have decided against pressing NatWest for a larger loan? **(8 marks)**

  b Outline the main risks being faced by the venture capital investors. **(8 marks)**

2 **a** Copy out the cash flow table, filling in the data for months 2–6. State at least two assumptions you are making. Check that your month 6 total equals £245,000. **(10 marks)**

  b Consider the implications for D.B. Racing Gear Ltd of production delays resulting in the final customer payment being delayed by a month. **(10 marks)**

3 Explain why a company can suffer a fall in its cash flow position even when it is making a profit. **(8 marks)**

4 For the second six months, Doug is hoping for double the level of orders. He believes he can supply that with the same staff and facilities he has at the moment.

  a Calculate the profit he would make in those circumstances. **(6 marks)**

  b Draw a graph showing revenue, fixed costs, variable costs and total costs, marking clearly the profit made at £600,000 of revenue and £1,200,000 of revenue. **(10 marks)**

CREDIT FACTORING

AS
FINANCE

CONCEPTS NEEDED:

Factoring, Cash flow

SiteCo is a site investigation company. It is hired by property developers to test the soil structure on a site, to see if it is suitable to build on.

The firm started five years ago with two Directors/engineers working from one of their houses. They now employ six staff and have acquired an office and a laboratory. The company's development can be seen from the following record:

	Sales turnover £	Profit £
Year 1	16,835	174
Year 2	27,348	5,336
Year 3	82,488	1,536
Year 4	142,540	16,102
Year 5	251,310	44,531

Although delighted with their recent progress, the Directors were frustrated that they could not generate enough cash to buy the equipment they needed to cope with their expansion. So, for example, they had to subcontract sulphate testing, which was expensive and time consuming, as an average of four trips were needed per week to the outside lab. At present the testing was costing them £175 per week. This would be cut to £25 per week if they could find the £6,000 needed to buy the machine. However, this was just one among many pieces of capital expenditure that seemed pressing, and it had to join the queue.

All rapidly growing firms have a strained cash flow position, but the particular cause of SiteCo's difficulties was the Directors' inefficiency with paperwork. Both enjoyed the testing work, and the relationship with their customers, but neither liked dealing with administration or the job of chasing late payers. So the busier they were, the more reasons they found for not processing the paperwork. As a result, the last time they checked they were owed £60,000 by customers.

Now, rather than going to their bank manager to ask for their overdraft limit to be increased, they called in a management consultant. After a few days of investigation, she concluded that there was no point in looking for a solution that would have to be implemented by the current staff. Nor could she believe that the appointment of a Credit Controller would be worth the expense, as it would still be essential for the Directors to cooperate fully with the administrative system. Hence her recommendation that SiteCo should use the Credit Factoring service of one of the major banks. She suggested that they should use the full service, including 80% of invoiced amounts paid within 24 hours; sales invoice management and analysis; debt collection; and insurance against bad debts. This service would result in a charge amounting to 5% of sales turnover.

Both Directors loved the idea of someone else being responsible for debt collection, especially as their business was so dependent on good relationships with clients. Yet the cost did concern them, so they needed to be convinced that the cash flow benefit would be large enough to enable them to make several of the cost saving investments they had planned.

Based on their sales forecast of £360,000 in the coming year, and on their current three month lag between invoicing and receiving payment, the consultant made a back-of-the-envelope calculation. She estimated an immediate cash benefit of £72,000, being whittled down to £54,000 in the following 12 months. That reassured the Directors fully, so after the bank had made the necessary checks into SiteCo and its customers, the new system became operational. Within a month both Directors were convinced that it was a great success.

Questions
(50 marks; 60 minutes)

1 On the basis of the information given, how many weeks would it take for the purchase of the sulphate testing machine to pay for itself? **(7 marks)**

2 Explain why 'all rapidly growing firms have a strained cash flow position'. **(8 marks)**

3 Outline three ways in which SiteCo's Directors might benefit from using the service of sales invoice management and analysis. **(9 marks)**

4 Attempt to reproduce the management consultant's 'back-of-the-envelope' calculation of the cash generated by factoring. **(8 marks)**

5 Identify three types of firm that would probably not find factoring worthwhile. Explain why. **(9 marks)**

6 Analyse the effects upon the cash flow of a firm of a decision to stop using the services of a Factor. **(9 marks)**

THE FURNITURE SHOP

AS
FINANCE

CONCEPTS NEEDED:

Profit, Cash flow

Harrogate Furniture Ltd was as well established as the town itself. After 100 years of trading, however, the owners were very concerned about its future. New furniture multiples such as DFS were taking business away. Recently, sales of £100,000 a month had to cover fixed overheads of £50,000 plus the cost of buying in furniture from the suppliers. Pricing was on the basis of marking up variable costs by 100%.

The family owners of Harrogate Furniture Ltd (HFL) were very gloomy about the future, but Katie, the young manager of Sofas and Chairs, refused to admit defeat. She came up with three different ideas for boosting demand and then carried out a survey of 80 existing and past customers. One idea proved the best by far: offering customers three months' interest-free credit on all purchases. This should double sales!

The owners were delighted by the findings, especially when they calculated the effect on profit. They were all set to start the offer when, by chance, they had their annual lunch with their bank manager. When they explained the offer, the bank manager did some quick cash flow calculations on his napkin. He pushed the napkin across the table and the owners went white. Later the manager was to joke that the £50 lunch bill was the best investment they had ever made. He asked how much cash they had in the bank at the moment; they replied £50,000. There and then they came to an agreement about an overdraft facility to tide the business over the next months.

On 1 February the offer started. It worked exactly as Katie's forecast had suggested, generating sales of £200,000 per month. After five months, the owners decided to stop the offer, so from 1 July, sales dropped back to £100,000. Now they could sit back and consider what to do next.

Questions
(60 marks; 75 minutes)

1 a Calculate the monthly profit being made by HFL before
      the offer was started.   **(4 marks)**

   b Calculate the monthly profit when sales doubled to
      £200,000 per month.   **(4 marks)**

2 Katie's research had a sample size of only 80, yet the findings
   proved very accurate. Discuss why this might have occurred. **(10 marks)**

3 a Work out the bank manager's cash flow forecast for HFL,
      using the format set out below. For now, just work through
      to the end of June.   **(12 marks)**

£000

	Jan	Feb	Mar	Apr	May	June	July	Aug	Sept	Oct
Cash at start										
Cash in										
Cash out										
Net monthly cash flow										
Cumulative cash										

   b Now complete your cash flow forecast with the figures for
      July to October, based upon the offer ending in June.   **(8 marks)**

4 Draw a line graph to show cumulative cash and cumulative
   profit over the period January to October. Label the graph
   carefully, then shade in the area that indicates the difference
   between profit and cash flow.   **(14 marks)**

5 Using the graph and the rest of the evidence available,
   explain the importance of distinguishing clearly between
   cash flow and profit.   **(8 marks)**

PLASTICAN LTD

CONCEPTS NEEDED:

Budgeting, Cost and profit centres

Like many instinctive entrepreneurs, Paul and Jo Granger have a knack for spotting a business opportunity. Theirs is the production and sale of plastic containers, which are used to hold many products, ranging from shampoo to soft drinks. With no great originality they named their company Plastican, on the basis that it says what they are and make.

In some ways the production of the containers is a nightmare. Some have twist tops, some screw tops; some are tiny, whilst others can hold half a litre of liquid; some have a protective cover inside the top, whilst others don't. Although such diversity creates

production problems, it makes it a dream for salespeople. Paul, the company's salesman, is able to go from one manufacturer to the next, not only taking orders, but also suggesting other areas where Plastican containers might be used. This dynamic relationship between salesman and client is something Paul is keen to encourage, because he believes that it is their best protection against the competition. As he often says: 'They might be able to match us on price, but not on creativity.'

Unfortunately, Paul's enthusiasm for variety is not always matched back in the factory, where Jo's organisational ability is under increasing stress. She has room for six product lines, each making a different-sized container. Within each one she has some flexibility in terms of the type of top that will go on, but every time the top is changed, the line workers have to reset the machine. This takes time and so loses valuable output, not only during the change but also immediately afterwards, when quality checks show more errors. It also upsets the workers, whose morale drops the more machine alterations and resettings there are. Indeed it was the workers who eventually prompted Jo to tackle Paul on the issue of production.

'Listen, Paul,' she said, 'We're making too many different products. Because we lose so much time and production every time we change over, we can't be making much of a profit on some of them. I know your concern about our 'dynamic relationship with customers' but now it's time for a change. The business has just grown and grown and we've been happy for that to happen because we've been making a pretty good living out of it. But we must introduce more controls. I suggest we need to identify and introduce cost and profit centres, so that we know exactly where we stand.'

'I do accept that we need to have more information, if only so I can promote our most profitable lines more than the others,' replied Paul. 'But in the long term we've got to make sure the customers are happy. What do you suggest?'

'It seems to me that because we can work out the costs and the revenue from selling each type of container made on different production lines, we can make each of the six lines a profit centre. My idea is that we promote one of the people on each of the lines and make them responsible for production on that line. After a few weeks we can set targets for each one and start paying bonuses if the targets are exceeded.'

'And what about changing settings for different tops?'

'Initially we continue production as at present, but compare the profitability of each line depending on the number of changes they have to make. Then we will have a more precise indication of the cost of changing, compared to the benefits of selling a wider range.'

'Well, that's all very fine, but what about my role as salesman? I don't actually make any profit directly, and what about our two administrators and our cleaning and maintenance staff?'

'Well, we'll just make these head office expenses into a cost centre, then we'll have to find a way of allocating these costs, as well as others like heating, lighting, insurance and so on. At this point the simplest thing would be to take all of them and divide them equally between the six profit centres.'

'That makes sense,' Paul responded. 'Anything else?'

'Well, yes, there is actually. At the same time I also think we should do something about controlling our costs through budgets.'

'We've already got budgets,' said Paul slightly wearily. 'I know I have.'

Jo made a face in response and then replied: 'Come on, Paul, you've got a budget for your petrol and other expenses, but if you under-spend or over-spend, what do we do about it? Nothing. We either say "great" or "boo-hoo", but we never ask why. And this applies across the entire factory. We know that raw material costs went up last year, but was that simply because we produced more, or did the price go up across the board or just from one supplier, or what? We need to break down our activities and then produce monthly budgets for each. Then when we have either a positive or a negative variance we will be in a better position to take some action.'

'Sounds like a lot of work to me,' said Paul.

'Yes,' replied Jo, 'Setting budgets is never easy, and because we've never done it before we won't have last year's to go on. Perhaps we should start with zero budgeting, what do you think?'

'I think I'd better put my golf clubs away for a while,' replied Paul, only half jokingly.

Twelve months later, and Plastican has reduced its product range to 12 different-sized containers, each with a maximum of two types of top. Of these combinations, eight containers have been found to be the most profitable and Paul is amazed to find that his 'dynamic relationship' with his customers often leads him to suggest the adoption of one of these eight! Profits have risen by 48% over the year, helped by costs which overall fell by 7%. Levels of absenteeism have fallen, as have recruitment costs.

Manufacturing budget, Plastican Ltd – Year to 31 August

	Budget	Actual
	£000	£000
Raw materials	70.0	55.0
Direct labour	140.0	145.0
Direct expenses	2.5	2.0
Total direct costs	**212.5**	**202.0**
Rent	10.0	10.0
Maintenance	5.2	6.1
Heating/lighting	2.8	2.6
Maintenance wages	22.0	20.3
Other factory overheads	11.0	11.5
Total factory overheads	**51.0**	**50.5**
Total factory costs	**263.5**	**252.5**

Questions
(50 marks; 70 minutes)

1 **a** Explain the meaning of the term 'direct costs'. **(3 marks)**

b Both the raw materials and the direct labour costs varied from the budget. Offer one possible reason why in each case. **(4 marks)**

2 **a** What do you understand by the term 'zero budgeting'? **(2 marks)**

b Give two reasons in favour and two against setting zero budgets. **(4 marks)**

3 **a** Calculate the adverse and favourable variances for Plastican Ltd in each of the categories in the firm's manufacturing budget. **(10 marks)**

b Why is it likely that Plastican's variances will reduce in future years? **(5 marks)**

4 **a** Describe the state of morale amongst the production line workers before the introduction of the profit centres. **(6 marks)**

b Explain how establishing cost and profit centres may have helped to improve morale. **(10 marks)**

5 What do you think is meant by the sentence: 'Of these combinations, eight containers have been found to be the most profitable and Paul is amazed to find that his 'dynamic relationship' with his customers often leads him to suggest the adoption of one of these eight!' **(6 marks)**

BUDGETING IN HARROGATE

AS
FINANCE

CONCEPTS NEEDED:

Budgeting, Variance statements

Cleeton is a long established family firm based in Harrogate, Yorkshire. Its production of ropes and cables began in 1863 and has changed little since then. The only striking change in recent years has been the appointment of a young Finance Director, given the task of masterminding a steady increase in the firm's profitability.

Last December he brought in a new computerised budgeting system to provide managers with a monthly print-out of actual, compared with forecast, revenues and costs. At the same time, he encouraged the Sales Director to introduce a more flexible pricing policy, allowing sales representatives to offer discounts in order to get business.

Now, in April, he is reviewing his initiatives at the monthly Board meeting:

'**O**ur policy changes have been working very well. Sales are up, market share is up and profits are up ... Our new budgeting system has been especially successful, encouraging staff to keep costs down (though variable costs, I am delighted to say, have been pushed up by our buoyant sales level). With the economy of our major export market, Germany, so strong at the moment, the future looks very bright.'

Other Board members, still unfamiliar with the format of the budgeting spreadsheet, could only nod their approval.

Budget and variance statement – Cleeton Ltd

£000

	January *B	A	V	February B	A	V	March B	A	V
Sales revenue	80	92	12	100	110	10	120	122	#
Materials	40	48	(8)	50	57	(7)	60	63	#
Other direct costs	10	12	(2)	13	15	(2)	15	17	#
Overheads	20	21	(1)	24	24	–	27	24	#
Profit	10	11	1	13	14	1	18	#	#
Year to date	10	11	1	23	25	2	41	#	#
Profit last year		5			20			40	

*B = Budget   A = Actual   V = Variance

Questions
(40 marks; 60 minutes)

1   What benefits might Cleeton hope to receive from implementing a budgeting system such as the one in the table above? **(9 marks)**

2   Identify and explain the profit variance for January given that sales volume was 15% above budget. **(9 marks)**

3   Calculate the March figures omitted by a computer error. Instead of the numbers, the computer has printed a # symbol. **(8 marks)**

4   To what extent does Cleeton's performance this year justify the Finance Director's statement to his Board of Directors? **(14 marks)**

INVESTMENT DECISION MAKING

A2
FINANCE

CONCEPTS NEEDED:

Average rate of return, Pay-back

Zentek had enjoyed a splendid financial year. At the start it had budgeted for £2.6 million of sales turnover and £1.8 million of direct costs. With £0.4 million of forecast indirect costs it would have produced a £400,000 profit. In fact, with 10 months of the year completed the Managing Director had just found out that the firm had already met sales targets, and she now expected the end of year profits would approach £600,000. This was especially pleasing as she knew that a Japanese competitor's first British plant would be opening within a few months, so it would be useful to have some extra funds in the kitty.

When chatting to the Finance Director about the profit forecast, she also learned that there was still £80,000 left in the capital expenditure budget for this financial year. So a memo was sent to all department heads inviting proposals for the investment of this sum.

The first bid was from the distribution department, which proposed buying four new

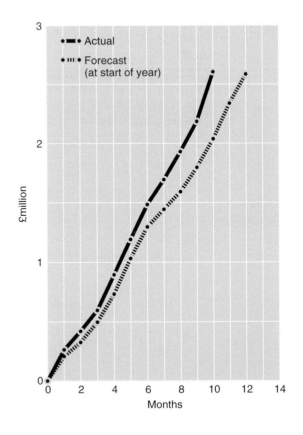

Zentek cumulative sales revenue – forecast and actual

fuel efficient lorries as replacements for eight year old ones. Each would cost £20,000 and should last four years, after which time it would have a second hand value of £4,000. The new lorries should save £8,000 each per year on fuel and maintenance costs.

The only other detailed proposal came from the marketing department, requesting the establishment of a new customer services department. It would cost £80,000 to set up,

and its £20,000-a-year running costs should generate extra contribution from sales amounting to:

Year 1 £20,000   Year 2 £40,000
Year 3 £80,000   Year 4 £80,000

As the year is running out, a speedy decision is needed, so the Managing Director has asked the Finance Director to write a report for tomorrow's senior management meeting.

Questions
(30 marks; 45 minutes)

Taking the role of the Finance Director, write a report to the Managing Director covering:

a which investment is more attractive on financial/numerate grounds alone;

b any further information you would like from each department to help you make a final recommendation.

Mark allocation: **a** 16 marks   **b** 10 marks   **Report format** 4 marks

THE BUSINESS PLAN

A2
FINANCE

CONCEPTS NEEDED:

Cash flow forecasts, Profit and loss accounts, Balance sheets

Fresh from college, Karen could not wait to put her Business Studies theory into practice. Careful saving during her work experience year, plus a £5,000 legacy, meant that she had the £10,000 she thought necessary as **equity capital**. The work year had been at Thomson Holidays and that – plus her love of travel – convinced her to start up a travel agency. Not just any one, mind, for she believed a market gap for adventure travel existed in her home city of Birmingham. She had been taught to make decisions on the basis of evidence, not hunch, so she had tested out and validated her hypothesis over the past two years by visiting every one of the 140 agencies listed in Birmingham's *Yellow Pages.*

Now Karen had to prepare the documentation for the business plan to persuade her bank to lend her the extra **fixed capital** and **working capital** she would need. The keys to this, she knew, were a credible

sales forecast, a cash flow forecast, a projected profit and loss account for the first six months, and an estimated six months' balance sheet. To forecast sales she visited comparable agencies in London, relying on her charm and the lack of threat of competition to persuade someone to volunteer their early sales performance. Two days of being charming yielded the information given below. Karen decided that averaging the figures for all three firms would give her a realistic sales forecast.

The main start-up costs were estimated by her as follows:

Purchase of 5 year lease on shop	£2,500
Fixtures and fittings (to last 4 years)	£6,000
Advertising prior to launch	£3,500

The advertising would be treated as revenue expenditure, and therefore charged in full against the profit and loss account for the first trading period. All the start-up costs would be paid before the start of trading, i.e. in month zero. Fixed assets would be depreciated on a straight-line basis.

Running costs would include the 90% payment of revenue to the tour operator (as travel agents work on a 10% commission), plus overheads amounting to £800 a month. The 90% would be paid to the tour operator in the month after being received from customers. Overheads start in month 0 and must be paid in the month they are incurred.

Sales revenue data for the first year's operation of three adventure travel agencies

	Adventure Hols Streatham	Go-Go Travel Hampstead	Action Vacs Acton	Average of all 3
Month **1**	£2,400	£5,800	£800	**£3,000**
Month **2**	£3,400	£8,200	£2,500	**£4,700**
Month **3**	£5,800	£12,200	£4,800	**£7,600**
Month **4**	£6,400	£16,800	£6,200	**£9,800**
Month **5**	£7,200	£19,100	£7,300	**£11,200**
Month **6**	£7,400	£20,700	£7,900	**£12,000**
Months **7–12**				
Monthly average	£8,000	£23,000	£9,500	**£13,500**

Questions
(60 marks; 90 minutes)

1 Explain the meaning of the following terms (in bold print in the text):
equity capital
fixed capital
working capital   **(9 marks)**

2 **a** Construct a cash flow forecast for months 0–6 on the basis
of the above, assuming that the bank is prepared to grant a
£3,000 medium-term loan (ignore interest charges).   **(14 marks)**

    b What level of overdraft facility appears to be needed (if any)?   **(1 mark)**

    c Outline two alternative methods of raising business finance
that Karen might consider.   **(4 marks)**

3 Draw up a Profit and Loss Account for the period up to the
end of month 6. Then use it, plus the other information
available, to forecast the firm's Balance Sheet for the last day
of this first trading period.   **(20 marks)**

4 Discuss whether Karen should go ahead with the enterprise.   **(12 marks)**

INVESTMENT WITHIN FINANCIAL CONSTRAINTS

A2 FINANCE

CONCEPTS NEEDED:

Published accounts, Financial ratios, Investment appraisal

ScanCo is a medium-sized producer of X-ray machines. Last year its sales were £4.5 million at a gross margin of 60%. It expects sales growth of £0.5 million per year for the coming five years, with gross and net margins staying constant.

ScanCo's Research and Development manager has just come up with a new product idea for a portable scanner that will require an investment outlay of £400,000. Each machine will cost £4,000 to make and will be priced at a 100% mark-up on direct costs. It will be ready for launch at the start of next year. Forecast sales and overheads are given below.

The target market for the new X-ray scanner is the oil industry, to check the accuracy of pipeline welds. The Research and Development manager decided on the sales forecast after discussion with an expert on North Sea oil technology.

ScanCo's Directors must decide whether to approve the £400,000 investment at their next Board meeting.

Year	Sales forecast (units)	Forecast overheads (£000)
Next year	150	600
1 year later	250	700
2 years later	250	750
3 years later	250	750

ScanCo balance sheet Dec 31st	
	£000
Fixed assets	1,900
Stock	450
Debtors & cash	150
Current liabilities	700
Net current assets	(100)
ASSETS EMPLOYED	1,800
Loans	720
Shareholders' funds	1,080
CAPITAL EMPLOYED	1,800

Discount factors		
	4%	6%
Year 1	0.96	0.94
Year 2	0.92	0.89
Year 3	0.89	0.84
Year 4	0.86	0.79
Year 5	0.82	0.75
	8%	10%
Year 1	0.93	0.91
Year 2	0.86	0.83
Year 3	0.79	0.75
Year 4	0.74	0.68
Year 5	0.68	0.62

Questions
(50 marks; 60 minutes)

1 Explain the meaning of the following terms:
overheads
fixed assets
shareholders' funds   (9 marks)

2 a Given that ScanCo's overheads were £1.8 million, what was
the firm's profit and trading profit margin last year?   (6 marks)
   b Comment on the firm's return on capital last year.   (6 marks)

3 a Use two appropriate investment appraisal techniques to
analyse the Research and Development manager's proposal
(stating any necessary assumptions). What would you
recommend purely on the basis of the numerate data available? (18 marks)
   b Discuss what other factors the firm should consider before
making a decision.   (11 marks)

THE STING

A2
FINANCE

CONCEPTS NEEDED:

Published accounts, Financial ratios, Overheads, Working capital

---

Sadaf bought the shares after seeing the company featured on *The Clothes Show*. She had wanted to invest part of the £4,000 inherited from her grandfather, and this company seemed just right. Brilliant clothes designers with shops in all the major high streets, Sting plc was now expanding into Europe. At only 40p each, Sadaf considered the shares a bargain; she bought 2,000.

As the economies of Europe picked up during the spring, Sadaf felt increasingly confident about her investment. When the share price hit 56p in July, she was tempted to sell and enjoy a 40% profit.

Then in August the share price dropped back unexpectedly. Two days later the Chairman issued the following profit warning:

'Poorer than expected trading in Britain plus a disappointing first season in Europe has led to a profit downturn. I remain convinced that our move into Europe will be in the long term interests of your company. Full details will be available in the interim accounts, to be published within two weeks.**'**

By the time the accounts arrived in the post, Sting shares were quoted at just 18p.

Sadaf wondered whether to sell while her investment still had some value. So she looked at the accounts with great interest. Did the company's finances look strong enough to survive a period of poor trading, while still expanding into Europe?

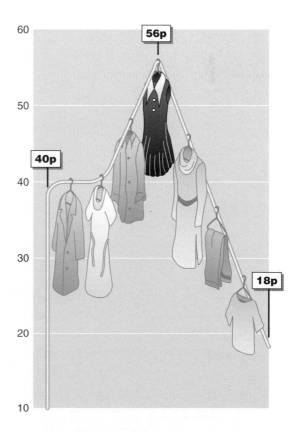

Interim accounts for Sting plc, Jan–Jun (unaudited)

Profit and loss account		Balance sheet (June 30th)	
	£m		£m
Sales turnover	34	Property	16
Cost of sales	26	Machinery	4
GROSS PROFIT	8	Vehicles	4
Overheads	10	Stock	6.5
TRADING PROFIT	(2)	Debtors	4.5
		Cash	1
Taxation	3		
NET PROFIT	(5)	Current liabilities	11
Dividends	1	Working capital	1
RETAINED PROFIT	(6)	ASSETS EMPLOYED	25
		Loans	15
Note: Issued share capital of 50 million 10p shares		Shareholders' funds	10
		CAPITAL EMPLOYED	25

Questions
(50 marks; 70 minutes)

1 What might Sadaf conclude about the short term financial health of Sting plc from these accounts? **(9 marks)**

2 A recent newspaper article mentioned that Benetton's stock turnover was about 12 times per year. What does this suggest about Sting's management of its working capital? **(6 marks)**

3 The Chairman's statement that accompanied the accounts said: 'We intend to conduct a vigorous exercise in overhead reduction.' Give examples of items that might be affected, and outline the possible effects on the firm of the proposed cuts. **(9 marks)**

4 **a** What dividend yield is Sadaf receiving on the sum she invested? **(4 marks)**
   b What real rate of return does that represent, given the current rate of inflation? **(4 marks)**

5 Why may Sting plc be continuing to pay a dividend even though it is making operating losses? What risks does this action carry? **(10 marks)**

6 For what reasons might Sadaf's reliance on these accounts prove ill founded? **(8 marks)**

TOO GOOD
TO BE TRUE

A2
FINANCE

CONCEPTS NEEDED:

Published accounts, Gearing, Business plan

I n the eight years between 1983 and 1991 the share price of High Tide rose 2,900%, making fortunes for the early investors. The company had been founded in 1979 by Steve Dray and Frank Thomas, quickly becoming a leading producer of self-assembly conservatories. Through the 1980s High Tide became a stock market darling, famous for its rapid rise in annual earnings per share. It even managed to keep profits rising during the recessionary years of 1990 and 1991. Yet by 1993 fame had turned to notoriety for poor accounting practices, allowing the *Financial Times* to repeat an old stock market cliché: '*If a thing looks too good to be true, it probably is.*'

High Tide's troubles became public when, in late 1992, it announced accounting problems at a subsidiary. Two months later a follow-up statement warned that 1992 profits would be significantly below 1991. Further warnings followed, pushing the share price lower and lower. Eventually the company's large institutional shareholders (such as pension funds) forced the firm to appoint a new senior management team.

By September 1993 the new Finance Director and Chairman were able to quantify

and comment on previous management mistakes. Accounting changes meant High Tide declared a pre-tax loss of £36.4 million for the half year to July 1993. This compared with an equivalent figure for 1992 that had, at the time, been stated as an £18.4 million profit. Now the 1992 total was recalculated at £8.2 million, changing the profit figure by

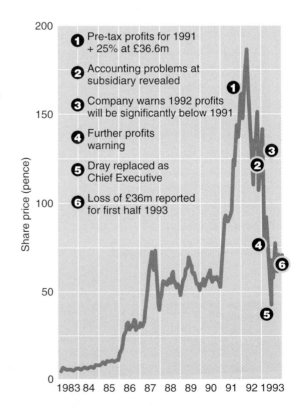

① Pre-tax profits for 1991 + 25% at £36.6m

② Accounting problems at subsidiary revealed

③ Company warns 1992 profits will be significantly below 1991

④ Further profits warning

⑤ Dray replaced as Chief Executive

⑥ Loss of £36m reported for first half 1993

Share price (pence)

1983 84 85 86 87 88 89 90 91 92 1993

£10 million at the stroke of a pen. The group, previously believed to have a positive net cash position, also revealed debts of £43.9 million, giving a gearing level of 39%.

The new Finance Director described the previous accounting practices as 'very aggressive'. For example, to mask poor trading in 1992, sales were being booked early towards the end of the financial year. In other words goods that would normally have been delivered in August or even September were being rushed to customers in July. This distorted the 1992 figures for the six months to July, making sales and therefore profits look higher than they really were.

There were two underlying causes of the difficulties. One was that 'Senior management did not want to recognise that the recession had happened' and imposed unrealistic targets on the line managers. It was as if High Tide could not bear to lose its status as a super-growth company. So the managers felt forced to produce high 'profits' to meet their targets and keep their jobs.

The second cause was an expensive diversification into the start-up of two businesses in 1992, Victorian Greenhouses and Edwardian Doors. A total of £46 million was invested in Victorian Greenhouses alone, yet the two operations lost over £6 million in the first half of 1993. The new Chairman was especially scathing that his predecessors had permitted these businesses 'to commence trading without the benefit of definitive business plans, and without an adequate appreciation of the technical, production and marketing issues surrounding their early development.'

In September 1993 several of the former Board directors were encouraged to resign, including the founder Mr Dray. The firm's auditor was also replaced. The new Finance Director said that the auditor's performance 'was not perfect but they were not responsible for the worst things'. As with many fallen 1980s star performers, High Tide's self belief led it to push its accounting systems beyond prudence towards optimism or worse; its auditors proved unable to protect the company from itself.

Sources: Financial Times, The Guardian

Questions
(50 marks; 70 minutes)

1 High Tide's experience shows that company accounts cannot
   always be relied on.
   a In what ways may accounts mislead the user?   **(8 marks)**
   b Outline the pressures on companies that may result in
      misleading accounts.   **(8 marks)**

2 Approximately how much money would have been lost by a
   shareholder who bought £5,000 of High Tide shares when the
   1991 profits were declared, and sold when Mr Dray was
   replaced? Show your workings.   **(6 marks)**

3 a What would you expect a business plan for a new
      operation to contain?   **(6 marks)**
   b Discuss the problems that might result from starting up
      without one.   **(12 marks)**

4 It was only in 1993 that it became clear that High Tide had a
   gearing level of 39%. What does this mean, and how might
   the company reduce this figure in future?   **(10 marks)**

THE SOFABED SAGA

A2
FINANCE

CONCEPTS NEEDED:

Profit margins, Asset turnover, Return on capital

The Sofabed Company Chief Executive was examining her firm's accounts in comparison with those of her nearest rival, SofaSogood. She found that margins were similar, but her return on capital (ROC) was markedly worse: 21% compared with 30%.

This was a worry because the current economic downturn made it likely that future trading conditions would be poor, so the weaker of the two might be forced out of business. The subject came up at the next Board meeting, where the Finance Director and the Sales Director put forward alternative methods for boosting the ROC.

The Finance Director spoke first: 'At present our net margins are 14%, which is only 1% below those of SofaSogood. So our real problem is asset turnover. I propose that we negotiate a sale and leaseback on our head office. That will bring in £400,000 that we can use to pay off some of our long term loans. Our assets employed will be cut by 25%, boosting our asset turnover and therefore our ROC.'

The Sales Director replied: 'Paying off our debts may be sensible, but I am more concerned about our margins. Two years ago they were 17%, last year 14%. What of the

10%   20%   30%
Return on capital

Sofabed

SofaSogood

coming year, given the recession? Our sales staff are under constant pressure to give bigger discounts to customers. If they give an extra 7% discount our margins will be halved! So my proposal is that we should boost our advertising spending with a highly distinctive campaign, in order to make demand for our products less price sensitive. That should protect our share of this falling market.'

The Finance Director was unimpressed with this argument from Sales. He said that point of view 'just holds gross margins up at the expense of net margins'.

Eventually the Chief Executive decided on a third option: to open up a sixth outlet in rented premises in a different town. It would use stock from existing outlets, the same distribution lorries, advertising budget and office staff. Therefore 'our assets can be made to work much harder'.

Questions
(50 marks; 60 minutes)

1   Calculate the asset turnover ratio for:
    a The Sofabed Company
    b SofaSogood   **(8 marks)**

2   Explain the logic behind saying:
    a 'If they give an extra 7% discount our margins will be
        halved.'   **(5 marks)**
    b 'Just holding gross margins up at the expense of net
        margins.'   **(6 marks)**

3   Outline two weaknesses of the Finance Director's approach.   **(10 marks)**

4   **a** Discuss how well the Chief Executive is making use of the
        concept of asset turnover.   **(12 marks)**
    b Assuming her plan works, and that the sixth outlet achieves
        sales and profits comparable with the other five, what will
        be Sofabed's ROC?   **(9 marks)**

TAKEOVERS AND PUBLISHED ACCOUNTS

A2
FINANCE

CONCEPTS NEEDED:

Balance sheets, Profit and loss accounts, Ratio analysis

The spectacular growth record of the fromage frais dairy sector looked unending – from £15 million two years ago to £36 million last year, and industry analysts were forecasting £48 million this year. Little wonder that Zee Co was interested in buying a firm, English Dairy, boasting a 20% market share. English Dairy had been the first British firm to spot the product's potential, and although its share had slipped from the 50% it once held, the growth in the market size ensured that its own sales volume kept rising.

When he heard a rumour that English Dairy's shareholders were thinking of putting the firm up for sale, Zee Co's Chairman immediately phoned his merchant bank to ask for a report. The bank soon returned with a detailed analysis of English Dairy's three most recent years' accounts. The summary read as follows:

1 The chilled dairy products market is growing in volume by 8% per annum and should reach £750 million this year.

2 English Dairy had sales last year of £6 million – all in the booming fromage frais sector. Their gross margins of 45% and net (pre-tax) margins of 10% were better than most dairy product firms.

3 In their latest accounts, English Dairy's key ratios were as follows:

Liquidity	1.7
Acid Test	0.8
Gearing	40%
Return on Assets	30%

We believe these to be encouraging.

4 With its £1,200,000 of shareholders' funds, its high profitability and the value of its brand name, we recommend that you offer £1.20 for each of the 1.5 million ordinary shares. This will give their shareholders a chance

to sell at a 30 pence premium over the most recent price at which English Dairy's shares were traded.

5 The purchase of English Dairy could be financed by a sale and leaseback of your £1.4 million head office, and by bank loans that we will provide. Our fees will amount to just 4% of the purchase price plus a £4,000 arrangement fee for the loans.

The Board of Zee Co found this satisfactory, and authorised the takeover to be carried out by the merchant bankers. The Financial Director was a little worried about the high combined gearing level after the merger, but reasoned that English Dairy's high stock levels could be cut back – thereby generating the cash to repay some of the borrowings. Appendix A shows the balance sheet for Zee Co at the time of the bid.

With the merger completed on the financial terms outlined above, a small team of Zee Co executives went in to learn about English Dairy's business. Within a fortnight they began to realise that not all was well. The factory looked impressive, but the stockpile of finished, refrigerated fromage frais was worryingly large.

Worse came when it emerged that English Dairy had three separate distribution depots – all equally full of finished product. When Zee Co's cost accountant explained this to his marketing colleagues, they analysed English Dairy's sales figures carefully. Four days later the position was quite clear.

After its years of spectacular growth, the fromage frais market had been hit by an unexpected problem this year. The switch in consumer demand towards skimmed milk had led to such excess supplies of cream (skimmed off the milk) that the bulk supply price of cream had fallen by 20%. As a result, many manufacturers were launching real dairy cream versions of their yogurts, mousses, and ice creams. These new products took market share from fromage frais.

This setback had occurred at a very awkward time for English Dairy, since it had just completed a factory expansion programme designed to cope with a forecast of £10 million of sales next year. In order to keep its stated profit high, the company had kept production levels up, even though demand had slipped by 10%. This had led to stockpiling but because it kept the apparent fixed costs per unit down, it enabled the firm to declare what appeared a healthy profit figure. Now – too late – Zee Co had found out that the assumptions it had made were based on misleading figures. The Board considered taking legal action against the Directors and Auditors of English Dairy, but they knew this would succeed only if they could find evidence that the deception had been deliberate. Otherwise, the defendants would just plead that they had misjudged market conditions, i.e. that theirs was an honest mistake.

Once Zee Co's accountants had finished a complete audit of English Dairy's position, they concluded that it had in fact made no profit last year, and was making substantial losses currently. As a result, English Dairy's gearing level was probably near to 80% at the time of the takeover. Now Zee Co had to try to retrieve something from its misguided investment.

Appendix A: Zee Co balance sheet

	£000	£000
Fixed assets	12,200	12,200
Stocks	4,800	
Debtors	3,600	
Cash	400	
Current assets	8,800	8,800
Assets employed		21,000
Long term loans		7,000
Shares	1,200	
Reserves	12,800	
Shareholders' funds	14,000	14,000
Capital employed		21,000

Questions
(80 marks; 100 minutes)

1 Outline the danger signs that Zee Co should have followed up more carefully before buying English Dairy. **(12 marks)**

2 **a** Explain the ways in which English Dairy's accounting ratios misled Zee Co and its merchant bank. **(8 marks)**

b What conclusions can you draw about the accuracy of published company accounts? **(10 marks)**

3 **a** What was the value of the goodwill element in Zee Co's bid for English Dairy? **(6 marks)**

b What percentage of the extra bank loans will be paid to the bank in fees? **(8 marks)**

4 Use the data available to help you analyse and discuss Zee Co's gearing position before and after the takeover. **(15 marks)**

5 **a** Outline three actions that Zee Co might take to 'retrieve something'. **(9 marks)**

b Consider how the Directors might decide between the three you suggest. **(12 marks)**

MATALAN'S MARVELLOUS MANAGEMENT

CONCEPTS NEEDED:

Ratios, Marketing strategy

On 13 May 1998, under the headline 'Matalan Just Not Worth The Chase', the *Daily Telegraph* wrote sceptically about the stock market flotation of Matalan PLC. The paper cast doubt on 'the justification for floating on a historic price earnings multiple of 20 – up there with Marks & Spencer'. The journalist concluded that Matalan shares were 'not worth chasing'. By implication, it would be wiser to invest in Marks & Sparks.

On the day of its flotation, Matalan shares were priced at 47p (including a bonus issue); mighty Marks & Spencer stood at 580p. Embarrassingly for the *Daily Telegraph*, its advice proved spectacularly wrong. As the graph shows, by November 2000 Matalan's shares had risen tenfold while Marks & Spencer shares had fallen two thirds to 180p. £1,000 invested in Matalan would have become £10,000 in two years. The same sum in Marks & Spencer would have crashed to just £310.

Matalan Ltd was founded in 1985 by John Hargreaves. He had been a market stall trader, then opened his first shop. Its proposition was

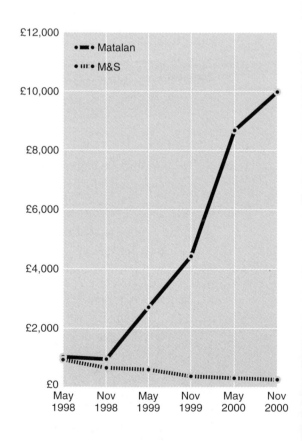

Performance of Matalan and Marks & Spencer shares 1998–2000

simple: fashion clothing at discount prices. Most High Street retailers have gross margins of around 50%, i.e. their products are priced by adding 100% to the purchase cost. Matalan would buy as cheaply as possible, but would also accept lower gross margins. The intention was to maximise sales per square metre of floor space. This would generate an acceptable return on capital by achieving high asset turnover rather than high profit margins.

As shown in the table below, in the year of its flotation Matalan's operating margins were less than half those of Marks & Spencer. Yet by attracting lots of customers the asset turnover was much higher than M&S. Consequently little Matalan was generating a higher return on capital than mighty Marks.

A further element in Matalan's strategy was (and is) to encourage shoppers to see themselves as part of a club. For a fee as low as £1, you can become a member of Matalan and can therefore shop there. This makes the shop slightly different from other retailers. By September 2000 over 4 million people had joined. The membership details give Matalan a database that can be used to obtain consumer profile data, and as a mailing list.

From its 100 outlets nationally, Matalan's share of the clothing market pushed up from 1.2% in 1999 to 1.9% in 2000. Its low prices and fast moving, fashionable clothing were drawing sales away from the middle market

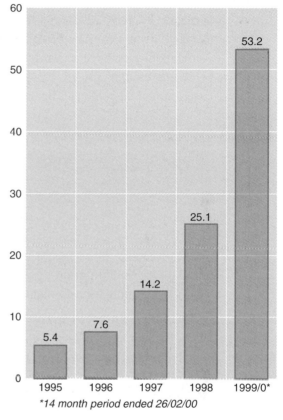

14 month period ended 26/02/00

Matalan annual operating profits (£m)

	Sales	/	Assets	=	Asset turnover
Matalan	£229.6m	/	£34.6m	=	6.6 times
Marks & Spencer	£8,243m	/	£5,091m	=	1.62 times

	Asset turnover	×	Operating margins	=	**Return On Capital**
Matalan	6.6 times	×	6.2%	=	**40.9%**
Marks & Spencer	1.62 times	×	13.4%	=	**21.7%**

retailers such as Marks & Spencer, C&A and British Home Stores. As the operating profit details show, there is no mystery about why Matalan's shares had risen by nearly 1,000% between 1998 and 2000.

Yet what was the secret of its trading success? By July 2000 the *Telegraph* had changed its position on Matalan. It wrote: 'Matalan buyers have a fashion sense that belies the clothes' prices. A market position based purely on price can be snatched away simply by charging less than your competitor; a position based on fashion – as Matalan achieves with its Gucci-esque jackets – takes more skill to break down.' The following month *PR Week* pointed out that the stock market was wrong to see the firm as a cut-price retailer of brands such as Nike: 90% of sales were Matalan own label products. The company itself was beginning to be a brand in its own right.

Sources: Matalan Annual Reports; *Financial Times*

Questions
(60 marks; 70 minutes)

1   A market share of 1.9% may sound small, yet Matalan made £53.2 million profit from this in 1999/2000. How may it be benefiting from its niche market marketing strategy? **(12 marks)**

2   **a** Explain how a firm might achieve a high asset turnover. **(6 marks)**
    b Use the material in the case to assess the benefits to Matalan of its high asset turnover. **(10 marks)**

3   Most analysts regard Return On Capital (ROC) as the most important test of financial efficiency. Why do you believe this is so? **(6 marks)**

4   Consider the long term benefits to Matalan of 'beginning to be a brand in its own right'. **(10 marks)**

5   In its annual report for 1999/2000 Matalan stated that its sales and profit upsurge had come about from wider margins, sharply increased like-for-like sales and new store openings. Discuss which of these three sources should be considered the most important to the firm's long term future. **(16 marks)**

KAREN'S TAXIS

CONCEPTS NEEDED:

Marketing decisions, Pricing, Profit and loss account, Depreciation

'**Q**uite honestly, Bill, these interest rates are killing me.' Karen put down her cup, and stared at the far wall of the café in which she and Bill were sitting. She looked sad, as well she might. Her taxi company had started so well just over a year or so ago, when she had decided to follow a niche market strategy.

Karen's original idea had come from Bill, who had run a small taxi firm in Leicester for years. She had used the figures for his firm, based upon buying a fleet of eight Ford Mondeos, which in his words, did '100 thousand miles in two years, and are then so worn out that they are only worth, at most, £3,000 – and that out of a purchase price of £12,000.'

Bill estimated that the cars each brought in £4,000 per month, but out of that, half went on the taxi drivers' wages and £1,000 on fuel and maintenance. There wasn't much profit after allowing for the annual fixed overheads of £22,000 on administration, £2,000 per year per cab on insurance, plus the rapid depreciation mentioned earlier.

Karen had quickly calculated Bill's monthly profit and loss account, so she could clearly see his problem, but her solution was to go for

customers at the top end of the market. She could buy Mercedes limousines for around £30,000 each. These cars should always command a premium over ordinary taxis, and would be available for other work, such as weddings. Karen even thought about buying two white ones and two in black so that she could cover funerals as well.

Karen's first problem had been to raise the finance to start her business. She had drawn up a business plan, which included a projected budget, cash flow, profit and loss account and balance sheet, but encountered problems with all the banks she approached. Eventually she was able to gain agreement from a small local bank that demanded very high interest charges on the money she borrowed.

Her year started well enough. Karen was able to charge a 25% premium over normal taxi fares, although she had to spend £20,000 on advertising the new service in the first year. As she expected, some of her costs were higher than Bill's, in particular she had to pay 50% higher insurance premiums for each of her four cars and 20% more for diesel fuel. Nevertheless her wage bill was the same, as were her overheads.

The major problem for Karen as the year went by was a sharp rise in interest rates. Higher mortgage payments hit consumer spending, which dampened demand for upmarket services such as hers. At the same time the bank's interest charges jumped even higher, giving her problems in keeping up with the payments. She started to realise why so many banks had been so reluctant to lend to her in the first place. Bill reassured her that 'better times might be just around the corner', but it was hard for Karen to look much further ahead than next month's bills.

Questions
(50 marks; 60 minutes)

1 It is not clear how Karen arrived at her pricing policy of a 25% premium over ordinary cab fares. Explain how you think she *should* have come to her pricing decision. **(10 marks)**

2 **a** Explain the meaning of the term 'depreciation'. **(3 marks)**

  b How much should Bill allow for the depreciation of his taxis using the Straight Line Method? **(5 marks)**

  c Apart from the purchase price, what information does Karen need to know about her Mercedes taxis in order for her to calculate the depreciation on her fleet? **(5 marks)**

3 Draw up a simple annual profit and loss account for Bill's business. **(12 marks)**

4 If you were lending Karen the money to start her business, discuss the factors you would take into account in granting or refusing her request. **(15 marks)**

PRODUCTION AND STOCK SCHEDULING

AS
OPERATIONS
MANAGEMENT

CONCEPTS NEEDED:

Stocks, Cash flow, Capacity utilisation

The Marketing Manager of a lawnmower manufacturer forecasts the following sales pattern for the coming year:

Monthly sales (000 units)	
Jan	55
Feb	60
Mar	95
April	140
May	110
June	80
July	70
Aug	65
Sept	75
Oct	80
Nov	60
Dec	45

Maximum production capacity is 90,000 units per month and only 80,000 units of finished stock can be stored. The management aims to keep a minimum (buffer) stock level of 40,000 units at all times; so the year starts and should finish with that amount of stock. The Production Manager must schedule output for the coming year bearing all these factors in mind.

With a view to the longer term, though, the Production Manager believes she must discover whether a different strategy would be more profitable. At present, it is inevitable that the expensive factory overhead costs are being fully utilised for only part of the year. Perhaps it would be more economic to sell off some of the machinery, convert part of the factory to warehousing, and then use a full-time workforce to produce flat out all year? Surely that would be more efficient than the time consuming and expensive process of recruiting and training temporary workers every winter.

She decided to spend more time planning out her idea, and then to discuss it with the firm's Chief Accountant.

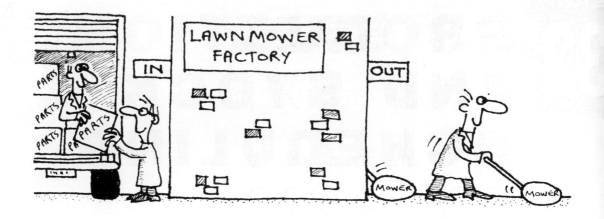

Questions
(50 marks; 70 minutes)

1 What production level do you recommend for each month, bearing in mind a general requirement for stable production levels where possible (to minimise the need for temporary staff or 'double-time' overtime payments)?
Use this layout to work out your answer: **(16 marks)**

	Stocks at start (thousands)	Monthly sales (thousands)	Production level (thousands)	Stocks at end (thousands)
Jan				
Feb				
Mar				
etc.				

2 **a** Draw a line graph of monthly sales and monthly production over the year. **(9 marks)**
b Shade in the areas on the graph that indicate when stocks are building up. **(2 marks)**
c Indicate the under-utilisation of the firm's 90,000 capacity. **(2 marks)**

3 **a** Is it possible to meet the desired buffer stock target at all times? **(1 mark)**
b How well do you think you managed to meet the constraints placed upon you by the terms of question 1? **(6 marks)**

4 What are the implications of the production manager's plan for the firm's future position regarding stock levels, cash flow, and responsiveness to changing customer demands? **(14 marks)**

33

BS 5750 AND THE QUALITY FANATIC

AS
OPERATIONS
MANAGEMENT

CONCEPTS NEEDED:

Quality assurance, Profit, International competitiveness

The management of the Kimber Wetsuit Company (KWC) had been considering adopting the BS 5750 quality standard for some years. What clinched it was when the Ministry of Defence turned down KWC's quote for 1,000 suits for Royal Navy divers. They lost the order to BJ Diving, which had just received its 5750 certificate.

As a former professional diver, KWC's Managing Director (Jim Stewart) had always

been fanatical about quality. This had helped in his development of a substantial export business, accounting for 75% of sales turnover. The level of quality that the overseas buyers looked for had been instilled by Jim into his workforce. So he found it hard to see what the British Standard could do to improve on the reliability of his wetsuits. Nevertheless he decided to hire a consultant to advise how to proceed.

The adviser spent a day following an order through from design, to materials ordering, cutting, bonding, assembly, styling, quality control and packing. Every piece of documentation was checked, as was the communication system and document storage method. The following day Jim Stewart received detailed feedback on what the firm would have to do to achieve the BS 5750 standard. He was horrified at the focus on paperwork, which included specific recommendations for at least 12 new pieces of record keeping or record storage. He told his wife after work: 'Not once did the clown mention the quality of craftsmanship or the care taken by every worker in my factory.'

After a few days, however, Jim calmed down and set about reading the documentation from the British Standards Institute, and re-reading the consultant's report. This enabled him to write his own report (see below), which he sent to every member of his staff.

Report to: All members of staff
From: Jim
Subject: Applying for the British Standard 5750 quality award
Date: March 17th

1 Background

We have recently lost out on a Royal Navy order that would have added 50% to this year's sales. BJ Diving won it because they hold the BS 5750 certificate that the Navy insists upon. As we all know, our quality is considerably better than theirs, so it would be foolish of us to allow this to occur again.

2 Proposal

I intend that we should achieve the required standard within nine months. The Italian Navy contract comes up then, and it is my plan that this should form the stepping stone to a far stronger presence in the European market. The BS 5750 is the same as the internationally accepted ISO 9000, so this should help our cause.

3 Detailed requirements

In order to be successful, we will need to cover four main areas:

3.1 Management responsibility: an organisation chart will be needed to set out the responsibilities of all staff who manage or carry out work associated with the quality of the product and customer service. Quality procedures must be written down in full detail.

3.2 Contract review: each customer's requirements must be defined and documented to establish that the necessary resources are available.

3.3 Process control: requiring documentation of how the process is to be carried out. Written instructions must be given to each employee involved and the process must be monitored. (Note to all: I do not know how this may affect our policy of self-checking.)

3.4 Document control: we must produce quality and procedure manuals to be kept in designated locations. Any changes to the system must be logged in the manuals.

4 Conclusion

I am as appalled as any of you at the amount of paperwork this will generate. It will cost us a great deal and will probably be very irritating to work with. Nevertheless, if important customers want us to hold this certificate, we must not only get on with it, but also trust that our customers are not fools. I will be very surprised if we do not learn a great deal from this process, and emerge an even stronger company as a result.

Jim decided that the best way to proceed was not through outside 'experts' or even as a purely management based exercise. His approach was to be bottom-up, i.e. employee centred.

The whole KWC staff received a huge boost when they heard, four months later, that the Navy had cancelled its order with BJ Diving on the grounds that the wetsuits delivered so far did not meet the Navy's standards. Gossip soon reached them that BJ's approach to obtaining BS 5750 had been so bureaucratic that the company was weighed down with paperwork systems. The process of producing high quality wetsuits had become secondary to producing high quality paper.

With BJ Diving rejected and KWC well on the way to its 5750 quality standard, it was no surprise when Jim received a telephone call from the Ministry of Defence. Within a fortnight KWC had the contract for producing the remaining 500 Navy wetsuits.

Questions
(50 marks; 70 minutes)

1 Why may a customer demand that a supplier holds a BS 5750 quality assurance certificate? **(6 marks)**

2 Jim Stewart decided to implement the BS 5750 requirements through a bottom-up approach. What is meant by that and how might it be achieved? **(12 marks)**

3 **a** Before getting the Navy order, the average cost of producing KWC's wetsuits was £124, comprising £74 of variable costs and £50 of fixed costs per unit. Calculate and comment on the effect on these costs of getting the Navy order. **(12 marks)**

 b Assuming a selling price of £195 per wetsuit, also calculate the effect of the extra order on KWC's profit. **(8 marks)**

4 Use the case as a starting point to discuss the reasons why high quality standards may be considered of particular importance in today's business world. **(12 marks)**

BRINGING IN QUALITY CIRCLES

AS
OPERATIONS
MANAGEMENT

CONCEPTS NEEDED:

Motivation, Resistance to change

'**B**ut we don't have a quality problem!' exclaimed the Chairman, evidently put out by Sarah's suggestion. He pointed to the very low rates of customer guarantee claim (just 1%); and to the advanced electronic testing system operated by the seven quality control inspectors. But Sarah continued to press her case for the introduction of quality circles:

'**T**here's more to quality than having fault-free products. Quality circles look at every aspect of a product's design and manufacture, with a view to providing a product the customer will be more satisfied with. Plus, of course, there are other vital areas such as delivery times. Quality means good service as well as good products.'

After some more, quite heated, discussion the Chairman agreed to provide Sarah with a £20,000 budget for a one year trial of quality circles within her own department. If her hedgetrimmer production line benefited, then perhaps the main lawnmower plant would follow. She would have to report to the Board

on progress in six months, and give a final assessment at the end of the year.

She began by calling a meeting of all her staff, to explain the test that was to take place, and the reasons why she had pushed for it. They were used to – and quite liked – her meetings, which often involved open criticism of her management of their section, so most were receptive to what she had to say. Some had moaned before about 'the waste of the skills and brains of the shopfloor workers' so they responded positively to a proposal to use those very attributes. The only groans came when Sarah explained that the group would meet after work, and would be unpaid. Her reasoning was that to offer to pay people would attract many who did not really want to participate, so it needed to be truly voluntary work.

By talking individually to all of her 85 staff over the following weeks, Sarah was able to construct a list of eight volunteers. Before their first meeting, she and they went on a weekend management training course on 'Setting up successful quality circles'. This had

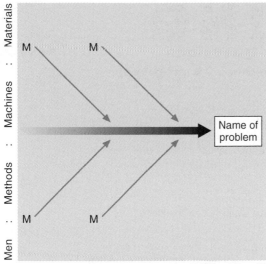

5 'W's and an 'H'

The problem (or effect) is identified in the rectangular box (right).

The four 'M's signify possible causes of the problem (Men, Methods, Machines, Materials).

A problem solving discussion then follows, based on the five 'W's and an 'H' (Why, When, Where, Who, What and How).

the desired effect of making them feel far more confident and far more motivated towards the scheme, and helped to knit them together as a team. All were especially impressed by the potential of the 'fishbone' diagram as a way of tackling problems (see above).

This invention of the Japanese management expert Ishikawa seemed easy to use. The problem to be solved is written in a box on the right hand side of a large piece of paper. An arrow is drawn across the sheet pointing towards the box, then the members of the circle suggest possible causes – which are put into one of the 'four M' categories: Men, Methods, Machines, Materials. Having agreed on the causes, a problem solving discussion follows, based on the 'five Ws and

an H' (Why, When, Where, Who, What and How). They were told that this technique is the one used most commonly by the two million quality circles operating in Japan. .

The first week's quality circle proved a disappointment, as the topic they chose to look at (late deliveries) was so wide that they became swamped by the number of different factors. In subsequent weeks they corrected this, and then began to generate some useful ideas. The first triumph was an idea for braking the hedge-cutting blades at the instant the user switches off. This was designed, tested, and then incorporated into all the firm's output. It was completed by the time the six month review took place, so Sarah felt very confident that the Board would congratulate her. In fact, she found that many Board members were worried about the implication of her work. The Production Director suggested that:

> **'T**he workers are already showing signs of believing that they know best. Two managers have reported insolence, and one has told me that some of his staff actually started changing the production process without his permission. I'd like this experiment abandoned.**'**

Fortunately for Sarah, the Marketing Director and the Chairman were so impressed by the improvement in the hedgetrimmer that they backed her for the other six months. She went away determined to overcome the resistance to change among the middle management, though not yet sure how to achieve this.

Source: The Independent

Questions
(60 marks; 70 minutes)

1 **a** Outline the strengths of Sarah's approach to the
   implementation of the circle.   **(8 marks)**

   b Examine two problems that might arise if the Chairman
   decided that the system should be implemented
   throughout the business.   **(8 marks)**

2 How, precisely, could successful quality circles boost the
   profitability of a firm?   **(9 marks)**

3 **a** Use the fishbone technique to tackle the problem of exam
   success at Business Studies. Group the causes of the
   problem under the 'four M' headings, and your thoughts
   on solutions within the categories: 'five Ws and an H'. Make
   your points as specifically as you can.   **(12 marks)**

   b Comment briefly on the potential of this technique as a
   focus for group work.   **(8 marks)**

4 Fundamental to a kaizen (continuous improvement) approach
   is the involvement of well qualified staff in suggesting product
   and process improvements. To what extent may the
   establishment of quality circles be sufficient to achieve
   successful kaizen?   **(15 marks)**

THE UZBEK HAT

AS
OPERATIONS
MANAGEMENT

CONCEPTS NEEDED:

Stock control, Opportunity costs, Profit

It started with Hatz, the 'new Spice Girls', according to *The Sun*. Their first record went to Number 2, and their *Top of the Pops* appearance featured great clothes, great dancing and – of all things – Uzbek hats. The girls had been frantically searching for clothes the day before the TV show and had stumbled upon this weird, wonderful headgear.

For S. Davis Ltd, the UK's only importer of these hats from Asia, the result was spectacular. The day after the Thursday TV appearance was bedlam as shops throughout Britain phoned through their orders. By mid-morning, sales were greater than for the three months since the company had bought two cases (10,000 units) and all the stock was sold. The previous order had come by truck from Asia, but now the company phoned to see whether an extra 50,000 hats could be flown in. Fortunately they were quoted just a three day delivery lead time.

Appearances by the girls on weekend morning TV shows raised the profile of the hats still further, and by Monday lunchtime it was clear that a further 50,000 needed to be ordered. This was more of a problem, as the supplier in Uzbekistan was now out of stock. The production lead time for these handmade

traditional hats would be as much as three weeks. Yet shops were clamouring for supplies immediately. In three weeks, would anyone still want these novelty items?

A further problem was that the Asian supplier would get the extra production under way only if he was paid in full for the recently completed order and paid 50% up front for the next 50,000 – all at a cost of £1.60 per unit. This would strain the importer's working capital position, as British retailers were used to receiving two months' credit. Nevertheless, as S. Davis was selling the hats to the shops at £4.80 each, the profit potential was irresistible. Sean Davis himself discussed the position with the company's bank manager and once overdraft facilities were agreed, the company could go ahead.

Nevertheless the S. Davis Ltd staff phoned the retailers to check whether they were willing to accept stock in three weeks. Several cancelled, but further orders (including reordering from shops supplied last Friday) gave the company the confidence to proceed.

On the Friday of that week Sean Davis asked to see the figures so far. All 60,000 hats delivered to date had been sold, and in addition there were firm orders for 70,000 more. The 50,000 extra delivery should arrive in just over two weeks, so there would need to be an extra order, but no one had managed to contact the Uzbek supplier for a day or two.

To everyone's surprise, demand for the hats continued to be quite high over the following weeks. Sean Davis was reluctant to hold a buffer stock, as he felt that demand would fall away suddenly, when fashion turned against the hats, Hatz or both. Yet after four weeks he decided to establish a 10,000 unit buffer. The figures for sales and deliveries are shown below.

At the end of the year, over a pre-Christmas lunch with the Chief Buyer from the Matalan retail chain, Sean told of the bedlam of the 'Uzbek hat crisis'. Both agreed that it had pushed their stock ordering and control systems to the limit, but that profitable crises such as this were a bonus to all concerned.

And Hatz? They proved a one hat wonder.

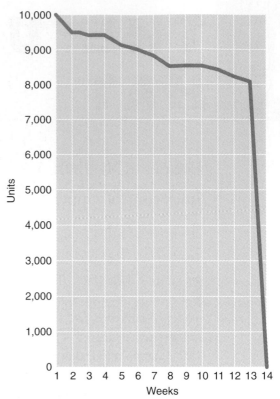

Uzbek hat stocks (first three months)

Stock and sales position, weeks 15–25

Week	Deliveries (at start of week)	Weekly sales	Excess demand (orders unfulfilled)
15	50,000	50,000	70,000
16	0	0	85,000
17	0	0	100,000
18	50,000	50,000	50,000
19	0	0	60,000
20	0	0	70,000
21	60,000	60,000	20,000
22	0	0	30,000
23	0	0	40,000
24	70,000	50,000	0
25	0	10,000	0

Questions
(60 marks; 75 minutes)

1 In this case the supply lead time varied between three days and three weeks. Why is it important for firms to have supply lead times that are fixed and are short? **(10 marks)**

2 Discuss the implications for S. Davis Ltd of being left with large stocks of 'novelty items', once fashion moved against the products. **(10 marks)**

3 From the graph and the text, answer these questions:
  a Approximately how many hats were sold in weeks 1–13? **(2 marks)**
  b What was the value of those sales? **(2 marks)**
  c What was the gross profit generated by the hat sales achieved in week 14? **(3 marks)**

4 Draw a graph to show the stocks of Uzbek hats held by S. Davis Ltd in weeks 15–25. Use the data in the Deliveries and Sales columns of the table. **(10 marks)**

5 Examine why Sean Davis may have decided on a 10,000 unit buffer stock for the hats. **(8 marks)**

6 **a** Explain the meaning of the term 'opportunity cost'. **(3 marks)**
  b Evaluate the business implications of leaving demand unfulfilled, as S. Davis Ltd did in weeks 15–23. **(12 marks)**

ROBOT HEL

CONCEPTS NEEDED:

Economies of scale, Capacity utilisation, Labour versus capital intensity

At first she said no. She was too young and wanted to concentrate on her law degree. When Carmen went home to Herefordshire at Christmas, though, old friends persuaded her to give it a go. The situation was that her father's death in June had left the family engineering business rudderless. All the shares were now owned by her mother, who was still coming to terms with bereavement. Carmen knew that 25% of employment within her village depended on the factory. With old school friends among the workforce, she felt she had to try. Exeter University proved surprisingly helpful about her request to delay continuing her degree for a year; in the meantime she would be a 21 year old Chief Executive.

Hereford Engineering Ltd (known as HEL by the staff) was in need of active management. It had invested heavily in robotic welding equipment in the mid 1980s, but machinery such as this was now unreliable and desperately slow. Carmen spent a morning in the welding section and was convinced by all the staff that extra investment was essential. She was lucky that one of the welders, Tim, was working during vacation from his Business Studies degree. He gave Carmen contact details for the

government's Benchmarking Index. For £150 Carmen was able to send off HEL's figures for productivity, machinery breakdowns and right-first-time production (among other indicators) and within 10 days knew the data for comparable engineering firms (see table opposite). In the meantime, she asked the welding section to come up with a shopping list for replacing the 20 year old robots. They were delighted to be asked.

Despite the figures, the level of work through the factory and the level of forward orders remained high. Occasional orders had to be turned away as HEL lacked the spare capacity to produce the goods within the timescale demanded by the customer. Current profitability was very low, but it seemed a bit of a miracle that the company was not losing money.

A visit to HEL's longest standing and biggest customer proved revealing. Carmen was told that the level of business was partly due to her father's reputation, but mainly because of booming demand from the UK railway industry and the car industry in mainland Europe. 'In truth,' he continued, 'we regard you as a second-line supplier. If a recession or a cutback in railway investment

Benchmarked data for HEL compared with other engineering firms

	HEL	Lower quartile	Median	Upper quartile
Labour productivity (units of finished output per worker per hour)	5.3	4.9	9.4	15.5
Machinery breakdowns per machine per week	0.85	0.75	0.31	0.04
% of production right-first-time	91.2	90.7	95.3	99.1
% of customer deliveries on time	74.8	76.2	87.1	97.5
% labour turnover	5.6	22.6	9.4	6.8
% absenteeism	2.7%	6.8%	4.5%	2.1%
Labour cost as a % of total cost	64%	60%	44%	29%

meant that we had to cut our number of suppliers, you'd be the first to go. Sorry, but HEL's our most expensive and least reliable partner. It's just that your competitors have no spare capacity at the moment.' It was a tough message to take, but it fitted in with Carmen's overall understanding of the position, so it helped complete the picture.

After eight weeks in the job, Carmen felt she understood enough about the business to know that medium to long term success (survival, even) required a dramatic change in efficiency, reliability and quality. Heartened by the clear evidence that the workforce was well motivated and well intentioned, she wanted to see whether the investment that was needed could also be afforded.

To prepare for a morning with HEL's part-time Financial Director, Carmen drove to Warwick to see Tim, now returned to university. He explained how to read a set of accounts and assured her that the business could comfortably raise £750,000. A couple of days later Carmen welcomed the Finance Director to her own office. He was very cautious, but eventually accepted that investment was essential. Carmen's plan would increase capacity by 25%, yet the labour requirement would fall by 15% over the coming year. The main targets, though, were to match the upper quartile results for quality and reliability. This would require an investment of £1.1 million in new robotic equipment, plus a further £200,000 in new stock and quality control software.

Happily, this proved possible, thanks to the Finance Director's helpful idea of a sale and leaseback on the factory premises, worth £600,000. The remaining £700,000 would come from a mix of internal and external sources. Within two days the Finance Director had put together a plan that should yield the required investment sum within 90 days.

Carmen now went with her works manager to visit several different producers or importers of multi-purpose robots. She soon learned that the world of industrial robots spoke of a 'rule of five', which suggests that every 10 years robots can do five times the number of tasks five times more quickly and for a fifth of the price (in real terms). She was very impressed, especially with the flexibility of these programmable robots costing £50,000 each. The works manager was especially excited by the thought that the robots could be reset to work through the night at the noisiest tasks – improving working conditions for all. It wouldn't be HEL to work there any more.

Eight months later, despite some difficult teething problems with some of the robots and all of the software, things were looking good. Two weeks of trouble-free, high quality production had led to 100% on-time delivery. No less importantly, Carmen had just had a quote accepted for a large, rush order at premium prices. Before, they would have been unable to complete the work in time. On its own, the profit on this order would pay for a robot. Very satisfying. So much so that Carmen felt for the first time that if she could find the right person to take over, she could return to her degree. In the meantime, she couldn't wait to spend another £150 to find out how the business was now performing against its rivals. Perhaps she would stay on a while longer.

Questions
(60 marks; 75 minutes)

1 Explain the importance to a company like HEL of:
  a 'benchmarking' **(5 marks)**
  b lacking spare capacity **(5 marks)**

2 Examine the positive and negative findings for HEL in the table. To what extent do the weaknesses outweigh the strengths? **(12 marks)**

3 Analyse the economies of scale that HEL might be expected to benefit from as a result of the changes. **(8 marks)**

4 Outline the evidence in the case 'that the workforce was well motivated and well intentioned'. **(6 marks)**

5 The investment will have altered the balance of HEL's production system away from labour intensive and towards capital intensive production. Evaluate the implications of this for the company. **(12 marks)**

6 Towards the end of the case it seems that Carmen is content that she has completed the task. Discuss why this may prove a short-sighted view. **(12 marks)**

THE END OF THE LINE

CONCEPTS NEEDED:

Lean production, Just-in-time, Kaizen

Brakes Ltd was just one among many companies hit hard by the travel chaos in the autumn and winter of 2000/2001. A number of rail crashes caused a nationwide examination of the tracks, and the consequent discovery that many were quite literally cracking up. The public outcry meant that Railtrack, the company responsible for the network's infrastructure, was required to undertake massive engineering work to replace worn out rails. This action caused chaos, not just while the work was carried out,

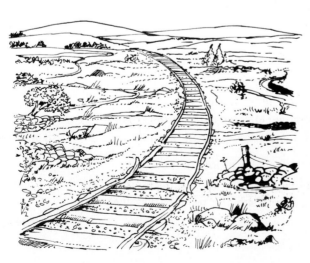

but also because speed restrictions had to be imposed beforehand. Just to make matters worse, November turned out to be the wettest for centuries, bringing flooding and further travel disruption. Because people no longer trusted the railways, Britain's already crowded roads faced even more congestion. The net result was that freight lorries frequently missed their delivery schedules.

For Brakes Ltd, the transport chaos was a major headache. The firm had embraced the concept of 'lean production' years before, adopting Tom Brakes's idea of a 'chain of customers'. Actually it wasn't Tom's idea at all, but since no one else had read Schonberger's work, there was no one to challenge him! What Tom, and Schonberger, meant was that by dividing up production into units, or 'cells', the line workers would feel a sense of pride in their work because the next cell in the process would hold them responsible for its quality. Eventually, the finished product would be sold to other firms, who were the more conventional and obvious 'customers'.

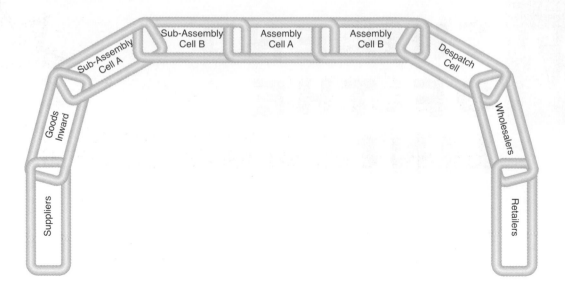

As part of the system of delegation to the shop floor, Tom also introduced 'just-in-time' production. This meant that as each cell used up its stock it called for more from the preceding one, hence the notion of 'pulling through' production. This system reduced levels of work-in-progress and costs of stock holding, but it did ultimately rely on suppliers delivering zero defect components *on time*, which is why the transport crisis hit Brakes Ltd so hard.

Questions
(45 marks; 60 minutes)

1 Explain what is meant by the following terms:
   a cell production
   b chain of customers
   c 'pulling through' production
   d infrastructure   **(12 marks)**

2 Outline two advantages and two disadvantages of 'lean production' as given in the case.   **(12 marks)**

3 Examine two ways firms might be affected by adverse transport conditions, other than delays in getting supplies.   **(8 marks)**

4 Discuss whether a firm moving to a JIT production system would be wise to do so through a process of continuous improvement, or whether it would be better to make a single, radical change.   **(13 marks)**

38

TIME BASED MANAGEMENT

CONCEPTS NEEDED:

Product life cycle, Just-in-time, Lean production

It was the mountain bike experience that led to the changes. Wheeler Bikes of Nottingham had been producing profitably until a flood of cheap Taiwanese bicycles saturated the market. The collapse in the market price of mountain bikes led to huge losses at Wheeler. During the worst period, four years ago, the company was close to liquidation. It survived due to ruthless cost-cutting and rationalisation.

Since then, its finances have recovered to allow a new growth strategy. The first phase was to reorganise the factory into cells. The continuous production line was replaced by a system of 19 work groups, each responsible

for a significant part of bicycle production or assembly. The cells represented 10 of the 12 links in the chain from raw material to customer (the other two being delivery and retail sale). Reinforced by flexible teamworking and just-in-time production, the company could regard its manufacturing as fully up to date.

Now Ann Raymond, the new Managing Director (MD), wanted to go one stage further. The firm could produce quickly and flexibly within its existing model range, but new products were still taking at least 18 months to get to the market. That slow pace increased the cost of new product development and restricted the firm's ability to respond to changing customer needs. A case in point was the new Wheeler 'City' bicycle, launched earlier this month. Started 20 months ago, it was conceived when the government Minister for Transport was offering subsidies to encourage local councils to create more bicycle lanes. Yet in this launch month for the Wheeler 'City', the company's main rival announced that its 'CommutaBike' had sold an impressive 50,000 in its first six months. Worse still, the government minister was being replaced by a car enthusiast.

Ann had recently attended conferences on time based management and simultaneous engineering. She felt ready to implement change. Her first step was to call a meeting of the heads of Wheeler's six departments. Ann explained that she wanted to set time based targets for future product development, such as 10 months from idea to retail sale. The head of engineering was concerned about the effect on design quality, but accepted the need for more speed. Ann assured him that she would finance the purchase of an advanced computer aided design (CAD) system, but urged everyone to think about how to coordinate better, rather than just to work faster:

'*I'm sure that the key is simultaneous engineering. For the City bike, John worked for two months on the design before Christine even started thinking about the structure and materials. If they had spent a couple of days together at the outset, surely both could have been working at the same time.*'

The MD showed what she meant by sketching a diagram of the stages they went through to produce a finished prototype of the City bike (see Diagram A).

The head of engineering looked admiringly at the diagram, but was puzzled at the shorter times allowed in Diagram B for tooling and making the prototype. Ann explained that this should be possible if the teams responsible for both operations were involved in the

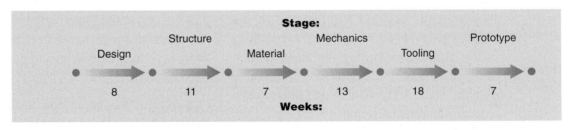

Diagram A: Development of City bike (64 weeks)

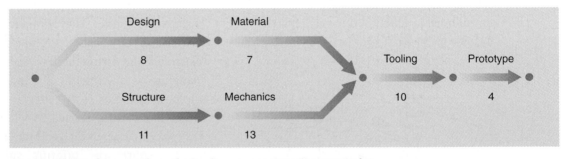

Diagram B: Development through simultaneous engineering (38 weeks)

earlier stages. That would enable them to plan their work in advance.

During the following weeks the department heads went on a series of training courses. They learned not only that their MD's summary was sound but also more about how to make time based management work.

The course leaders emphasised the importance of communications. Different sections of the firm could work simultaneously only if each knew exactly what the other was doing. Otherwise there would be considerable wastage of time, materials and money.

Questions
(60 marks; 80 minutes)

1 It is widely thought that product life cycles are becoming shorter.
  a For what reasons may this be occurring in a market such as bicycles? **(8 marks)**
  b What implications do shorter life cycles have for time based management? **(10 marks)**

2 Examine two financial implications for Wheeler of shortening the development time for new products from 64 weeks to 38. **(12 marks)**

3 **a** Explain the meaning of the term 'simultaneous engineering'. **(3 marks)**
  b Examine the value to a firm such as Wheeler Bikes of using this technique when developing new products. **(12 marks)**

4 As with other elements of lean production, time based management is about the elimination of waste. Discuss the importance of this in improving a firm's international competitiveness. **(15 marks)**

THE BLACK HAIR-DRESSERS

A2
OPERATIONS
MANAGEMENT

CONCEPTS NEEDED:

Critical path analysis, Profit, Break even

It was a Business Studies project that made Kim think seriously about opening the hairdressers. She had always enjoyed fixing friends' hair, but knew that hairdressing trainees were badly paid, so saw no sense in thinking further about such a career. Then came the project.

She had set herself the objective of identifying where and how to open a profitable new hairdressers in Sparkbrook (Birmingham).

A survey among 50 fellow students revealed that 40% went to hairdressers regularly, but few were satisfied with the standard and atmosphere of the salons. She noticed that several had scrawled on the questionnaire comments like: 'All hopeless with Afro-Caribbean styles', which was a view she agreed with heartily. So Kim began to research the prospects for a black hairdressers.

She knew enough about marketing to understand the pros and cons of segmenting the market in this way. If there were no rivals, she would have a good chance of dominating

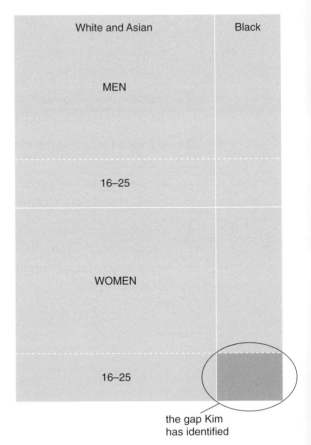

Segmentation of the market for hairdressing for adults

the niche, with all the profit potential that implied. However, if her clients were mainly young (as seemed almost inevitable), she might end up **segmenting a segment**, and thereby have a large share of such a tiny market that overheads would be impossible to cover (see diagram opposite).

A trip to the library told her that 40,000 over-16s lived in her part of Sparkbrook, of which 25% were believed to be of Caribbean origin (and 50% were women). Kim then roped three friends into spending a day interviewing people in the nearby High Street. They approached 140 black women, and managed to get 80 interviews. Kim felt sure that they supported her strategy, and that with 60% saying they would definitely try a new, black salon, she had a potential base of 3,000 customers. Kim was then able to forecast her revenue, on the assumption that half the potential customers would come once every three months, and spend an average of £15 per visit.

Now, a year after getting her A levels, her lifetime savings of £8,000 were to be sunk into the business (along with £4,000 from her parents and the same from the bank). She knew the site she wanted, but needed to make sure that her limited capital would cover not only the start-up period, but also the early months, in case custom proved slow to develop. Her bank manger advised her to set 40% of her funds aside for working capital, i.e. for the day to day running of the business. Given her tight cash constraint, Kim decided to plan the start-up period with great care. She realised that the shorter she could make that period, the less time she would suffer **cash flow difficulties**.

These were the stages she knew she must go through:

A obtaining the site; this would take 2 weeks and would have to be completed before any other activity could begin;

B designing the layout, decor and equipment (3 weeks);

C rebuilding and redecorating (6 weeks);

D buying the equipment ready for installation as soon as C was completed (1 week);

E installation of equipment (1 week);

F hiring staff; this would take about 4 weeks, but could be started after the site was obtained;

G training staff; this would take 3 weeks and could begin only once the equipment had been installed;

H advertising when the salon was to open (2 weeks);

I run a one week half price opening offer.

Adding these up came to 23 weeks, which seemed worryingly long, so Kim drew a **network** diagram to show how to schedule these events to enable completion to take the least possible time.

With just one week until opening time, Kim had just £3,500 left in the bank. Would this be enough to tide her over the half price week? She had calculated that her weekly overheads would be £900, but her £2 variable cost per customer would generate only £5.50 contribution this week.

Fortunately Kim pulled through the early problems and soon had a thriving ethnic hairdressers. Word of mouth proved her main advertising medium, and pulled people in from far enough afield to counteract the worries about segmenting the market excessively.

Questions
(50 marks; 60 minutes)

1 Explain the meaning of the following phrases (in bold print in the text):
segmenting a segment
cash flow difficulties
network **(9 marks)**

2 Show how the figure of 3,000 potential customers was calculated. **(6 marks)**

3 **a** Draw the network required by Kim, labelled to include the earliest start times and latest finish times of each activity. Indicate the critical path. **(15 marks)**
b Analyse two ways in which this diagram could help Kim. **(10 marks)**

4 On the basis of her forecasts, what weekly profit could Kim expect after the launch week was over (assume four weeks per month). How many customers would be required per week to break even? **(10 marks)**

DECIDING ON FACTORY LOCATION

A2
OPERATIONS
MANAGEMENT

CONCEPTS NEEDED:

Location, Break even, Contribution

In his large office in Hesketh House, London W1, James Drayton studied the wall map of Britain. He realised, with some surprise, that he did not know it very well. His 20 years of building up Jarton Electronics had made him familiar with the industrial districts of Japan, Taiwan and South Korea, so he felt he knew Singapore Airport better than he knew Newcastle or Glasgow. Yet having decided to build his first British factory, he knew he must adjust.

Jarton's Projects Director had already done the legwork, and the afternoon's Board Meeting was to discuss whether to choose Site A (Billingham, Co. Durham) or Site B (Rochester, Kent). As Chairman, James Drayton's opinion would probably be decisive. The Projects Director started the meeting by presenting a report on the financial implications of each site.

Report to: The Board of Directors
From: D. Springer, Projects
           Director
Subject: The Costs and Benefits of
           Sites A and B
Date: April 17th

1 Background and Objectives

1.1 Due to forecast excess demand next year, the Board agreed on 2nd March that a new plant should be constructed. It will produce up to 100,000 video cameras per year at a target cost of £225 each. With worries about the degree of import protectionism towards non-EU goods after the establishment of the single currency, the Board approved a proposal that the factory should be constructed in Britain.

1.2 This report sets out the costs of each of two alternative sites, broken down into fixed and variable.

2 The Costs

2.1 Based upon the best available evidence, the costs are:

	Site A	Site B
Fixed (per annum)	£000	£000
Rent and rates	1,240	2,100
Salaried staff	3,660	4,500
Depreciation	1,900	1,900
Interest charges	1,200	1,500
Variable (per unit)	£	£
Materials and components	£89.50	£80.00
Piece rate labour	£4.00	£5.00
Delivery costs	£14.50	£5.00
Travel and expenses	£10.00	£4.00

3 Recommendations

3.1 Final conclusions can only be drawn once the marketing department has made a firm sales forecast. The above costs have been calculated on the assumption that 50% of output would be exported to Europe via the Channel Tunnel. If the proportion changes in favour of UK sales, site A will become more attractive than suggested above.

3.2 If sales are 100,000 units with about half being exports, site B looks more attractive.

The Chairman asked the Personnel Director for comments and received the following reply:

'I have severe doubts about estimates such as these. I think they fail to allow for the problem of high labour turnover in the South. There are the measurable costs of staff turnover, of course, such as recruitment and training overheads. But I think it's still more important to allow for the impact on morale of having too little continuity. Both on the production and R & D side, what we need is experienced, loyal staff. In the long run,

I'm sure that County Durham with its 8% unemployment will serve us better than Kent with its 3%.'

The Marketing and the Finance Directors both spoke against this view. The Finance Director's views were typical of both:

'To succeed, we need first rate top management. If we set up in the North it will be a struggle to get high calibre people, because the best ones want to be in reach of London.'

The Personnel Director thought them ignorant and prejudiced. She was feeling rather isolated, and although the Production Director spoke up in favour of County Durham, it was evident that the majority wanted the factory in the South. She tried one last line of argument:

'Are we not being reckless by ignoring the possibility of a slump in demand for our product? After all, if sales fall sharply from 100,000 and perhaps the price slips from the £320 we anticipate, how will we cope with the high fixed costs in the South?'

The suggestion was greeted in silence, with the Finance Director appearing very angry at this stepping over what he regarded as the demarcation line between finance and the rest of the organisation. He reminded his fellow Directors that:

'Our duty is to our shareholders; it is not for us to allow emotion to cloud our judgement just because unemployment is temporarily higher in the North. At 100,000 units, site B will give us £400,000 more profit than site A. I move we vote for site B and then get on with the rest of our agenda.'

Questions
(50 marks; 70 minutes)

1   On a large scale, construct a break-even graph that shows the
    costs of both sites. Mark and state the point at which B
    becomes more profitable than A.   **(14 marks)**

2   If you were James Drayton and had all the above information
    available, which site would you choose? Explain your answer.   **(12 marks)**

3   How might the Projects Director have found out the
    information upon which to base the figures given in the
    report? How definite would they be?   **(12 marks)**

4   What other information should the Board be requesting
    before it makes a decision? Explain how each piece of
    information could be important.   **(12 marks)**

FINDING A EUROPEAN LOCATION

A2
OPERATIONS
MANAGEMENT

CONCEPTS NEEDED:

Location factors, Direct and indirect costs, Single European market

The success of Stun in the United States has already become a standard business case history. Started as an ethnic, black leisurewear business, it grew on the back of the athletics and basketball successes of its sponsored sports stars. Unusually for a fashionable sportswear firm, Stun had always used the slogan 'The value of style' to highlight that it offered the customer performance at reasonable prices. Sales of $380,000 in its first year ballooned to $56 million by year five. Now, two years later, with US sales still rising at a compound rate of 50%, the Stun directors want to make a decisive move into Europe.

Their strategy is to set up a single marketing and distribution centre which will be given responsibility for covering the entire European Union. The warehousing and transport systems must be capable of handling and storing large volumes of shoes imported from Mexico. The Directors believe that the single European market's removal of costly and time consuming border controls has opened up the opportunity of distributing

goods cheaply to a market of 320 million people. Stun's rivals such as Nike and Reebok operate on a national basis, with offices, depots and staff overheads in each country in Europe. So Stun wants to gain a competitive advantage by benefiting from the economies of scale associated with a single, large operation.

Their problem is to decide where. A consultant has collected data and provided a shortlist of four sites: Dover in south-east England, Hamburg in north Germany, Antwerp in Belgium, and Lille in north-east France. All four sites are near to ports that could cope with the shoes shipped from Mexico. They also have very good motorway and rail links. Yet there are many other points of difference. The consultant has set out the key points in a report; an extract from this is shown below.

From their research into potential European revenues, Stun's Directors forecast first year gross profits of $15 million, after allowing for direct production, distribution

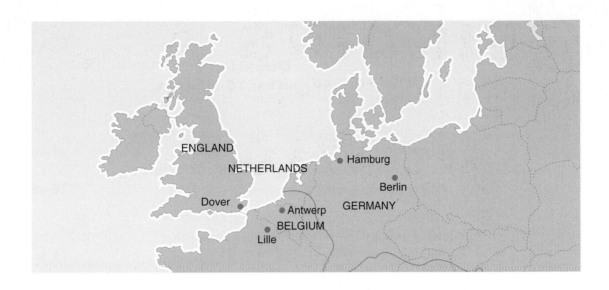

Main resource needs

Office space	10,000 sq feet	Marketing staff	45
Warehousing	80,000 sq feet	Warehouse staff	30
		Other staff	50

Main resource (indirect) costs

	Dover	Hamburg	Antwerp	Lille
Office ($ per sq ft)	14	10	8	8
Warehouse ($ per sq ft)	5	3	2	2
Marketing staff ($ p.a.)	32,000	52,000	40,000	45,000
Warehouse staff ($ p.a.)	15,000	25,000	20,000	18,000
Other staff ($ p.a.)	30,000	40,000	30,000	30,000
Overhead costs ($ p.a.)	570,000	575,000	450,000	500,000
Corporation tax (%) (tax on profit)	35%	48%	40%	38%

and marketing costs. In addition the Dover site would carry a cost penalty of an estimated $2 million for a year's time delays and charges relating to crossing the English Channel.

There are other, less quantifiable factors to consider. As more of the East European countries are allowed to enter the European Union, the nearness of the German site would be most useful. Dover also has its trump cards. The Directors are aware that, as the least regulated of all the member states, Britain would be the easiest location for redundancies or dismissals, should either be necessary. No less important is that senior American managers are more willing to move to England than to continental Europe. Offset against these advantages for Dover is this warning from Stun's consultant: 'Do bear in mind that Britain is a reluctant European Union member, and has not yet joined the euro.'

Stun's Directors have a few calculations and a great deal of thinking to do.

Questions
(60 marks; 70 minutes)

1 a To what level has Stun's annual sales revenue grown over the past two years? **(6 marks)**

b Examine the problems such a growth rate might cause in relation to factory and office sites. **(10 marks)**

2 Evaluate the advantages and disadvantages to Stun of operating with a single location for all its European distribution and marketing. **(14 marks)**

3 a On the basis of the numerical data available, calculate which of the four sites would be the most profitable for the company. **(15 marks)**

b State the assumptions you have made. **(3 marks)**

4 Discuss the reasons why Stun might choose a site other than the one identified on quantitative grounds in question 3. **(12 marks)**

WORK-FORCE PERFORMANCE AND THE SKODA SUPPLIER

A2
OPERATIONS
MANAGEMENT

CONCEPTS NEEDED:

Motivation theory, Accountability, Personnel performance, Change

Sadiq could hardly believe it. Only 15 months out of university and he had landed this plum project. His employer Lincoln McGee, Management Consultants, hired him straight from college in preference to 18 other shortlisted candidates. Three months of induction training were followed by a series of assistant roles in projects run by senior partners. Now Sadiq was being sent to Liberec, 80 km north-east of Prague. His task was to advise Floc, a supplier to Skoda cars, on the modernisation of its factory working methods and practices.

Lincoln McGee had been hired because of Skoda's threat to withdraw orders from Floc if the supplier could not guarantee performance improvements within four months. The specification laid down by Skoda is shown in the table below.

Problem	Measurement	Current rate	Target rate
Quality	Rejects per thousand	24.5	9.9
Lead times	Time from order to delivery	18 days	6 days
Delivery reliability	% of occasions delivery is late	23.5%	2.5%

Over the following month he came to know the Floc components factory intimately. Sadiq's excellent German made it easy to communicate with the Czech managers and supervisors, and his youthful appearance encouraged people to talk openly.

The Works Director told him that the whole assembly section of the plant had, until the late 1980s, been staffed by political prisoners. To minimise sabotage risks, production was reduced to many simple operations. The winding mechanism for a car window, for example, involved 18 different people, each recruited and trained to complete a task as quickly as possible. Such was the specialisation that workers who could carry out their own task in nine seconds per unit might take five times longer if switched to someone else's. This mattered little in the past, as the prisoners were not allowed to be absent. Now, with paid employees carrying out these tedious tasks, absenteeism had become a major worry.

Floc did not have conveyor belt production lines, so to ensure high output rates the payment structure was through piece rate. As each stage of production took a slightly different time and skill, a staff of 14 salaried clerical workers was employed to set, measure and calculate the piece work payments. Recently the factory workers had elected their own representative to negotiate the sums involved. There was even talk of joining the National Engineering Union. There were two main grievances: the piece rate wage loss caused to an individual by being forced to switch from their own post to that of another, absent colleague; plus the poor health and safety position within the plant.

The Floc factory was a huge, drab site with three corrugated iron buildings linked by pot-holed roadways. The machinery in most of the plant was 30 years old and revealed little concern for health and safety. There was no extraction system for the dust and fumes caused by the mechanical and chemical processes used. Not all the machines were guarded to protect workers from moving parts. Sadiq learned that the average accident rate was 9.5 per week, with serious injuries occurring at least once a month.

Sadiq spent the fourth week of his investigations visiting Floc's suppliers and customers. He wanted to find out their opinion of the company. The suppliers were understandably hesitant about criticising their customer, but Sadiq was able to learn that the Floc production staff had never met or even spoken to the supplier factory management. The only contact was through Floc's purchasing department. Skoda, the main customer, was complimentary about Floc's helpful customer service, agreeing to replace defective parts without a quibble. Nevertheless it did criticise the erratic deliveries and unreliable quality standards.

Lincoln McGee had a four week consultancy contract, so it was now time for Sadiq to present his findings to Floc's 13 Directors, and to make his recommendations for change. There would be one other participant at the meeting, as Mr Fraser McGee was flying out specially. So Sadiq spent a whole day preparing the slides for his presentation.

For a full two hours, Sadiq was on his feet going through a detailed account of Floc's strengths and many weaknesses. As lunchtime approached, he summarised his argument:

Main strengths:

- effective control of output and costs
- good recruitment and training procedures for the manufacturing system being used.

Main weaknesses:

- Absenteeism levels running at:

Monday	11.4%
Tuesday	9.1%
Wednesday	6.9%
Thursday (payday)	2.7%
Friday	10.1%

- ratio of direct (factory) labour to indirect (staff) of 1 : 1.6 compared with 1 : 0.6 in equivalent British plants, thereby generating a very high staff overhead cost

- a prevailing attitude (culture) of interest in high volume production at the expense of product quality, delivery schedules or customer satisfaction

- a climate of fear of detection; no one wants to be held accountable for mistakes, so errors are hidden and decisions delayed: 'There is always a bunch of signatures on every document,' says Sadiq.

With Sadiq's report over, they all went off to lunch. He felt delighted by how well the morning had gone, but knew that the hardest part had yet to come: the recommendations for action.

Questions
(60 marks; 80 minutes)

1 Examine the probable causes of Floc's poor performance at the factors identified in the table. **(10 marks)**

2 If Floc continues to operate as at present, what personnel problems might arise if Skoda requires Floc to change to higher technology production of a brand new product? **(10 marks)**

3 What actions might the company take to reduce:
  a the level of absenteeism **(7 marks)**
  b the proportion of indirect labour? **(6 marks)**

4 Analyse the underlying problems in terms of motivation theory. **(12 marks)**

5 Putting yourself into Sadiq's place, discuss the recommendations for action that you would make. **(15 marks)**

JUST-IN-TIME PRODUCTION – THE JAPANESE WAY

CONCEPTS NEEDED:

Communications, Stock control, Productivity, Objectives and constraints

As Redlin's new Group Production Controller, Paul Booth felt it important that he should make his intentions clear from the start. So he arranged a meeting with the seven senior and middle managers answerable to him, to announce his commitment to just-in-time (JIT) production systems. He put his case as follows:

'**G***iven the low profitability of our products in recent years, plus the threat of increased competition when we finally join the euro, we have to tackle our uncompetitiveness compared with the Germans and the Japanese. We have not got the demand to justify a fully automated flow production system, so we must ensure that we make the best use of our 500 staff and our financial* resources by moving towards the Japanese just-in-time (JIT) method. In other words production that operates so smoothly that waste of time, labour and resources is minimised, as each part arrives just in time for the next stage of manufacture.*'

Booth concentrated first on the suppliers, with three objectives in mind:

1 to minimise the need for raw material stocks;

2 to eliminate the need for goods-inward quality inspection;

3 good communications with suppliers to ensure their awareness of new product developments that may require them to redesign and retool.

To achieve the first objective, it was necessary to switch from the traditional system of infrequent deliveries of bulk orders, to very frequent – even daily – deliveries. To make that economic, one supplier had to be chosen to get the whole order instead of having competing suppliers. Before the JIT programme, Redlin had 330 suppliers with an average on-time delivery performance of 82%. As JIT relies upon 100% reliability of supply (since virtually no buffer stock is held), Booth began discussions with the suppliers with a view to cutting their number to one hundred of the most reliable.

For the second objective, since 207 of the 330 had already achieved 100% quality, Booth could act decisively to ensure that suppliers took their materials straight to the production line, rather than through a quality control inspector. The latter could be switched to checking the quality of Redlin's finished goods.

To improve Redlin's communications with suppliers in order to meet the third objective, Booth began an education programme for each: a factory tour, conversation with the workers using those materials, and a discussion between the New Product Development engineers and the supplier. After several months of close contact, he persuaded the suppliers that if they delivered a faulty component, they would have to pay for all the costs generated. In other words, if a 25 pence switch was discovered to be faulty after it had been built into a Redlin RangeVan, and it cost £40 of labour time to replace it, the supplier would have to pay Redlin £40.25 compensation. Both sides could see that such a strong incentive to supply 100% reliability would be to everyone's long term benefit.

Having completed the preparations for supplier reliability, Booth was in a stronger position to convince his manager of the opportunities provided. After all, if components could be relied upon totally, less labour would be needed to handle stocks, because the suppliers could deliver straight to the factory floor. The Assembly Manager also suggested: 'Less warehousing should be needed for stocks, so perhaps we could convert half the warehouse into the assembly line extension we need so badly.'

The Group Production Controller reminded them, though, that JIT would require some fundamental changes. Meticulous production planning would be needed, so that suppliers could receive their orders four days before delivery was needed. No less importantly, it would be essential to ensure that work flow in every section of the factory was uninterrupted. Previously, a temporary breakdown in one section would not stop work elsewhere in the factory, because semi-finished products were stockpiled at every stage of manufacture and assembly. Now the approach would be what the Japanese term 'Kanban', whereby good communications between production sections enable each to produce the right quantity of the right components for the next section to use. As a result, no stockpiling of work-in-progress should be necessary.

One senior production manager looked at Booth with disbelief, and said:

'**W**e're not dealing with Japanese machine-people out there, you know! On a Monday 15% of them will be "off sick", and we won't know which 15% until 8 o'clock that morning. What if they're mostly from one section, so we can't get any production of a vital component that day? Must we send the rest of the workforce home?'

This comment emboldened others to add:

'**A**nd what about machine breakdowns? The average one takes three hours to restart and we get at least a couple a day. After all, we've a good 180 machines on each production line.'

'**I**'m more worried about the power it'll give to the shopfloor workers. We'll be so dependent on each one of them that they'll have us over a barrel.'

Booth listened as one after the other criticised his proposal, then he fished some sheets of paper out of his briefcase which, without speaking, he handed to each of them. They quietened down as they looked at the contents (see opposite). After five minutes of silence he asked them if they accepted his view that the situation was critical, and needed drastic action. Glumly, they nodded.

Although that meeting had ended gloomily, over the following weeks Booth saw each manager individually to discuss how they should help move towards the Japanese JIT production method. Each came to realise that full cooperation from the workforce was an essential element in the process. Some saw this as a marvellous opportunity to adopt a different management style from the authoritarian one they had used in the past. Others, though, dreaded the changes involved; two sought early retirement and one asked for time off to look for another job. Booth agreed, knowing that full commitment among the management was essential.

After three months of intensive training on JIT the managers felt able to implement changes. One of the first was to negotiate a job flexibility deal with the trade unions. This would overcome the problem of individual absentees holding up production. If all workers could do each other's jobs, staff could be switched as necessary. After this change was achieved, Booth experimented by doing away with a component stockpile between the grinding and the plating departments. The plating team were made responsible for ensuring that the grinders had their 'orders' at the beginning of each day – so no overnight stocks were needed. When this process was running smoothly (after two months) it was introduced step by step through the factory. After two years, the improvements began to show through in dramatic productivity and financial gains.

Key facts on Redlin's competitive position

Redlin's market share

	UK	Europe	Rest of world
Last month	19%	8%	5%
1 year ago	23%	10%	8%
5 years ago	31%	12%	11%

Output per worker (productivity)

	Redlin	Average European rival	Average Japanese rival
Last month	24*	31	45
1 year ago	24	29	40
5 years ago	19	23	26

Units of output per month

Stockholding per worker*

	Redlin	Average European rival	Average Japanese rival
Latest year	£9,800	£6,500	£1,800
Previous year	£9,500	£6,600	£2,700
5 years ago	£7,100	£5,800	£4,900

Stock value divided by no. of workers

Questions
(70 marks; 90 minutes)

1   Outline the reasons why good communications are regarded
    as crucial to the success of JIT.   **(10 marks)**

2   Consider how Redlin's suppliers would view the changes being
    introduced.   **(12 marks)**

3   Explain the significance of the figures Booth provided.   **(13 marks)**

4   Examine the financial benefits Redlin might have received from the
    impact of the JIT system on their stock and productivity positions. **(10 marks)**

5   Booth overcame his management's resistance to change.
    Examine two other internal constraints he might have faced
    in the circumstances outlined.   **(10 marks)**

6   Traditional economic theory suggests that firms make
    decisions on the basis of short run profit maximisation.
    Discuss this in the light of the above text.   **(15 marks)**

HUMAN RESOURCE MANAGEMENT AND COST CONTROLS

CONCEPTS NEEDED:

Types of production, Standard times/costs, Single status

Dreeman Limited is a manufacturing firm employing 40 factory and 30 administrative/managerial staff. It is a major producer of smoke detectors, which it designs, assembles, tests and markets.

It regards itself as rather progressive in its personnel policies, with its close links with local colleges, and its **single status** conditions of service. So, whereas in many firms only the factory workers have to clock in, and have no sick pay and no company pension, at Dreeman the shopfloor staff enjoy the same rights as the white-collar staff. This system was introduced three years ago, when four factory workers with 80 years' service between them, refused to clock in any more. Now the Managing Director believes there is much more mutual trust and respect between workforce and management.

Each year, Dreeman makes over 100,000 smoke detectors, in 26 different models. The largest selling line – with 12,000 units – is produced continually, the remainder in batches. Having so many lines produced by batch production in the same factory, and largely by the same people, makes it hard to keep track of how long it takes to produce each item. Without accurate information, it is then impossible for the accountant to decide the true production cost; this matters because 60% of the firm's direct costs are on labour. In turn, it makes pricing a hit-and-miss affair. The other need for accurate production time information is to enable the supervisor to judge the output per worker. Annual bonuses can be based on this information, as can decisions to give warnings of dismissal to those considered inefficient.

At present, Dreeman's approach is two-fold:

1   Standard Costs are calculated when a new line is introduced. This entails a lot of work in measuring precisely how long it should take to carry out each task, plus the estimated wage, material, and fuel costs per unit. Yet it has the advantage of providing a yardstick against which shopfloor performance can be measured. Unfortunately, shopfloor resistance to the sight of anyone with a stopwatch means that once an item is in production, the Standard Times do not get updated. Some are as much as 10 years old.

2   The second element in their costing system is timesheets, on which the factory workers are supposed to record how long they spent on each batch of work. If these were completed accurately, it would be possible to calculate precisely the time spent per unit on each line made. This could then be compared with the Standard Times to assess efficiency. Unfortunately, the shopfloor workers regard timesheets either as pointless **bureaucracy** or as a threat, so

they fill them in only when the supervisor pressures them – too infrequently for them to be accurate.

Now a new Human Resources Manager has been given the task of setting up a computerised system of timesheet analysis that would print out actual production times per unit. Although a computer novice, he knows enough to warn the Managing Director: 'Computerising a defective system can only speed up the mess.'

When he starts talking the problem over with the two factory supervisors, he is surprised to find out that not even they know how the information is used to work out production costs and prices. What is clear, though, is that shopfloor resistance to the system is deep rooted. One supervisor suggests:

'*If you want a system that my crew will work properly, you've got to make it so that it cannot be used to measure their own performance. They can't abide snooping.*'

In fact, it is the Human Resources Manager's secretary who suggests the solution that is adopted. She suggests a timesheet that follows the batch round the factory floor, and is filled in anonymously by those who spend time on the batch. In that way, no one need object to filling it in, and therefore a training session on its importance should ensure that it will be completed with fair accuracy. As she says:

'*Better to have valid information on one thing than worthless information on two.*'

Questions
(60 marks; 70 minutes)

1 Examine the business significance of:
   a single status
   b bureaucracy   **(10 marks)**

2 **a** Outline three main benefits to a business of operating
      continuous/flow production, instead of by batch.   **(9 marks)**
   b What is the average output for the batch-produced lines?   **(3 marks)**

3 **a** Explain the term 'Standard Times'.   **(3 marks)**
   b What benefits does Dreeman's wish to obtain from using
      Standard Times?   **(6 marks)**
   c What is the significance of the information that some of
      the Standard Times are 'as much as 10 years old'?   **(8 marks)**

4 Comment on the secretary's solution.   **(9 marks)**

5 Discuss the company's view that it is 'rather progressive in its
   human resources policies'.   **(12 marks)**

KAIZEN – CONTINUOUS IMPROVEMENT AT OKI

CONCEPTS NEEDED:

Lean production, ISO 9000, Productivity

In 1992 a company only four years old won three prestigious awards. *Management Today* magazine named it the 'Best Electronics Factory in Britain'; ICL awarded it a total quality accolade; and it became one of the first companies to reach the government's standard as an 'Investor In People'. The management was delighted, but fearful that complacency might set in. So OKI (UK) Ltd redoubled its efforts to improve, continuously.

The Japanese electronics company OKI had decided to establish a dot-matrix printer factory in Europe in 1987. After brief consideration of Germany and Spain, the project leader, Mr Kojima, decided on Britain. This was due to the success of other Japanese firms in the UK, plus the familiarity of OKI staff with (American) English. Mr Kojima

OKI

settled upon Cumbernauld in Scotland for its air and sea transport and its closeness to numerous electronic component suppliers in the heart of 'Silicon Glen'.

Mr Kojima was appointed Managing Director of OKI (UK) Ltd and given the task of getting a new factory up and running within two months. Sixty experienced OKI staff were flown over to help commission a factory layout designed and developed in Japan. Meanwhile, Mr Kojima recruited new managers and supervisors and arranged for each one to spend at least a week in Japan. From the start, it was established that OKI would be a single status employer, with everyone paid on a straight salary basis.

By mid 1988 the Cumbernauld plant had 300 staff producing 2,400 printers per week. Twelve months later a doubled staff level made 6,000 printers weekly. Having coped with the pressures of rapid expansion, OKI's UK management team wanted time to think through the company's future. A series of discussions was held with managers and a hundred shopfloor representatives. All agreed that OKI should build its future around its staff rather than automation. Yet the highly competitive market for printers made it essential for costs to fall and for quality to rise each year. This pointed to the Japanese idea of 'kaizen' (continuous improvement).

OKI management translated kaizen as follows:

KAIZEN

'*The establishment of a process for continued improvement involving everyone – managers and workers alike.*'

This became the unifying theme that ran through the company's production and personnel practices.

Ian Smith, the production manager, realised it would be hard for each individual among many to see how to contribute meaningfully to OKI's overall improvement.

Therefore a system was needed to provide immediate, localised feedback on performance to each staff member. OKI followed a two-stage process to achieve this.

1 Cell production. The factory operation was split into five cells, each with its own suppliers and 'customers' (internal and external). For instance, completed printed circuit boards (PCBs) were delivered to the final assembly line, so the assembly line was the customer. If the 'customer' found any quality defects, these were reported back to the relevant PCB workers. An important side-effect of this system was that quality was checked several times over. In 1992, buyers of OKI's printers reported a defect rate of only 0.25% (one in 400).

2 Performance targets. Each section had a daily quality target (such as a maximum of eight reported defects per day). This was displayed on a large board to which was added, every hour, the 'customer's' report on quality performance (see below).

PCB Quality Performance Friday 24th					
FAULT	MAXIMUM	ACHIEVEMENT			
		9.00	10.00	11.00	12.00 →
Loose fit	1	–	N O	1	–
Cracking	3	–	D E F	–	–
Electrical fault	2	1	E C	–	–
Discolouring	2	–	T S	1	1

This system ensured that the PCB workers knew within an hour if a fault had slipped through to the assembly line. The individual responsible could be traced and the cause discussed. This might lead directly to a suggestion that would improve the production process. For example, workers suggested changing the height of work benches, criticised the quality of materials from certain suppliers and learned to spot when machines were starting to go wrong.

Improvement need not only stem from mistakes, however, so it was important to find ways of discussing how good methods could be made better. OKI's approach to communications began with a 5–10 minute meeting every morning. Problems concerning the previous day's production were discussed and possible improvements often emerged. Twice a year all employees had an appraisal interview with their immediate superior. This was not concerned with pay or bonus levels, but with any problems or ambitions the employee had. It was a form of more reflective communication.

Interlinked with OKI's approach to communications was its heavy expenditure on training. Within its £250,000 training area, OKI provided new recruits with full induction courses, including simulated conveyor belt production lines. Existing staff were encouraged to take between six and 15 days of training per year, primarily focused upon learning new skills. This created a more flexible workforce and provided the skills (such as public speaking) to foster the discussion and involvement that the management wanted. In addition to job training, the company was very proud that staff were taking Further Education evening courses up to degree level – sponsored by OKI.

In 1993 OKI piloted its first suggestion scheme, among the sub-assembly workers. A rule set from the start was that suggestions would be considered only if they related to the person's own performance. Suggestions on how others could improve were not welcome. The management team – all with experience of suggestion schemes in British firms – had debated about what type of financial rewards to offer. When raised with the pilot staff, however, this was treated with surprise. The staff felt that suggestions to improve people's working life or performance were worthwhile in themselves. The scheme got off to a strong start and was extended to other sections of the plant.

The result of all this effort was measured in two ways within the factory: quality defects and productivity. In 1988, 75% of completed PCBs passed first time when tested. After a year an 80% target was set, which was extended to 85% in 1992. With that having been achieved, the 1993 pass rate was pushed to 89%. This progress not only reduced the chance of a faulty product slipping through to the customer, but also reduced production time and therefore cost. Instead of 25% of all PCBs needing extra work in 1988, the target for 1993 pointed to only 11% failing first time.

The factory manager liked to measure productivity in a slightly unusual way. He concentrated on the time it took for a printer to be produced. In 1988 it took 120 minutes from the start of the final assembly line until packing. This included 45 minutes of 'robust test printing in extreme temperature conditions'. In 1994 the assembly target was 75 minutes, even though the test had not changed. This approach to improvement enabled output per worker to rise to 16 printers per week in 1993.

When asked about the company's management approach, Mr Kojima denied that it was purely Japanese. He made it clear that he preferred the plain speaking of his Scots staff to the respectful language of the Japanese. Yet as he sat with his blue jacket on – the same jacket as on the shopfloor – there was no doubt that he had brought Japanese thinking to Scotland; and it seemed to be a marriage of continuous improvement.

Source: Visits and interviews

Questions
(60 marks; 90 minutes)

1 Examine why OKI's management might be happy to build the company's future 'around its staff rather than automation'. **(10 marks)**

2 From OKI's experience, evaluate the main preconditions of establishing a successful kaizen programme. **(10 marks)**

3 **a** Calculate OKI's output per worker in 1988 and 1989. **(6 marks)**

    b Assuming an average wage of £150 per week in 1988 and £200 in 1993, what was the labour cost per unit in those two years? Express the change as a percentage. **(8 marks)**

4 Ian Smith tries hard to encourage a lean approach to production at the Cumbernauld factory. What does this mean and what examples of this are evident within the text? **(10 marks)**

5 OKI holds the ISO 9000 quality standard, describing it as 'a possible starting point for developing high quality products'.

    a Why may ISO 9000 not lead to high quality products? **(6 marks)**

    b Explain how OKI achieved the quality levels that won the ICL and *Management Today* awards. **(10 marks)**

46 PRODUC-
TION
MANAGEMENT

CONCEPTS NEEDED:

Stocks, Theory X and Y, Company objectives, Production management

Scott's arrival from the United States as the new Managing Director came after eight redundancy programmes within the previous 10 years. So the workforce of York International was understandably defensive, and job demarcation was rife. As a producer of air conditioning equipment, the firm's sales were dependent upon the highly cyclical construction industry – hence its hire-and-fire record. The poor morale among the 800 workers showed in the firm's poor delivery and quality performance. Sixty-one per cent of all deliveries were over 20 days late, and quality costs of £1.5 million a year were accounting for 14% of the total manufacturing bill. The major element in the quality cost was warranty claims, which implied further customer inconvenience and therefore dissatisfaction.

Scott's first statement to his staff was to promise no more redundancies, and to announce a three year programme for 'Order out of chaos'. At first, middle management was as sceptical as the workforce. The first

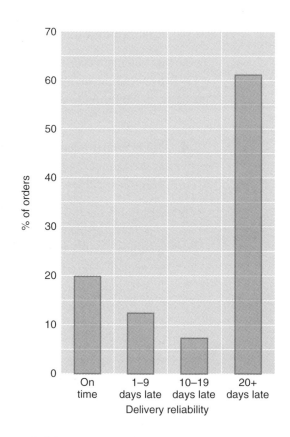

York delivery record before introduction of 'Order out of chaos' programme

action that made people take notice was Scott's order to the sales department to aim for steady growth. They were to refuse orders that would beat their sales targets, since that would disrupt the attempt to reorganise the production system. His second action was to set the factory the objective of establishing an efficient system of production control so that the whole production monitoring process could be computerised in 12 months' time. For Scott had quickly appreciated that York's fundamental problem was that it was locked into a chaos spiral. Disorganisation undermined production control, which reinforced the disorganisation; and low morale had become both cause and effect. The greatest surprise for the staff was that the third step was not to dictate how this objective should be achieved, as the previous management would have done. Instead, Scott encouraged middle management to work in teams with engineers and shopfloor workers to decide on the correct strategy.

The building of order required certain key building blocks.

1 Training was needed on the purpose of monitoring systems, so that it was possible to obtain accurate data. Before, maintenance men would have helped themselves to spare parts from the stores; now careful recording took place.

2 Meaningful production plans were needed to schedule people's work for each day. Variance analysis was used to check the accuracy of the planning, and major variances by individual workers were discussed openly between worker and foreman.

Within the 12 month target, York had production information of an accuracy that it had never enjoyed before; and production

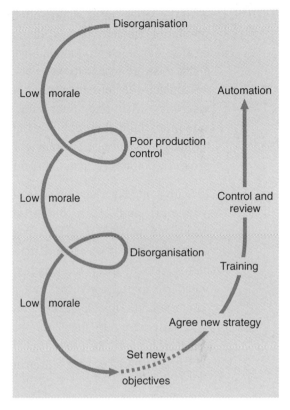

Order out of chaos

planning had emerged from the old-style crisis management. By the time the Manufacturing Resource Planning (MRP) computer was installed, Scott suspected that they had already achieved 80% of all the possible gains.

The computer monitored all material inputs and stocks, all production in each section of the factory (plus wastage) and finished goods quality and stock levels. It could also match this information with customer order quantities and delivery dates, enabling managers to anticipate when completion of a particular order would need to be speeded up. Within a year of the MRP computer's installation, on-time deliveries had risen to 85%, from 20% just two years before.

In the longer term, though, the computer's simulation capacity proved its most valuable facility. It enabled production engineers to get quick answers to questions such as 'What if we replace the four hand-operated pressing machines with one automated one?' The computer could show not only the direct cost implications, but also the impact on work-in-progress, on factory layout, and on overheads.

Scott's managerial skill was to use such print-outs not as a blueprint, but for discussion with the relevant engineers and workers. Often it was found that there were better ways of using the existing equipment (perhaps using conveyor belt transfer of components). This encouraged the workforce to participate in decision making, and therefore to work to prove that the decision they had initiated or backed was the right one.

The higher motivation of the workforce showed through in product quality. From representing 6.5% of the total manufacturing bill, the cost of guarantee claims fell to 1%.

The next stage in the company's production-led revival came with the appointment of an expert in just-in-time manufacturing as the production director. When interviewing, Scott made sure that candidates were not only qualified technically, but were also committed to a bottom-up approach to employee involvement. Authoritarian, top-down managers were rejected. For Scott was convinced that active participation by the workforce was essential if further changes to working practices were necessary.

Source: Machinery and Production Engineering

Questions
(70 marks; 90 minutes)

1 Explain why Scott felt the need to announce a programme for 'Order out of chaos'. **(10 marks)**

2 How would the preparation for – and installation of – the MRP computer have helped York's stock position? **(10 marks)**

3 Discuss the management styles outlined in the text in terms of McGregor's Theory X and Y. **(15 marks)**

4 **a** How might the computer's 'What if?' facility be used to improve further the product and service quality received by customers? **(10 marks)**
  b Why would such achievements be important? **(10 marks)**

5 In what ways could the success of Scott's approach be measured other than the ones listed in the text? In what circumstances would such approaches be especially important? **(15 marks)**

MONEY AND MOTIVATION

AS
PEOPLE IN
ORGANISATIONS

CONCEPTS NEEDED:

Profit, Remuneration, Motivation theory

The Walton Furniture Company is a long established, highly profitable business. Its sales turnover averages £15,000 per week. Given that it operates on a 200% mark-up (quite normal in furniture retailing), its £7,500 of weekly overheads are covered with ease. The owners have always believed that much of their success has been due to the incentive scheme they operate; the 2% commission on all sales provides a carrot of about £300 per week for the staff.

Recently, however, the owner/managers (Mr and Mrs Vine) have seen takings hit, following the departure of the only two full-time staff. Over the past eight weeks, sales have averaged only £10,500. Mr Vine believes it is just a temporary problem, as the two new full-timers find their feet. Mrs Vine decides to talk to each of the six staff members to find out their views.

Joyce, a 55 year old part-timer, has no doubts:

‘It's the commission system that's causing the problem. Both the full-timers left because of it, and I'm totally fed up with it as well ... The problem is that you pay commission only to the

person who writes out the customer's bill. So no one wants to do any of the other jobs such as checking deliveries, chasing up special orders, or pricing new stock. You keep asking me to do these jobs because you know I'm reliable; but that prevents me from getting commission.’

Eileen, a 22 year old part-timer, is even more forceful:

‘I can't stand Grace (another part-timer), because she's always robbing me of my commission. Yesterday morning, I spent two hours discussing sofas with a customer. After she'd settled on two £1,100 leather ones, she felt she should bring her husband along for a second opinion in the afternoon. And what happens? When I come back after my afternoon break I see them just leaving, and Grace has written out the bill for £2,200. So she makes £44 for doing damn all, while I do the work and get nothing. I'm still fuming, and I refuse to work with her again.'

A shaken Mrs Vine then sees Margherita, one of the new full-timers (and the deputy manager). She is hardly reassuring:

'I've never known such a touchy, bitchy staff. I'm seriously thinking of quitting. I got Joyce to do some pricing this morning, and for the rest of the day she's been grumbling about Eileen getting a £1,000 order from a regular customer of hers. I can't see that £20 is worth all the fuss.'

Questions
(40 marks; 60 minutes)

1 Remembering the commission, what profit would the Vines have made last year? **(8 marks)**

2 Outline three problems with the commission system operated by the Vines. **(9 marks)**

3 What alternative payment systems might work better, and why? **(8 marks)**

4 Analyse and evaluate the behaviour and attitudes of staff using a motivation theory of your choice. **(15 marks)**

MANAGE-MENT STRUCTURE

AS
PEOPLE IN
ORGANISATIONS

CONCEPTS NEEDED:

Management hierarchy, Company objectives, Span of control

The new Chief Executive of British Aircraft Technologies (BAT) was a straightforward man. He thought it was his job to know how all the divisions of the business were doing. 'But how can I,' he complained, 'when there are twelve divisions – each answerable to me?' He intended to set a **corporate objective** of cutting costs by 30% over the next three years, but was concerned about his own ability to monitor progress. As the objective was fundamental to BAT's survival in the competitive environment for high technology products, he decided a complete organisational restructuring was needed.

After several months of discussion with divisional senior management, it became clear that eight of the 12 could be merged into four new divisions – each headed by a Chairman. Of the remaining four, the managers in three were implacably opposed to any loss of independence. Yet the involvement of all three in military production suggested the solution that a Chairman be appointed to oversee the three

independent divisions. The 12th division fitted poorly with any of the others, so it was kept separate; it, too, was to be run by a new Chairman.

Within this new hierarchy, the divisional Chairman would be answerable to the Chief Executive, who would in turn be **accountable** to the Board of Directors. The Chief Executive would agree corporate objectives with the Board, then decide divisional goals and budgets in consultation with each Chairman before the start of each year. The Chairman would then have complete autonomy to work within the agreed constraint, and each division would be a **profit centre**.

The new structure proved highly successful. The Civil Aircraft division set its own priority as the reduction of production time, in order to speed up deliveries to customers. This, it reasoned, would increase demand and thereby enable existing capacity to be utilised more effectively.

Within two years the assembly time on the executive jet had been cut from 26 weeks to 12. This was achieved by reorganising the factory layout, automating the more repetitive tasks, and retraining staff to use existing equipment more efficiently. These changes were implemented only after very full consultation with the workforce; indeed some of the most valuable ideas came directly from the shopfloor. It was clear that the division would achieve its cost reduction target, and at higher output levels than many had thought possible.

Four of the other divisions adopted more conventional cost cutting measures, which also looked likely to achieve the 30% cut the Chief Executive demanded.

The Military Products division, though, struggled badly. Its Thames Valley production site for Guided Weapons was losing many high quality, technologically educated staff to local computer firms. Labour turnover was averaging 35% a year on its 2,000 employees. Given that new employees were costing an average of £4,000 to recruit and train, the annual cost was enormous.

The Chairman of the Military Products division argued that the site should be moved to Derby, where the larger pool of skilled labour should ensure longer term employment. The Director of Guided Weapons refused to allow this, however, and reminded the Chairman that he had delegated to him the details of the restructuring. Six months after this, a reorganisation was announced for the Military Products division, in which the post of Director of Guided Weapons became redundant.

Questions
(50 marks; 70 minutes)

1 Explain the meaning of the following (in bold print in the text):
corporate objective
accountable
profit centre
(9 marks)

2 What was the Chief Executive's span of control before the
reorganisation? What evidence is there that it was too wide? **(8 marks)**

3 Draw a chart to show the organisational hierarchy after the
first restructuring. **(8 marks)**

4 Discuss why it is considered so important for organisations
to have a clear structure, with clear lines of authority. **(10 marks)**

5 How might careful consultation help in the reorganisation of
the factory layout? **(6 marks)**

6 Discuss whether BAT's retraining of factory staff would have
been more likely to succeed if carried out on-the-job or
off-the-job. **(9 marks)**

A BMW AT TWENTY-THREE

CONCEPTS NEEDED:

Mayo, Maslow, Leadership styles

Yin Fan had a wonderful time at the school reunion. It started as soon as she turned up in her BMW. She happily told all the inquirers that it was her company car. 'A BMW at twenty-three!' gasped one. Throughout the evening she was grilled about her career, with many of her former classmates eager to know where she was working and at how high a salary. Several others had made good starts to their working lives, but none as glitteringly as Yin Fan.

When asked for details, Yin Fan explained that her advertising agency job involved planning and buying multi-million pound media campaigns for the agency's clients. She had to liaise with the marketing managers of advertisers such as Cadbury, Heinz and Dixons to find out the target market they were aiming for and then decide which media to use – TV or newspapers? If TV, how much on ITV or Channel 4 or on satellite? How much in each ITV region? And so on. Yin Fan's working life was one of meetings, business lunches and a frantic social life revolving around an advertising agency staffed by young, well paid people.

Back at her desk the following Monday, Yin Fan found herself enjoying the work more

than ever. She smiled at the thought of her school friends' amazement that she had a PA (personal assistant) and a trainee working for her. The day's work revolved around an important negotiation for Cadbury on Channel 4. She met her boss, the Media Director, for 20 minutes to discuss tactics.

Tony was an unusual boss; from the day he hired Yin Fan two years ago, he had hardly ever told her what to do. On that day he gave her the Cadbury and Heinz business to run, and since then had done little more than to offer her the huge Dixons account as well. At first she had been daunted by her total responsibility for decisions involving millions of pounds. She knew that her predecessor had been fired, reputedly because one of the clients had talked about him unenthusiastically to Tony. Yet as the weeks passed she felt liberated by the freedom to make instant decisions. At her previous agency the Media Director had fussed over every aspect of the job, frustrating Yin Fan by interventions that seemed to cause more mistakes than they cured. Occasionally she and Tony talked over work at lunch, but otherwise he focused on his own clients and his Board responsibilities.

So her visit to talk things over with Tony was unusual. She wanted advice because the Sales Manager she would be dealing with at Channel 4 was an old friend of Tony's. With a planned budget of £500,000 for Channel 4, a discount of as little as 10% would represent a lot of money to hand back to Cadbury. So she wanted to establish the right approach to the negotiations.

Despite the pressures of the day, Tony found the time not only to advise Yin Fan, but also to ask her generally about how things were going. She took the opportunity to tell him how she had struck a deal giving Heinz £150,000 of extra, free TV airtime in Scotland, and about a costly mistake on a new business presentation. After 50 minutes she left Tony's office feeling invigorated. By mid-afternoon she had a 16.5% discount rate from Channel 4 and a rather smug smile.

Questions
(50 marks; 60 minutes)

1 Analyse Yin Fan's working life in relation to Maslow's hierarchy of needs. **(12 marks)**

2 **a** Examine Tony's leadership style, using relevant theory. **(9 marks)**
  b In what circumstances might such a style be ineffective? **(8 marks)**

3 **a** What is meant by the term 'Hawthorne Effect' and when did it occur in this case? **(6 marks)**
  b The motivational importance of the Hawthorne Effect was identified over 70 years ago. Discuss why many managers still appear to ignore it. **(15 marks)**

MR McGREGOR

AS
PEOPLE IN
ORGANISATIONS

CONCEPTS NEEDED:

McGregor, Herzberg, Induction, Delegation

It was all the more frustrating for Gemma because of his name – Mr McGregor. She did not know his first name, but felt sure it wasn't Douglas. The other depressing aspect of it was that Gemma had spent ages looking for this job. After leaving college with three reasonable A levels, she had specifically wanted employment in a bank. With jobs so hard to find locally, it had been a huge thrill when the call came through to say she could start the following Monday.

The week's induction programme had been great. Held at a regional training centre, it had been wonderful to meet other keen beginners like herself. The training was well planned and quite interesting; and of course there was the delicious thrill of practising counting money – masses of it.

Then came the first day in the branch and the first meeting with the Deputy Manager, Mr McGregor. To be fair, he made a bit of an effort on that day, but by day 2 a clear pattern had emerged. Mr McGregor kept his door shut, except on the all too frequent occasions when he came round to check up on staff, or to demand to see someone about a customer complaint. All the staff were scared of him. That was not a problem in itself, as fear

brought them together. Gemma would have had little in common with the middle aged staff around her had it not been for their shared dislike of the Deputy Manager.

The real problem was the way it started to affect her. Just 10 days into the job Gemma's two-bus journey into work was disrupted by a bus breaking down in driving rain. Late, soaked and stressed, she was greeted by a long lecture about self discipline and reliability. Later that day she was called in to Mr McGregor's room to be told that he was unhappy at Gemma's slowness at serving customers. She tried to protest that she was still learning, but was cut short. She left feeling like a naughty schoolgirl. Later, a silver-haired colleague said, 'Don't worry pet, he makes me feel the same and I haven't been at school in a long time.'

The frustrations were huge. Not only did Gemma get nervous, always making mistakes when Mr McGregor was around, but also she had hoped to learn about banking, and that seemed no part of the process. Mr McGregor, the Bank Manager and different managers from the regional office seemed to deal with all the interesting issues. The staff knew nothing of the business side. If a customer asked to open a business account, the counter staff had to call Mr McGregor. For a Business Studies student such as Gemma, this was all too disappointing.

By Christmas Gemma noticed that she was getting irritated and tearful not only at work but also outside it. Then at a school reunion session at a local bar, her old friend Roger told her enthusiastically about what a great three months he had spent at his job. His colleagues were great, with lots of evenings out together and the work was really interesting. He was learning about share dealing and credit checks. Where do you work? asked Gemma, and was sickened to hear that it was her own employer, but at a different branch.

After another ear-bashing from Roger on New Year's Eve, Gemma resolved to see her Bank Manager on her first day back at work. She would tell him about her disappointment,

about the satisfaction and enthusiasm shown by Roger and how she wanted to enjoy work and feel she was learning and developing, not just earning a wage. She might even tell him about Douglas McGregor's theory.

When she was ushered into the manager's office, though, she saw with horror that Mr McGregor was sitting there. The manager said, 'I've asked Mr McGregor to pop in to help talk things through, my dear. Now sit down and tell us what this is all about.' That evening, Gemma phoned Roger and told him tearfully about how she had chickened out. He cringed for her as she explained her embarrassed, stammering exit from the room. He promised to have a word with his Branch Manager the following day. He would do his best to find Gemma a job at his branch. The sooner Gemma was away from Mr McGregor the better.

Questions
(50 marks; 60 minutes)

1. Outline two factors that might lead to an authoritarian style of leadership being established in a workplace. **(6 marks)**

2. Analyse Gemma's situation at work using Professor Herzberg's two-factor theory. **(10 marks)**

3. The Mr McGregor in this case had no use for delegation or consultation. Discuss how the running of the bank might have benefited from either of these management approaches. **(12 marks)**

4. Gemma's induction training took place in a regional centre, not at her new workplace. Examine the arguments for and against this method. **(10 marks)**

5. Evaluate the managerial attitudes displayed at Gemma and Roger's workplaces, using McGregor's Theory X and Y. **(12 marks)**

PUTTING HERZBERG INTO PRACTICE

AS PEOPLE IN ORGANISATIONS

CONCEPTS NEEDED:

Productivity, Profit, Herzberg, Conflict and change

Although Professor Herzberg's researches date back to the late 1950s, it was still unusual in the mid 1980s for British businessmen to have heard of him. So Frazer Park was a rare Managing Director, not only to have studied Herzberg, but also to be determined to implement his recommendations. His target was the semi-skilled workers producing his firm's main product: plastic-coated wire bindings. He knew he was taking a risk, because Herzberg's researches into job satisfaction were conducted on white collar and engineering jobs. There had always been some dispute, therefore, about whether the theories could be applied to semi-skilled and unskilled factory work.

At the time Frazer Park became Managing Director of Russell Gray Holdings (RGH), the production of the wire bindings (the kind used on calendars and computer manuals) was divided into five tasks (see opposite). He

saw his first job as combining these functions. In that way, each worker would have a complete unit of work; they could follow an order through from its arrival to its dispatch. All the operatives would be trained to check the quality of the wire on arrival from suppliers, and the quality of their own finished products. Any sub-standard goods sent out would be traceable, because every box sent out was to be signed by the worker. This began as a sensible monitoring process, but quite soon clients started to ask for specific operators by name, which provided recognition for achievement.

This reversal of the classic process of division of labour did cause a short term reduction in output, especially from those workers whose previous, specialised jobs had higher status than that of machine operator. To counter this, Park knew that he would need to enlist the help of the employees to improve working practices and methods. So problem

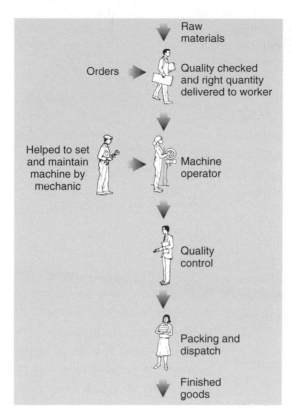

Raw materials

Orders

Quality checked and right quantity delivered to worker

Helped to set and maintain machine by mechanic

Machine operator

Quality control

Packing and dispatch

Finished goods

The five person production system, prior to the change to a complete unit of work

solving groups were established. Typically, they would consist of two operators, an engineer, and one person from each of Purchasing and Sales. Problems tackled and solved included strengthening the packaging, designing a new wire-pressing machine, and tackling the problem of late deliveries caused when workers were ill or on holiday. Russell Gray Holdings (RGH) had this system in place long before quality circles became trendy.

When asked about the value of these groups, the Works Manager said:

'**T**he more angles and options you can get to make the decision from, the nearer you are to a correct solution ... and involving the people in the factory creates interest – a break from the normal routine – a chance to think ... One of the biggest problems a manager has is getting people to change their ways of working. Involving people in making decisions helps to overcome resistance to change.'

Having addressed the higher order needs of the workforce, Park tackled the hygiene needs. Productivity bonus schemes were phased out, so that factory workers could be put on the same salaried basis as office and managerial staff. The foremen were very apprehensive about this, as they imagined it would be much tougher driving a workforce that no longer had a financial incentive to work hard. In fact, this problem arose with a mere handful of the 60 workers, and most of those chose to leave within a month.

In the longer term, RGH found that moving people from piece rate to time rate helped focus on the need to raise productivity by better machinery or methods, rather than by 'harder work'. Furthermore, Park made it clear that he intended his workforce to be paid at the top end of the local pay ranges, and for a share of any productivity gains to be used to increase real earnings further. These policies helped to bring about an atmosphere in which raising productivity could be viewed as a common aim.

By 1989 Park felt the confidence to remove a standard complaint among industrial workers – the differences in conditions of service between them and 'staff'. So the shopfloor workers were given pension rights and sick pay, while for the first time clocking-in was stopped for all employees (though new white and blue collar staff had to clock in for their first 12 months until they had earned the right to staff status).

As Herzberg's study highlighted, for many employees the major source of dissatisfaction is not related to status or pay, but is due to a feeling of being over-supervised. Frazer Park's own trust in his workforce, and his establishment of enlarged jobs with self-checking, both pointed to the need for a streamlined management structure. So, in consultation with staff, he cut the layers of hierarchy from five to three over a number of years.

This led to a wide span of control, which forced supervisors to delegate more, and check up less on their subordinates. Throughout the organisation, people were expected to take responsibility for their own decisions.

A further benefit of the new management structure was the reduced number of intermediaries between shopfloor and Boardroom. This helped Park to achieve what he felt certain was a key piece in the jigsaw – the achievement of good communications. He wanted the workforce to understand fully not only what was going on currently (and why), but also what was planned for the future. Monthly briefing meetings were established, and a company newsletter was distributed every week.

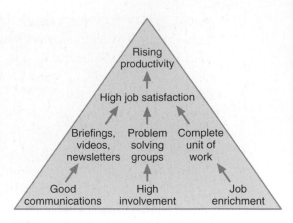

The Russell Gray Method

He felt particularly strongly that staff (even managers) tended to misunderstand the nature of 'profit'. By the early 1990s, RGH's profit was approaching £750,000 per annum on a turnover of £5 million, so there was a lot of scope for employees to feel that someone was getting very rich from their efforts. So Park bought a video camera, and made – each year – a film to explain where the profit had come from and how it was going to be ploughed back into the business. All employees were given an hour off work to see the film and talk about it.

RGH's style of management proved highly successful. After initial teething problems, product quality, delivery reliability and productivity all rose. Yet higher productivity can represent a threat to jobs, unless rising demand allows output to rise. This could have undermined Park's whole programme, as no one would discuss labour saving or cost cutting measures if they were talking themselves out of a job. In RGH's case, the ending of long standing patents during the 1980s meant that maintaining market share and output was a real struggle. So a strategy was needed to absorb the extra labour time being generated.

At first, RGH retrained staff to work in-

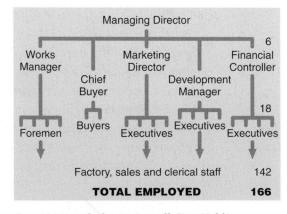

Organisational Chart – Russell Gray Holdings

house on processes that had previously been subcontracted. When there were no more jobs that could be done internally, the managers looked for new product opportunities. One such was the Snakey toy (the rings that walk downstairs), which was produced in a variety of bright colours for firms such as Habitat and Hamley's. For the management, Snakey represented a business opportunity; for the workforce it represented an outlet for their extra productivity – in other words, job security.

By 1995, with sales of over £7 million and profits topping £1 million for the first time (a better profit margin than ICI), it appeared that RGH's model of management was set for long term success. Then to the complete shock of the workforce, Frazer Park 'resigned'. The reasons for this remain unclear. Probably either RGH's American owner decided that Park was becoming overly absorbed in his design of a perfect employee centred company, or they demanded that he generate higher short term profits than he thought wise. Visiting the factory soon afterwards, it was clear that the workforce was deeply sad to lose him. The Personnel Manageress who had helped implement many of his ideas left soon afterwards. The new Managing Director had a tough act to follow.

Questions
(60 marks; 90 minutes)

1 a Outline the features of Frazer Park's policies that fit into Herzberg's two categories: motivators and hygiene factors. **(10 marks)**
  b Why might it be a mistake to tackle one but not the other? **(6 marks)**

2 Why might one expect that a reversal of the process of division of labour would lead to a reduction in output (apart from the status problem mentioned in the text)? **(7 marks)**

3 Discuss the benefits and costs of 'involving people in making decisions'. **(12 marks)**

4 a How might employees misunderstand the nature of 'profit'? **(5 marks)**
  b Why is it important to management that the term should be understood fully? **(8 marks)**

5 a Why can productivity be a source of conflict between management and workers? **(6 marks)**
  b How did Frazer Park attempt to turn it into a common aim? **(6 marks)**

52 THE NEW LASER SCANNING SYSTEM

AS
PEOPLE IN
ORGANISATIONS

CONCEPTS NEEDED:

F. W. Taylor, Remuneration, Motivation

When the laser scanning system was first mentioned, Suzanne felt the same sense of mild anticipation as the other check-out staff. The management explained that because it would do away with individual item pricing, it would prevent friction with customers over missing or incorrect prices. Furthermore, the fact that it was modern technology might make it easier to get another job in the future.

In the lead up to the changeover, all the staff went on a two day training course. This was interesting and gave Suzanne a chance to get to know her fellow workers far better than ever before. So by the time it was installed, her attitude to the system was very positive. This was strengthened further in the early weeks, when managers came round regularly to ask her how it was going, and when customers chatted about their likes and dislikes of the high speed service.

The first moment of doubt came when she overheard managers discussing 'IPMs'. The Store Manager was telling the Human Resources Manager that:

'**T**hree of the staff are so far down on their IPMs that they're dragging the store average down. You must sort them out.'

It soon became clear that IPM stood for Items Per Minute, and that the computerised tills not only checked out groceries, but also checked on staff. When managers realised that information was spreading on the grapevine, they called a meeting to explain how this information was to be used. All the staff were given a copy of the computer print-out from the previous week, as shown opposite.

Week 4 Summary of check-out operator productivity (rear of store operators only)

Operator	Hours worked	Total items	Average IPM	Operators' variance from their average	
				IPM in best hour	IPM in worst hour
Trudy S.	22	31,680	24	32	17
Simon G.	36	38,880	18	33	13
David W.	14	14,280	17	23	14
Tracy F.	35	52,500	25	30	21
Sonal S.	35	48,300	23	26	20
Suzanne P.	18	31,320	29	38	22
Jane H.	35	40,000	19	23	16
Steve H.	20	25,200	21	27	17
Eileen L.	38	57,000	25	36	16
Mutlu M.	24	31,700	22	34	13
AVERAGE	27.7	37,060	22.3	30	17
UK AVERAGE	24.5	36,450	24.8	30	20

The 10 check-out staff were told that head office set a minimum IPM target of 22 per head. Any who failed to achieve this would be retrained, moved to other duties, or be asked less often to work extra hours. Steve asked if there was any way the till could give them a running score of how they were doing, but apparently there was not. At the end of the session, the Human Resources Manager asked Jane, Steve, Simon and David to stay behind.

Suzanne was pleased to see how well she had been doing, and wondered whether the company might introduce a bonus scheme based upon IPM performance. She did feel disturbed, though, to think that this clever monitoring device had been sprung upon them. What came as a shock, however, was the pressure she found herself under at break time. Steve and Simon (both students at her college) told her bitterly that their performance had been compared directly with hers. Simon finished off by saying:

'**W**hat are you doing it for? They're making massive enough profits anyway. You ought to stop crawling and think of your mates.'

Over the following weeks Suzanne tried to slow down her workrate, but she found this surprisingly hard; she preferred to work at her natural, fast pace. Nevertheless, anything was preferable to poisoning her relationships with her work and college friends.

After four weeks, Steve and Simon had pushed their productivity level up to 22, while Suzanne's had slipped back to 25. The store managers held another meeting, though, because they were getting pressure from the Regional Manager to boost the IPM score up from the 22.8 level it had now stabilised at. The Deputy Store Manager showed clear signs of stress as he shouted:

> **'W**e've flogged ourselves sorting out all the teething problems with the new system. You don't know the half of it. All you have to do is to work reasonably hard. We're the ones with the hassles – don't make me pass them on to you.**'**

As Suzanne's productivity slid back up towards the 30 IPM level, she began to realise how much her back ached after a busy Saturday. During a dull Geography lesson the following Monday, she scribbled some numbers down on paper.

Saturday hours

8.30 – 12.15 am	=	$3\frac{3}{4}$ *hours*
1.00 – 3.15 pm	=	$2\frac{1}{4}$ *hours*
3.30 – 6.00 pm	=	$2\frac{1}{2}$ *hours*
		$8\frac{1}{2}$ *hours*

$8\frac{1}{2}$ *hours* × 60 *mins*	=	*510 mins*
510 × *30 IPM*	=	*15 300 items*
15 300 × (*say*) $\frac{1}{2}$ *lb*	=	*7650 lbs*
7650 lbs	=	*5.3 tons a day!!*

5.3 tons lifted for wages of £32.30!

Over the following months several of the original staff left. Many complained about back pains; some also said that migraines were ruining their evenings. All felt that the scanning machines had made their job even more repetitive than before. With new, inexperienced staff being recruited, the IPM average for the store worsened. The Deputy Manager began to pressurise the older hands to work more hours; and when Steve slipped back to an IPM of 19 in the week of his mock A level exams, the same manager bellowed at him. It was all too much; Suzanne handed in her notice that night.

Questions
(60 marks; 70 minutes)

1 Analyse the mistakes, if any, you believe the store management team made. **(9 marks)**

2 How might a follower of F.W. Taylor view this introduction of laser scanning? **(12 marks)**

3 Analyse how managers with a more people centred approach might have made use of the IPM summary table. **(12 marks)**

4 Discuss Suzanne's thought about basing a bonus scheme on IPM performance. **(15 marks)**

5 Apart from monitoring productivity, the computers controlling the scanning check-outs provide daily print-outs of the number of sales of each of the 8,000 lines stocked. They also pass this information on to the head office mainframe computer that shows national figures and trends. Examine the use management might make of this information. **(12 marks)**

RECRUITING A MANAGER

AS PEOPLE IN ORGANISATIONS

CONCEPTS NEEDED:

Human resource management, Recruitment, Organisational hierarchy, Motivation

Imran had been looking forward to it. Up until then he had built up his staff largely through friends and family. Now the time had come to recruit on a more professional basis. He liked the idea of a new challenge. Would he be as good a human resources manager as he was an entrepreneur?

Before getting going he bought a book called *How To Recruit Successfully In A Week*. It was quite short, but still surprised him with just how many stages were involved. Undaunted, he set to work.

The first stage was to write a job description. For Imran's software business, the job of Sales Manager would be a very broad one, requiring skills not only with customers, but also in feeding customer ideas back to the software developers and in managing the sales and after sales service teams. In addition, the ideal Sales Manager would have the charisma to establish new, major customers. As Imran's software was focused upon the needs of major investment and merchant banks, the typical potential customer was a senior banker earning perhaps £400,000+ per year, and located in London, Frankfurt or Paris.

With that task done, a job (person) specification came next. The personal qualities required seemed quite obvious to Imran, so he spent just 10 minutes jotting down some points.

Then came the job advertisement. He had already decided to place large advertisements in the *Daily Telegraph* and the *Financial Times*, partly because he hoped his own customers would notice and be impressed. He had always been alert to the importance of his customer image, as the software systems he sold were highly complex, very expensive (between £60,000 and £450,000 each) and highly confidential. Therefore his banker clients had to see his business as professional and reputable.

The book told him to keep the job advertisement brief, focusing upon the opportunities rather than the details. So that is what Imran did. Unfortunately he had not really thought about the implications of the book's proud boast that 'this approach will maximise the number of responses'. The day after the advertisements appeared the phone lines were nearly jammed by people eager for an application form. So Imran had to produce one pretty quickly!

Usefully the book provided a disk containing an outline application form; Imran asked his assistant to help tailor it to his own requirements. After three hours of intensive work, a four page application form could be printed and sent out. Within a week over 180 forms had been mailed out, together with the job description and job specification.

Then came the replies. By the deadline date 67 job applications had arrived. Important though the appointment was to Imran, the thought of wading through all 67 was daunting – especially as the very reason for recruiting the Sales Manager was because business was booming. While he spent three hours devising the application form, 14 e-mail messages built up. Even if he spent just 10 minutes reading each application, it would still take more than 10 hours to get through them all!

Imran decided to give the shortlisting task to his assistant, Sue. He explained that he wanted three piles: no-nos, possibles and 10 top goodies. And he asked his assistant to concentrate on three qualities: bright/sparky; sales success; and success at managing people. For the assistant, the next two days were a delight. She was thrilled to be given the responsibility and also fascinated by the different approaches taken by the different applicants. Some seemed desperate for the job, which was quite off-putting. Others were extraordinarily sloppy, with messy amendments (one crossed out English GCSE C, changing it to an A!) or lazily brief personal statements. Yet at the other end of the scale were some really impressive applications. One woman with experience only in confectionery sales made a superb case for why she would be the right person for selling complex software to bankers. Even stronger was the application from a young man who had run climbing holidays in South America before joining a major merchant bank.

Imran went through the 10 top goodies with Sue. He was not keen on two, but delighted with the other eight. Sue sent invitations to interviews the following week: two per day for Monday to Thursday. Each of the eight would spend half an hour with Software Development Manager Khalid, another half hour with one of the three Sales Executives and then 45 minutes with Imran.

Disappointingly, only six of the eight agreed to come for interview, but the sessions still proved a great success. At the end of each day Imran got together with Khalid, Sue and the Sales Executives and talked over their feelings about the people they'd seen. Imran was impressed with Sue's contributions, because although she had no formal part in the process, she often had to look after the applicants while they were waiting around. One had talked so much about himself that she was totally put off; how would customers take to him? Another had seemed quite cold and distant, yet a good Sales Manager should be able to charm everyone at the client end, not just the bosses.

After seeing them all, Imran took his interview 'panel' to a nearby bar with a private room for hire. They took 10 minutes to reject three, but two hours arguing about the other three. Eventually it was Sue who came up with a solution: 'Let's see if we can settle it this way. Let's agree on six main qualities we want from the candidates. Then rate each of the three out of 10 marks on each quality. Then add up the marks and see whether we have a clear-cut winner.'

After some wrangling, the following table was eventually arrived at. 'Voting power' was awarded to Khalid, the Sales Department, Sue and – of course – Imran. So the maximum possible mark was 40 per quality.

Sue settled back in her chair with a slightly

smug smile when the results emerged. It was just clear-cut enough to have made the exercise worthwhile. Imran smiled at her, then declared he was delighted that Cara was the winner. Indeed, he took out his mobile and phoned Cara on the spot. The others all heard her whoop of delight as she received the news. As he drove home that evening, Imran reflected that Sue had shone almost as much as Cara in the recent events. Tomorrow he would give her a pay rise and resolve to delegate far more to her in future.

	Matt	Cara	Sadiq
Charisma	38	39	34
Intelligence	34	37	40
Evidence of sales success	35	30	37
Evidence of management skills	29	38	32
Good references/employment record	38	39	38
Appropriate manner for our clients	40	38	33
TOTAL (max 240)	214	221	214

Questions
(60 marks; 70 minutes)

1 The position of Sales Manager would form a new layer in the hierarchy of the Sales Department. Outline two problems this might cause the business. **(10 marks)**

2 Imran wanted a new Sales Manager as part of a comprehensive human resources plan for the next two years. Explain two factors that might have influenced this plan. **(10 marks)**

3 Outline a likely job specification for the post of Sales Manager at Imran's business. **(10 marks)**

4 Use motivation theory to evaluate why Sue was so pleased at her involvement in the recruitment process. **(15 marks)**

5 Discuss the pros and cons of the recruitment process undertaken by Imran. **(15 marks)**

HUMAN RESOURCE MANAGEMENT

A2
PEOPLE IN
ORGANISATIONS

CONCEPTS NEEDED:

Division of labour, Trade unions, Labour turnover, Motivation

The ABC Company was proud of its reputation as a no-nonsense employer. The TGWU had once organised a six week strike over union recognition but the strikers had eventually given up. 'We want to make money, unions want to take money,' ABC's Chairman had once said.

The factory was organised with very high division of labour, in order to ensure that relatively unskilled workers could be used, yet output would be high. For the same reasons the factory was highly automated.

Now the Directors were having to admit that things were not working properly. Absenteeism (at 15%) and labour turnover (at 40% a year) were nearly three times the national averages, and were making it impossible for production to keep up with the demand for their products. Even more alarming was that the local Job Centre had told them that jobseekers were refusing to go for interviews at ABC because of its poor reputation.

The Board of Directors met to discuss the situation. The Production Director said:

'It's simple; we need much greater financial incentives. An extra £20 for every full week of attendance, a £500 bonus for each year of completed employment, and a £50 signing on fee.'

The Marketing Director disagreed:

'I think we need a new approach. Our products are pretty poor quality, and my customers complain that if they phone the factory to check on deliveries, our people are very off-hand with them. It's not just a matter of money, we need to give our workers the job satisfaction that will lead to a more responsible attitude by them.'

The Managing Director had a different solution: 'If we moved to the North-east, the level of unemployment would mean people really want to get jobs and keep them. We could sell this factory, and with the proceeds could buy a factory in Newcastle plus management offices here in Bristol. So only Production need move.'

Questions
(50 marks; 60 minutes)

1   Explain the term 'division of labour'. How might it lead to lower production costs per unit? **(6 marks)**

2   In what ways might the ABC Company have been in better circumstances if a trade union had been allowed to represent its workforce? **(8 marks)**

3   Explain the meaning of 'labour turnover'. Outline two major costs that would be caused by high labour turnover. **(6 marks)**

4   Re-examine the Production Director's proposals. Discuss their advantages and disadvantages for the firm. **(12 marks)**

5   Examine three other human resources-based considerations in the decision on whether to move to Newcastle. **(6 marks)**

6   a   What elements might one introduce into the ABC factory production methods if one wanted to create more job satisfaction? **(6 marks)**

    b   What constraints might operate that prevent these from succeeding? **(6 marks)**

BOOMTIME FOR BANKCHECK

A2
PEOPLE IN
ORGANISATIONS

CONCEPTS NEEDED:

F. W. Taylor, Herzberg, Delegation and Consultation, Communications

It had been a marvellous recession for Iain Truscott. His company BankCheck supplied ultraviolet banknote scanners, and demand soared as a wave of forged notes hit Britain. At first BankCheck's 40 employees were delighted at the job security implied by the firm's success. Then they found themselves overstretched as more and more orders needed to be processed. After three months of hectic work, mistakes began to be made with deliveries and invoices, so Iain advertised for more staff: two sales and two clerical, plus three distribution workers. The result was an unwelcome deluge of 600 applicants.

By the time the new recruits started work, demand was already forcing still more appointments to be made. Iain could see this process continuing, so he hired a human resources officer to look after these matters. Yet with every extra appointment Iain was frustrated to find that even more of his time was required to induct the individual into his business and his ways of working. The

situation became even worse when he found that the new human resources officer was failing to recruit the right kind of people. BankCheck's success had been built up by experienced, practical workers; yet many of the new recruits were graduates who had bright ideas but were unenthusiastic about applying the procedures that Iain had laid down.

Meanwhile, several of the original staff found jobs with competitor firms that were willing to offer responsible managerial posts to people from BankCheck. To stop this exodus, Iain offered substantial bonus payments to key staff based on workload (as measured by the number of subordinates the manager was directly responsible for). This worked well at first, but less so as staff numbers rose towards 70.

The situation came to a head at the company's finest hour. Iain had just signed a £2 million contract with the National Dairy

Federation to supply a portable banknote scanner to every milkman in the country. The extra work involved in supplying and training each milkman proved too much, and two key managers fell ill. Neither had kept their staff informed of their wider plans, so it was very hard for anyone to take over.

After eight weeks of chaos, in which Iain dashed around the country trying to keep things running, the Dairy Federation warned that if BankCheck could not sort out its administration, the contract would be cancelled and the firm would be sued. Other clients were just as angry, including some very long standing ones.

Iain knew he must act fast, but felt too drained to think clearly about what to do, so he called in a management consultant.

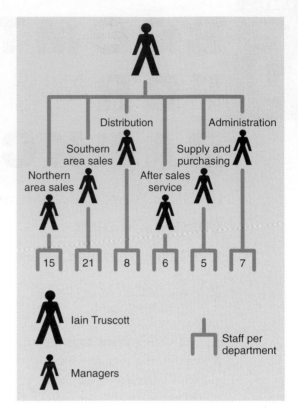

Questions
(50 marks; 60 minutes)

1 **a** Distinguish between delegation and consultation. **(5 marks)**
  b Outline the causes and effects of poor delegation within BankCheck. **(12 marks)**

2 One factor in BankCheck's difficulties was poor communication.
  a What organisational structures might have been set up to improve the internal communication? **(5 marks)**
  b What difficulties might these structures have presented to such a fast growing small firm? **(7 marks)**

3 **a** Faced with Iain's situation, discuss the practical advice that might be given by a follower of *either* Professor Herzberg *or* F.W. Taylor. **(12 marks)**
  b Examine the problems that might be faced in carrying out this advice. **(9 marks)**

THE TRENCH

A2
PEOPLE IN
ORGANISATIONS

CONCEPTS NEEDED:

Health and safety, Government intervention

'Gary Wilson was very lucky. He suffered a collapsed lung and a broken pelvis, but others have died in similar circumstances ...' began the Magistrate as he summed up the evidence he had heard.

It began with Gary's decision to have a year off between A levels and college. He wanted to earn money quickly so that he could spend the spring in America. As the local builder (Lancashire Houses) offered the highest wages, he started there as a general labourer earning £7 an hour.

Lancashire Houses had been enjoying a local housing boom caused by the arrival of a large Japanese electronics factory. From a two man business, the firm had taken on 45 employees on three different sites – each building eight houses. The two directors were finding it very hard to keep control over the sites as they had to spend so much time sorting out the problems of financing the £500,000 investment. To get round this problem, they hired site managers for each development and offered each one a £10,000 bonus if they could complete the work by a specified target date. (One week late would mean £8,000, two weeks late £6,000 and so on.)

Gary was shocked from the start at how hard the foreman worked him. In his first week he had shifted mounds of bricks, dug drainage holes, put up hundreds of feet of security wire fencing and cut dozens of metal pipes to length with a fearful metal-cutting saw. Shattered at the end of the week, he looked upon the weekend's driving rain with some optimism, hoping that the site would be too wet to work on Monday. Such illusions were soon dispelled by the foreman's orders, and Gary's day was spent carrying supplies to the bricklayers who were building up the walls in the rain.

The following day a JCB dug a three metre trench for laying drains. The foreman called Gary over to help him. Gary saw that water was running into the hole, but the foreman assured him that it was 'as safe as houses'. Both went down into the trench to lay the pipe. Gary was unaware that the correct procedure is to drive strong timbers into the ground at the sides of the hole, to create a wall. The foreman knew, but had not been supplied with the right type of wood, and felt that it was not worth hours of delay for what he considered to be the tiny risk of earth slippage.

Without warning, one of the sides collapsed. The foreman just managed to scramble out, but Gary was trapped. As another side gave way, it looked as though Gary would be buried alive. Miraculously, the wet mud kept just below his neck. After an hour he was free and taken to an intensive care unit in hospital. He was fit to be released only after three weeks, and then needed two months in a nursing home. The collapsed lung would be a permanent disability.

Lancashire Houses was prosecuted by the Health and Safety Executive under the 1974 Health and Safety at Work Act. By failing to support the trench sides it had committed an offence under the construction regulations. It had also failed to notify the safety inspectors of the start of any of the three construction projects, and had no written safety policy as required by the law. The Burnley Magistrates Court found the company guilty on all charges. The company director in the dock apologised to the court, and explained that since the accident, they had sent their foremen on safety courses. A fine of £2,250 was imposed, plus costs of £56.50. During the hearing it emerged that the company had not had a visit from a factory inspector for three years.

Gary's friends urged him to sue the company for negligence, but when he went to a solicitor he realised that his father earned too much to be able to get legal aid, but far too little to afford the legal costs. The solicitor also made it clear that such cases can take years to come to court, by which time the company might have gone into voluntary liquidation. It was no help to be told by a friend that he should have joined a trade union, which would have taken up his case for him.

Although his accident caused some delays, better weather helped two of the sites to be completed within the bonus deadline. One of the two was the site where Gary's accident took place.

Source: Legal reports in *Health and Safety at Work* magazine

Questions
(50 marks; 60 minutes)

1   Statistics show that young people suffer far more accidents at work than any other group. What might be the reasons for this?   **(10 marks)**

2   With the benefit of hindsight, what research or checking might Gary have done before taking the job?   **(10 marks)**

3   Discuss the underlying causes of this accident.   **(15 marks)**

4   Evaluate the arguments against having more factory inspectors and bigger penalties for companies that break safety laws.   **(15 marks)**

BRITISH MANAGE- MENT TECHNIQUES UNDER FIRE

A2
PEOPLE IN
ORGANISATIONS

CONCEPTS NEEDED:

Leadership, Industrial democracy, F. W. Taylor, Herzberg

A research study of British and German management styles and practices has highlighted many differences. It found that in Britain, attitudes to leadership and consultation showed a personalised, one way view which is more suited to a traditionally authoritarian kind of organisation.

British attitudes to the workforce showed a stronger tendency to emphasise the **'Economic Man' approach** associated with F.W. Taylor. There tended to be more **layers of hierarchy** in Britain and more **differentiated conditions**, e.g. in canteens, rest rooms, and employment contracts. Researchers found that engineers and production people had a lower status in the United Kingdom, and tended to occupy fewer of the top management positions than the marketing and finance professionals. Furthermore, there

was less training and education among the workforce in the UK than in Germany.

To develop this analysis further, they decided to compare British and German management within the same company – a German manufacturer with a large British subsidiary. This would remove certain variables (such as different production processes) and help to focus on factors such as management style, leadership and consultation.

The company selected was very forward-thinking – much concerned with employee job satisfaction. It had already done away with high division of labour assembly lines, and provided clean factory conditions. The latter point struck one researcher most forcefully in Britain, 'where standards in factories are so much lower in general than in Germany'.

It emerged that the main contrast was between the British subsidiary and other local British firms, rather than between the British and German branches of the same firm. The company's British workers liked the absence of assembly lines and the payment by salary; one said: 'At other places it's a rat-race because of the piece work.' They also appreciated the more equal treatment: 'Usually office workers are better looked after than us; here the management are pretty decent.'

The comparison with Germany did yield some useful points though:

1 In the German branch, a Works Council had been operational for 20 years, with great success. It provided a regular meeting point between management and elected worker representatives to discuss future plans and any immediate problems. The workforce considered it much more valuable than the contact they have with the boardroom via their two Worker Directors (all German firms have elected Worker Directors – by law).

2 The relationship between management and trade unions seemed much more mature in Germany, as was revealed in this quote from a German manager: 'Here, during the recession, the unions were very reasonable. The company placed all their accounts and statistics before them – not only the annual accounts . . . it's no use to employers having dissatisfied workers.'

3 The firm's German managers seemed more aware of the psychology of management and of the need to delegate. The idea of German authoritarianism proved a myth.

Questions
(60 marks; 70 minutes)

1 Explain the meaning of the following (in bold print in the text):
   a the 'Economic Man' approach
   b layers of hierarchy
   c differentiated conditions **(9 marks)**

2 What evidence is there that the British managers were more inclined to an authoritarian management style? **(9 marks)**

3 Discuss the possible effects of engineers and production people having a lower status in the United Kingdom. **(12 marks)**

4 Professor Herzberg said: 'The worst way to pay people is on piece rate . . . reinforcing behaviour. The best way is a monthly salary.' Consider the likely reasons for this view. **(12 marks)**

5 a Outline two ways in which a firm might benefit from a successful Works Council. **(6 marks)**
   b Evaluate why this might provide more effective consultation than Worker Directors. **(12 marks)**

MRS AHMED'S COUSIN

A2
PEOPLE IN
ORGANISATIONS

Concepts Needed:

Mayo, Piece work, employment discrimination, Data Protection Act

Mrs Ahmed shrieked when the needle hit her finger. As her cousin helped her to the medical room, she realised that she had nodded off at her workbench. The rushed order for 15,000 pairs of jeans had meant 10 hour days and six day weeks for the past month. Mrs Ahmed had not even wanted the extra work, for although the money was needed, a 40 hour week was as much as she could cope with. When she turned the overtime down, the proprietor of Mile End Textiles (MET) had threatened her with dismissal. With no shortage of clothing machinists seeking work locally, she had to accept.

At their 30 minute lunch break, the other workers asked anxiously about the damaged finger and talked yet again about the harshness of their working lives. Half were on the minimum wage of £4.20 per hour, while the others were on piece work. The biggest staff grievances were that none received holiday pay and there was no bonus rate for overtime. Mrs Bradfield thought it typical of the manager's meanness, while Mrs Ahmed's cousin pointed out that:

'**I**t makes little sense, as it means that we are always tired and never have anything to look forward to.'

As the discussion continued, Mrs Ahmed turned to her cousin and asked her to tell everyone what she had learned about the wage differentials in the factory. This was risky, as her cousin was supposed to keep secret the things she found out in her new post as office assistant. She hesitated, but was soon persuaded to say that:

'**T**he men are all on much more than the women. In the warehouse they earn

£5.50 an hour and the mechanics are on £6.80. It's the same in the office, with Dave the bookkeeper getting more than Sarah, our materials buyer.'

The all-female machinist section was outraged to hear that the warehousemen were earning so much extra. Making jeans was hard, skilful work, whereas the warehousemen could work at their own pace and the forklift trucks took most of the physical labour out of the job. Several muttered about joining a union, but they all knew that the MET management would never give it recognition.

That afternoon the cousin was summoned to see the proprietor. He said straight away that her conversation had been overheard and that she was being dismissed for breach of trust. She pleaded to have her job back, as it had taken her four years at MET to make the switch to the office. Her regrets were too late.

After 10 months of applications, interviews and rejections, it was a radio programme that made Mrs Ahmed wonder whether her cousin had been placed on an employers' blacklist. She persuaded the cousin to write to the local Textile Employers' Federation for a copy of any computerised files held on her. To her surprise the Federation did send information, and it contained a damning comment about 'her disruptive influence'. Clearly, to have any chance of getting another job in the industry she would have to get that phrase removed. In despair, she turned to the Citizen's Advice Bureau.

Questions
(50 marks; 60 minutes)

1 **a** On what grounds could the company be taken to court for sex discrimination? **(5 marks)**

   b How might the women proceed in this action? **(6 marks)**

2 Discuss how Mile End Textiles' management approach might have been viewed by a follower of Mayo's Human Relations school. **(12 marks)**

3 What is the business significance of:

   a keeping pay differentials secret **(6 marks)**

   b a management not giving union recognition? **(6 marks)**

4 Consider what advice the Citizen's Advice Bureau might have given Mrs Ahmed's cousin about her legal position. **(15 marks)**

TEAM-WORKING – THEORY AND PRACTICE

CONCEPTS NEEDED:

Recruitment, Discrimination

'I'*m Ronnie Stannard, very pleased to meet you.*'

Ronnie sat down and looked carefully at Yeisho's three man interview panel. They all looked friendly, but very formal. Earlier that day she had undergone three hours of aptitude and attitude tests; she felt tired, but now had to be at her best.

'Ronnie is, um, unusual. Is it your full Christian name?' asked one of the men in suits. She assured them that it was hers from birth. Later, one asked suspiciously about 'the reference on your form to Fulham Ladies' Football Club'. He needed reassurance that women's football was increasingly widely accepted. Despite these concerns about whether Ronnie would fit in with the other staff members, the interviewers soon decided that she was an ideal recruit. Her astute

answers to questions about her commitment, ambitions and attitude to work came across very well. She impressed them with her explanation of how she had become Fulham's coach as well as player. To her great delight she was offered the supervisor job on the spot.

That night she ran the training session for her football team. It was, as usual, a quick-fire mixture of hard exercise, skills training, short five-a-side matches and banter. After 90 minutes all the team were laughing and sweating in equal measure. After a shower they pulled on their Fulham tracksuits and went out for their customary curry.

During the meal, talk turned to their previous coach, Terry. He had been tough on discipline, but the harder he tried to teach them a new skill, the less confident they felt in their own abilities. He made them feel that their only role was to get the ball to the team's star player – and she never passed it to anyone. Their season had been tense and unsuccessful. Ronnie had changed all that. The star had relaxed into being a proper team member, and the exact same players as last year's relegation contenders were now third in the National Women's League.

The following Monday Ronnie started work at Yeisho Electronics. She was to be the supervisor of the finished assembly production cell, though her first week would consist of induction training. She listened with amusement to talks about the company's teamwork philosophy, its morning exercises, the company uniform and its continuous improvement (kaizen) groups. Yet whereas Ronnie looked happier and happier as the week progressed, the other staff on the induction course looked less and less so. When, on the Friday, they had to come in 15 minutes early for a team briefing and

exercises, most had surly faces. Ronnie positively glowed.

The next Monday would be her first day on the production line. She arrived at 7.30 to prepare herself for the 7.45 team briefing session. To her surprise the first worker strolled in at 7.55 and most came in together at precisely 7.59. All Ronnie could do was to insist that they arrive promptly tomorrow and then hurry them on to the production line for the start of the 8.00 shift.

That week proved the most stressful of Ronnie's life. She was being ignored by the men she was supposed to be supervising. Gradually, though, she pieced together what had happened. The previous supervisor had been promoted from the shopfloor and had built up a team spirit based upon contempt for the 'Japanese gimmicks'. The unit had worked effectively until quality problems emerged. Then an audit of the cell's methods of working revealed how far it was from the Yeisho approach. Foolishly, though, the Factory Manager had not told the Human Resources Department about the problem before going on holiday. So Ronnie had been totally unprepared for the inevitable hardships of taking over such a team.

Saturday's fixture against Doncaster was a great relief for Ronnie. Her teammates realised that she was tense and, on the coach journey up the M1, dragged the story out of her. They felt that she should dump the problem on the Factory Manager's lap, but they also worried that people might see the situation as a woman unable to manage a group of men. Over coffee at a service station they agreed that she should:

1 explain the situation to the Factory Manager on his return from holiday the following Monday;

2 call each person, in turn, off the production line for a private chat about the situation, warning each that without cooperation she would have to issue formal warnings about insubordination;

3 keep the Factory Manager fully informed at every stage.

Coming to this conclusion was a great weight off Ronnie's mind. She was able to play a full part in the afternoon's 2–2 draw and slept more deeply on the coach home than she had done for days.

At 7.40 that Monday Ronnie went to see the Factory Manager. She was astonished to find two of her production line workers there already. The manager asked her to wait outside 'for a few minutes'. A quarter of an hour later she was called in to be asked how she had managed 'to upset the men so much in such a short time'. Although furious, she controlled her temper enough to put her side of the case and to state her three point plan. The Manager listened coldly to what she had to say, and just said, 'Leave it with me.'

Ronnie went to the Human Resources Manager who had been on the selection panel and had inducted her. She explained the whole story but he seemed embarrassed to hear it. All he said was: 'Graham's the Factory Manager and what he says goes, I'm afraid.' She left in a daze, with her mind swirling with thoughts of teamwork and team management. Where should she go from here?

Questions
(50 marks; 70 minutes)

1 Examine the strengths and weaknesses of Yeisho's recruitment and induction procedures. **(12 marks)**

2 Discuss the degree of similarity between Yeisho's stated human resources management policies and Ronnie's approach to running the football team. **(12 marks)**

3 Use the text as a starting point to assess why discrimination exists in certain workplaces. **(14 marks)**

4 What is your assessment of how these events actually ended? In other words, what happened next? **(12 marks)**

60 A DAY IN THE LIFE OF TERESA TRAVIS

CONCEPTS NEEDED:

Communications, Delegation

Teresa sat down at her desk and switched on the PC. It flashed up two memos, one from the accounts department and another from the Manchester office. As she read them, her assistant came in with coffee and the mail. 'Deal with Manchester please, Anne,' she said, nodding at the screen.

Anne went over to her desk and called up the memo, to puzzle over its contents and a suitable response. As usual, Teresa had handed on a task that Anne knew little about;

and if she quizzed her boss about it there was likely to be a sharp retort about 'showing responsibility'. The manager of the Manchester office wanted to know the progress being made on the job for Graylink plc, as the deadline for completion had passed two days ago.

Meanwhile Teresa had rummaged through the post to find a letter from her biggest client. It was a message of congratulation for his satisfaction with the new Sales Director that Teresa had found. She scanned the letter into the internal computer network, to circulate it to her fellow Directors, then composed an elegant reply to the client. Teresa enjoyed great success at Park Lane Headhunters, the recruitment agency for senior management personnel, and was not shy about keeping others informed.

Before she had been through the rest of her letters, a telephone call from the Managing Director summoned her to an emergency meeting. A letter had arrived from a long standing client threatening legal action for negligence over a disastrously unsuccessful appointment. The absence from the meeting of the executive responsible showed the extent of the Managing Director's displeasure. Teresa put forward the view that even though their contracts with clients denied liability for their recommendations, they could not afford the bad publicity generated by a court case. Both of her fellow Directors agreed with this, but the Managing Director eventually said: 'I don't think we can afford to set a precedent. We'll have to brazen it out.'

Back at her desk, Teresa went through the rest of her post, then called up the computer's 'Pending' file. It contained the names and phone numbers of the firms she had decided to contact that week. Part of her job was to press for new clients and therefore extra sources of sales revenue. Teresa decided which companies to try, while Anne phoned to find out the right person to contact and then sent a standard introductory letter. This was later followed up by Teresa phoning to suggest a preliminary meeting, possibly over lunch (depending upon how promising the contact sounded). She decided that she would try three of the numbers that morning.

The first of the contacts was in a meeting, but the second proved promising. Yes, he often needed to appoint senior staff, and indeed newspaper advertising often failed to get the right calibre of applicant, and yes, he was free for lunch next Thursday. The third call was to the Human Resources Director of a large construction company. It began well,

but started to go wrong when the Director referred to 'the necessity for higher job quality delivery within the Field Installation section and the Attachment Materials Pipeline'.

As Teresa was grappling mentally with this, he asked whether she had experience in finding 'Unix-based Quality System Auditors'. She mumbled an apology and rang off.

It was with some relief that she went off to her lunch appointment with a long standing client. Nahdia Khan ran a chain of 15 exclusive, high fashion clothing outlets. Teresa recounted her story of the construction company to hoots of laughter from Nahdia, setting the tone for a relaxing lunch. Over coffee it was interrupted, however, when Teresa's mobile phone rang with an urgent message from the Managing Director, demanding that she return to sort out 'the Manchester problem'.

The afternoon turned quite unpleasant as Teresa blamed Anne for being unable to deal with 'a minor query from Manchester'. The atmosphere worsened when Teresa saw a copy of the fax that her assistant had sent. It made it plain that work on the Graylink account had all but ceased. It was honest but hardly tactful. Teresa phoned the head of the Manchester office to apologise for Anne's 'bizarre' fax, and to assure her that several contacts looked promising. The remainder of the day was spent in a frustrating and fruitless chase for Graylink's new Head of Finance.

To round off Teresa's day, just as she was about to leave a call came through from the Accounts Department: 'About that memo . . .'

Questions
(50 marks; 60 minutes)

1 Outline the main barriers to effective communication within the case. **(9 marks)**

2 Consider how Teresa could delegate more successfully to Anne. **(9 marks)**

3 To what extent does Park Lane Headhunters make effective use of modern, electronic forms of communication? **(10 marks)**

4 Use the case as a prompt to compare the advantages of written and oral communications. **(10 marks)**

5 Research has shown that managers spend over half their working day communicating with others. Discuss how this proportion might be reduced without damaging the effectiveness of the organisation. **(12 marks)**

61 A PAIN IN THE JOINTS

AS
EXTERNAL
INFLUENCES

CONCEPTS NEEDED:

Trade cycle, Unemployment, Technological change

Carl was a craftsman. He'd never been very good at studying, but he had a talent for working with wood that was the envy of many of his friends. It was almost inevitable, therefore, that when he left school, with few qualifications, he would become a carpenter.

For a while, things went well. Carl found steady employment, mainly on building sites, and although he was frustrated that much of the work he did lacked any creative input, he did at least have cash in his pocket at the end of each week. Indeed, when times were good, house builders and industrial constructors, exhibition organisers and ordinary house-holders all competed for his services. As a result he made very good money indeed. He didn't save much, as spending was part of the building site culture. Anyway, Carl was an advertising executive's dream. Any new gadget he saw, he bought immediately, regardless of cost.

From time to time Carl suffered periods of unemployment – that was part of the culture as well. Bad weather in the winter inevitably meant he was laid off on occasions, which was not something he minded particularly. After all, the work was hard and it was no joke

getting up at five in the morning if it was freezing cold or tipping down with rain. But of course not having the cash caused problems, not least in keeping up the repayments on his state-of-the-art widescreen television and DVD player, as well as various other items that he'd never quite had the money to pay for outright.

It all went seriously wrong one year, right in the middle of summer. Carl was informed by 'Chalky' White, a builder he had worked for regularly, that he would be laid off from the end of the following week. Naturally Carl asked how long this period of unemployment was likely to last, and Chalky said that he would be unlikely to be able to offer anything until the following spring at the earliest.

This prediction proved correct, because the rest of the year saw Carl having to travel further and further in search of work, and on many days and even weeks he had nothing at all. He was not alone in this – by the end of the year there were often three or four carpenters going for the same job. Even if Carl was lucky enough to be employed he had to accept a much lower rate per hour than he had been earning only 12 months earlier.

The simple fact was that almost no one was building factories or houses, and householders couldn't afford any improvements to their own. Interest rates had been climbing for a year; people were struggling to pay their mortgages and firms to pay their overdrafts. This meant that the demand for houses and industrial units was low and so building firms had little work. Indeed, as time went by increasing numbers of them went into liquidation. For Carl, like many others in the trade, the effect was far greater than he expected. Of course he had to give up many of his prized possessions, but also, frustratingly, he noticed that the papers were increasingly filled with advertisements for those flashy types of goods he enjoyed so much, and seemingly at a fraction of their earlier price. But all this was, to a certain extent, to be expected, and Carl reckoned that he would be able to afford them the following year, once the building trade picked up again.

Christmas was depressing because Carl had no money to spend on presents, but he still went to the pub as often as he could afford, in order to talk to his old mates. One night he ended up talking to Chalky White, his old employer, who delivered a nasty shock. Chalky told Carl that even if things improved in the New Year, he would still be changing his building techniques in favour of more standardised, prefabricated materials. These were constructed in factories, largely by machine and then transported to the building site 'just-in-time', as required. The days of the carpenter on building sites, especially skilled ones, were numbered, said Chalky, and Carl had just better get used to the idea. Was there anything else he could do for a living?

The answer to that question troubled Carl. He had no formal qualifications, and even his carpentry skills were largely self-taught or acquired through watching others. Yet the months of enforced idleness opened up another possibility, though at first only a faint one. He had started wood carving, using waste material from earlier building jobs. Initially it was simply a no cost way of passing the time, but he had become more and more involved in its creative possibilities. He loved the work and, amazingly, he found that people were keen to buy his finished pieces. Of course he wasn't earning anything like the money he had made previously, but it was enough to keep him in the basics.

Oddly, he found himself needing such possessions as the television and the DVD less and less. This was because he often found himself working well into the early hours of the morning in what he jokingly called his 'studio', which was actually a garden shed. He was so absorbed in the work that he simply didn't notice the time. Indeed, when winter turned into spring, and he was offered a month-long exhibition in an art shop in Suffolk in August, he didn't hesitate for a moment. The economy had started to turn round, interest rates were falling and houses and units were being built again, but all Carl could think of was getting out his chisels and heading for the coast.

Questions
(50 marks; 60 minutes)

1   **a**   Sketch a 'trade cycle'. Label the axes and identify the main points on the cycle.   **(6 marks)**

     b   Identify points in Carl's story that correspond to points in your diagram.   **(4 marks)**

2   **a**   Consider why the building trade is often hit especially hard during a downturn, but enjoys booming conditions during an economic upturn.   **(10 marks)**

     b   Explain how Carl has been affected by these cyclical extremes.   **(6 marks)**

3   Carl experiences three types of unemployment in the story. State and explain each one by reference to the text.   **(6 marks)**

4   Carl sees a new technical process as a threat, but he turns it into an opportunity.

     a   Name an industry currently under threat from technical change, explaining the circumstances.   **(6 marks)**

     b   Discuss whether it might be possible to turn its difficulties into new opportunities, explaining how it might be done.   **(12 marks)**

62 PANDA WOK

CONCEPTS NEEDED:

Company aims and objectives, Internal and external constraints

Panda Wok was started five years ago by Laura Piper and Chris Spence. It was Laura's idea to create a Chinese restaurant with a difference. Customers fill a bowl with ingredients chosen for themselves from a huge range of carefully sliced meats, fish, prawns and vegetables. After adding the flavourings, sauces and cooking oil, they hand their creation to one of three cooks who stand by a huge griddle in the middle of the restaurant. Within three minutes the food is cooked and the onlooking customers take the meal back to their table. People are welcome to repeat the process as often as they like.

From its opening day in a blaze of panda balloons and media publicity, Panda Wok was a success. Chris had planned to break even in the second or third year, but from the first night the restaurant made money. He was content to enjoy the profits, but Laura was determined to make Panda Wok a national name. Using bank borrowings and the business's cash flow, the company expanded at a furious pace. As the diagram shows, new restaurants were opened with increasing speed. As Laura put it: 'We're steadily turning the country black and white.'

Just 12 months after day 1, with annualised sales running at £2 million, Chris managed to sit Laura down to talk things over. He knew she was working from seven in the morning to eight at night, and then going on to visit a

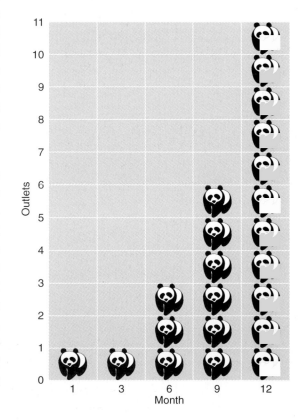

different outlet every day. He half-hoped to see signs of exhaustion on her face, but all he detected was shining enthusiasm: 'I want us to be the first national chain of Chinese restaurants ... the Tesco's of catering.'

Chris tried to persuade her that their company was not capable of more expansion: 'Our accounting system can't cope, our bank balance goes ever deeper into the red, and we cannot find the time to look carefully at alternative new sites ... we must consolidate ... we have no middle management ... if we keep on like this our quality control will go and so will our reputation.'

Chris thought he had got through to Laura, but the buzz of satisfied customers at the Brighton outlet that night switched her back to her growth targets.

It took two more months for the first shock to hit the firm. Panda Wok's bank, with little warning, demanded that its £400,000 overdraft be halved within six weeks. This forced a desperate reappraisal. It quickly became clear that the company's contracts to buy new properties made it impossible to cut back spending so quickly. To avoid liquidation, Laura and Chris had to accept a refinancing package which included the bank taking a 40% shareholding in the company. Chris wondered whether this was the time to diversify away from such an income elastic service as a restaurant, but Laura convinced him to keep concentrating on their core skill.

Having survived this phase, Panda Wok returned to its growth path. Its 120 sites were, by now, yielding annual profits of £500,000. Yet this was soon to be dented by a series of difficulties. A direct competitor with better restaurant locations was taking away some trade, while the whole market was affected by a sharp VAT increase on restaurant food. Then came the scandal. The St Albans outlet was prosecuted under the Food Safety Act of 1990 for sloppy hygiene leading to cases of food poisoning. This was picked up by the BBC's South-east news, and then by the national press. Takings dived. The company almost went under during the following six months, but then began to recover. This time, Laura was much more cautious. She accepted now that building up the company's quality image was more important than constant expansion.

Questions
(50 marks; 70 minutes)

1 Analyse Panda Wok's company objectives during the timespan covered by the case. **(10 marks)**

2 **a** Why do firms usually agree their aims and objectives at Board level? **(6 marks)**
   b How might Panda Wok have benefited from this exercise? **(8 marks)**

3 Examine the internal and external constraints faced by Panda Wok. To what extent could they have been foreseen? **(14 marks)**

4 Evaluate two other constraints the firm might face in future, as the business matures. **(12 marks)**

THE THROW
OF THE
DICE

AS
EXTERNAL
INFLUENCES

CONCEPTS NEEDED:

Niche market, Income elasticity, Inflation, Expectations

John knew the marketing power of an acronym, so he settled on Dice, which stood for Domestic Internally Controlled Environment. Using the image of rolling dice in his advertisements, along with the line 'Take the gamble out of home heating – and cooling!' he was able to promote his new product in a straightforward and effective way.

Dice was a modified, ducted-air central heating system, but with the capacity to cool as well as heat. In itself this was not new technology, though fairly unusual in Britain. What was new was the control device that John had developed. Each room in a customer's house contained a sensor that fed data into a central box, which would respond either automatically or manually depending on the setting. The box used components imported from a number of countries, mostly in Asia.

Sales last year were good and progressing well. The economy continued to improve, with low levels of unemployment and inflation, and John considered that air conditioned houses would have a **high income elasticity of demand**, and would appeal to consumers who were increasingly used to having air conditioning in their cars.

The challenge John faced was keeping his costs and prices down, though at the moment he had few competitors in his particular segment of the market. Based on current demand, the unit cost of a control box was as follows:

Part	Source	Cost (£)
Microchip components	Japan	2.50
	Taiwan	1.30
	China	0.60
Moulded box	Germany	0.60
Switches	France	0.20
Others	UK	1.00

Total cost of parts	£6.20
Cost of assembly	£3.30
Total	**£9.50**

At the start of this year, John had a number of concerns regarding his costs. Firstly, the political situation in parts of Asia was increasingly uncertain, with relations between China and Taiwan steadily getting worse. Because of this confrontation, as well as other factors, inflation in both countries was already into double figures and looked likely to rise. Secondly, John was having increasing difficulty recruiting the quality of workers he needed at current wage rates. He estimated he would need to increase pay by 10% in the coming year, despite overall inflation of around 3%. Thirdly, there was the relationship with Europe. Throughout last year the pound had been very strong against the euro. Most experts agreed that this was an over-valuation, so the likelihood was that it would fall by at least 5% in the current financial year.

John's meeting with his Finance Director to decide prices for the coming year was crucial, therefore. 'As I see it,' he said 'we'll have to bump up our prices by 10%, otherwise we could be making a loss on each unit by the end of the year. I'm pretty sure we won't lose too many sales if we do; I've been ringing around and it looks like everyone thinks more or less the same way …'

Questions
(50 marks; 70 minutes)

1 How do you know that Dice is operating in a niche market? **(3 marks)**

2 Outline two advantages to John of being in a niche market. **(8 marks)**

3   **a** What is meant by the term 'high income elasticity of demand' (in bold print in the text)? **(3 marks)**

  b Examine the concerns John might have about being reliant upon a product with high income elasticity of demand. **(8 marks)**

4 Is John justified in saying he should put his prices up by 10%? Support your answer with numerical data. **(12 marks)**
Note: In order to answer this question you may have to make some assumptions. Make sure you explain them clearly.

5 If 'everyone thinks more or less the same way' about prices rising:
  a Outline the likely effect. **(6 marks)**
  b Discuss why it might be considered a 'bad thing'. **(10 marks)**

54 ECONOMIC CHANGE AS AN EXTERNAL CONSTRAINT

AS
EXTERNAL
INFLUENCES,
OBJECTIVES AND
STRATEGY

CONCEPTS NEEDED:

Inflation, Interest rates, Value of the pound, Capacity utilisation

Rawsthorn Clothing had enjoyed three years of high profitability, thanks to a consumer spending boom that guaranteed high output and generous **profit margins**. By the third year it was looking to expand.

From its base in Burnley, the firm had been supplying the womenswear market for 80 years. Now the Directors had decided to diversify into children's clothing, for they thought an opportunity existed for a producer of high quality, classically styled childrenswear.

Despite their recent high profits, it was still necessary for them to borrow a substantial sum to establish a highly efficient new factory.

The Directors were not concerned, however, because their large retail customers had given enthusiastic verbal support to the scheme. Only the Production Director dissented from the Board's decision, on the grounds that:

'The labour content of a child's garment is only a little lower than that of an adult, yet the price of the finished product is far lower.**'**

Just five months before the new factory was due to open, however, the economic climate began to worsen. Signs of rising **inflation** had led the Bank of England to push interest rates up, and the pound had risen as a result. By opening day, Rawsthorn was starting to detect a reduction in orders throughout its product range. The salesforce made it clear that this was due to three factors:

1 Retailers wanted to cut stock levels to reduce the finance cost.

2 Customers were buying less as rising mortgage rates cut their **disposable incomes**.

3 Those who were still buying tended to buy imported goods that were now more price competitive.

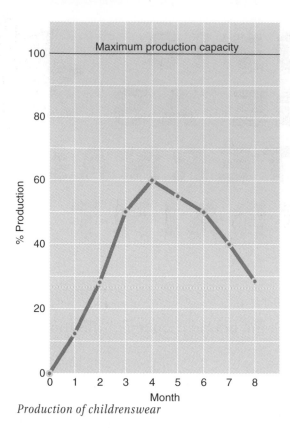

Production of childrenswear

Even more worrying were reports from its overseas agents that Rawsthorn's recent price rises had hit sales more sharply than anticipated.

The poor trading conditions made retailers reluctant to stock Rawsthorn's new childrenswear range. The *Financial Times* monthly Retail Survey had just revealed that most shop managers expected weak consumer demand to persist for at least a year. Shopkeepers felt that its high quality, high price proposition was inappropriate to the current marketplace. Eight months after opening, the children's clothing factory was producing at only 30% of single shift production capacity, causing heavy losses. Even the womenswear division could do no better than to break even, so the company as a whole was trading in the red.

Questions
(60 marks; 70 minutes)

1 Explain the business significance of the following (in bold print in the text):
profit margins
inflation
disposable income **(9 marks)**

2 Explain how the salesforce's comments relate to the economic circumstances outlined earlier in the paragraph. **(10 marks)**

3 **a** What was the significance of the reporting of the expectations of the retail trade? **(7 marks)**
b Outline two other ways expectations can affect business realities. **(8 marks)**

4 Examine the impact on profitability of 'producing at only 30% of single-shift capacity'. **(10 marks)**

5 Evaluate alternative strategies you believe the Directors could adopt to bring the company out of the red. **(16 marks)**

65 STORMY WEATHER

AS
EXTERNAL
INFLUENCES,
OBJECTIVES AND
STRATEGY

CONCEPTS NEEDED:

Business organisations, Corporate strategy, Ethics

The first summer of the millennium was not a good one. April and May were exceptionally wet; June was dry but lacked sunshine, whilst July was the dullest since 1992 and the wettest since 1993. For some firms this spelt disaster. Perhaps the most obvious ones to suffer were ice cream makers, who for many years had been trying, with some success, to extend their season, but who still relied on hot weather for the bulk of their sales. Similarly, firms that targeted summertime activities such as gardening faced problems. Indeed, Hozelock, a manufacturer of garden hoses and sprinklers, had already suffered badly some years earlier,

when two wet summers in a row had sent their shares tumbling, encouraging the management to return the company to private status.

Another sector to suffer badly was the retail trade. Sales were flat because people tend not to go shopping anyway for clothes in bad weather, but unsurprisingly the cold and wet conditions depressed summer fashion sales even further. The retailer New Look reported sales down 3.9% in the first four months of its financial year up to July, whilst Marks & Spencer continued the trend that it had experienced over the winter months, with sales down nearly 8% on the previous year.

The wet weather of the early summer also brought more surprising effects. For instance, Railtrack reported that more train delays had occurred in April and May because it had been too wet, which reminded some people of the 'leaves on the line' justification for autumnal delays some years earlier. In the autumn the situation became much, much worse, when appalling weather combined with a huge railway track maintenance programme following a tragic crash at Hatfield.

For the traditional British holiday resorts it

simply added to a trend that had been apparent for a number of years. In 1973 nearly 40 million holidays were taken in the UK (one holiday equals four or more nights away) but by 1997 it was down to 30 million. In August 2000 a government minister toured seaside resorts in an effort to encourage more people to return to traditional 'bucket and spade' family holidays, but the appeal of guaranteed sunshine overseas threatened to make this a futile effort (in the same period, 1973 to 1997, holidays abroad increased from around nine million to 28 million).

On the other hand there were more positive stories. Although Marks & Spencer had poor clothing sales figures, their sales of winter 'comfort' food such as oven ready Cumberland pies, Roast beef meals and Bangers and mash were exceptionally high. Similarly, the energy producing companies found demand strong, with National Grid reporting a 6.6% increase in demand at peak times during July. As the saying goes: 'Every cloud has a silver lining.'

Questions
(50 marks; 60 minutes)

1 **a** Outline two key differences between private and public
limited company status.　**(6 marks)**

 b Why may Hozelock have decided it was in its best interest to
return to private company status in the late 1990s?　**(9 marks)**

2 Examine two strategies ice cream manufacturers might adopt
to extend their season and therefore become less dependent
upon summer weather.　**(10 marks)**

3 At the end of the case it was suggested that the poor summer
weather was not necessarily bad for all firms. Indeed it is often
true that a threat to one business becomes an opportunity for
another. Suggest two firms that might benefit from:
 a a recession
 b an overvalued currency
 c high interest rates
 d stricter laws on health and safety at work
 e increased road congestion　**(10 marks)**

4 External shocks such as severe weather conditions can
undermine firms' profitability, making them consider drastic
action such as redundancies. Discuss whether it is ethical to
make staff suffer for something that is not their fault.　**(15 marks)**

BUILDING
A BUSINESS

AS
EXTERNAL
INFLUENCES,
OBJECTIVES AND
STRATEGY

CONCEPTS NEEDED:

Stakeholders, Law, Business objectives, Economic data

'**J**ust hammer it in!'

'But ...'

'No buts, just hit it. Come on!'

Not for the first time, Steve was shocked. After his redundancy from British Motors he had been put on a training programme with Mason & Sons Ltd and had expected to learn how to become a professional builder. Instead he seemed only to learn how to take short cuts. Ted Mason was ruthless about cutting jobs down to the quickest possible time, even if it meant hammering screws into place, or skipping the 'unnecessary' undercoat before painting window frames.

Ted was also no great fan of scaffolding. He hated the time spent putting it up and taking it down. So ladders were often used when permanent scaffolding might have been wiser. One Friday lunchtime, over a relaxing pint, Ted explained more of his business approach to Steve:

'*In upturns like this, you have to make good money. I'm not interested in repeat business and all that guff. Customers don't remember who their last builder*

was. If they get you out of Yellow Pages this time, they're just as likely to pick you next time, even if you let 'em down ... I believe in putting in low quotes to win the business, then getting the job done double quick so that there's still a decent profit margin. Customers are as likely to thank you for a botched job as they are for a quality one, so why bother? Keep their place clean, talk a good game and keep smiling – and they'll think you're a master craftsman!'

After six months, Steve decided to investigate the chances for a new building firm locally. Surely there would be room for a building firm that treated customers with more respect than the Masons. Steve started with *Yellow Pages* and the local paper, noting every builder in the town. Then Gemma, his wife, phoned every one, asking if they would be able to do either or both of two jobs: a new roof and a new, luxury bathroom. Six claimed they could do both, though most made it clear that they were very busy, so an early completion date would be difficult.

Further investigations at an estate agent revealed that only two local builders were held in high regard and both were 'very expensive, but worth it'. Encouraged by the evidence of a market for good quality work, Steve looked into the costs of starting up (see Appendix A). His savings could cover most of the total, but he knew he would need sufficient extra capital to pay for materials and labour until customers paid up. He popped along to his bank to discuss the position with the Small Business Adviser, but was irritated by the adviser's pessimistic warnings about the possibility of 'a recession leading to **excess capacity** and cut throat competition, especially among **tertiary businesses**'. The adviser even gave Steve a copy of a graph he'd seen recently (see Appendix B).

The following day at work, Ted Mason seemed especially friendly. Steve was wondering why as he climbed the ladder to continue the roofing job after lunch. When the ladder slipped, things happened so fast that he knew no more until he woke up in hospital. Steve could just about hear a doctor tell Gemma: 'He won't be working again for a while, I'm afraid.'

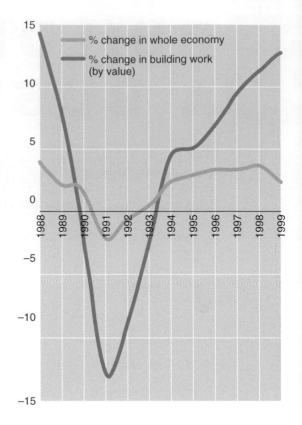

Appendix B: Graph to show building industry demand compared with the economy generally

Appendix A: Steve's estimate of start-up costs	
Start-up costs:	
Leasehold premises:	£8,000 plus £12,000 per year rental
Van:	£11,000
Tools and equipment:	£18,500
Office furniture:	£5,500
Other costs:	£4,000
TOTAL	£47,000

Questions
(80 marks; 90 minutes)

1 Explain the meaning of the terms (in bold print in the text):
   a excess capacity
   b tertiary businesses   **(8 marks)**

2 Examine Appendix B. To what extent is such data relevant to a small business such as the one Steve is considering?   **(15 marks)**

3 Discuss Mason & Sons Ltd's approach to its stakeholders.   **(15 marks)**

4 Examine the practical problems of start-ups for businesses such as Steve's.   **(12 marks)**

5 To what extent can a case such as this be taken as proof that laws are needed to regulate businesses?   **(15 marks)**

6 Use the case study as a starting point to discuss the reasons why some firms operate with short term and others with long term objectives.   **(15 marks)**

A SCRAP IN SOUTH WALES

AS
EXTERNAL
INFLUENCES,
OBJECTIVES AND
STRATEGY

CONCEPTS NEEDED:

Leadership, Law, SWOT analysis, Stakeholders, Ethics

Dai Evans started his South Wales scrap metal business in 1956. Before that he worked briefly in a steel mill, but soon became frustrated by having to take orders from supervisors. In all honesty he did not like taking orders from anyone. Dai was known to all around as a 'hard man'.

The scrap business suited Dai. It was tough, dirty, uncompromising work. People used to say, very quietly behind his back, that that was the reason why he liked it. But there was no denying that with the addition of his brothers, Peter and Simon, Dai had a formidable team. Certainly the company was a success, with scrap metal being sold to produce lead or copper ingots or steel rods, which were then exported around the world.

By the 1980s, Evans Brothers occupied a 30-acre site close to the main road linking Cardiff to the M4. The firm offered much needed employment to 60 people and so at the time the state of the yard was not overly criticised. Nevertheless, it was in a very poor and unsafe condition, with dangerous looking pieces of metal lying around, mobile cranes ploughing through what was often a sea of mud and the workforce rarely bothering to wear safety helmets. Unsurprisingly, there were often accidents. Indeed in one, the harness on a crane failed, allowing a container to crash through and destroy a building, which was unoccupied, luckily. People wondered why the local authority hadn't stepped in during this period. There were persistent rumours that Dai and his brothers had made generous 'gifts' to certain councillors, as well as unspecified threats to officials, in order to make sure that the business continued unhindered.

At the same time, trade unions were quite simply banned. One union official who tried to enter the gates was 'discouraged' from doing so by Dai and his barely constrained, enormous and apparently very hungry guard dog! Despite this intimidation, conditions were so bad that the workers staged an unofficial strike in December 1985. This was easily crushed within two weeks by the firm. Most were frightened into returning almost immediately by the threat of losing their jobs permanently. Those who stayed out on strike were replaced by new workers.

The 1990s brought change. The first was in scrap metal prices. Cheap steel from Poland and other countries in eastern Europe flooded the market, causing the price to drop from £200 to £60 a tonne. Similarly, competition for scrap aluminium, copper and other metals increased, so the Evans brothers found they were losing some of their best customers. At the same time, collecting and delivering metal was getting more and more expensive due to the rising cost of diesel fuel, with the result that margins were cut still further.

Then there were the changes to the labour market. The days were over of a seemingly endless supply of unemployed, unskilled labour that asked no questions. It was not only that other jobs existed; it was also the fact that they were in far more pleasant surroundings, often in warm, safe factories, newly built in the South Wales corridor. The only way people could be persuaded to work for Evans Brothers was by paying them relatively high wages, but even then few staff stayed for long. Dai's attitude didn't help. Now into his 70s, he liked to think he was still a hard man, but his verbal bullying didn't work any more; the men either ignored him or left – either way morale was extremely low.

Finally, there was the *Express and Mail*. A young reporter, Jacqui Thomas, who was the daughter of one of the workers who had led the strike in the 1980s, had written a series of articles attacking the firm. She wrote about the poor working conditions, Dai's management style, and hinted at the possibility of shady deals in the past. What she was as yet unaware of, but the Evans brothers suspected, was that there was serious soil contamination at the site. This was potentially damaging enough on its own, but there was an additional concern that the contamination might spread to the surrounding land. If the *Express and Mail* got to hear about it, Dai thought the publicity could be the end of the firm.

All was not yet lost, however. Nearly 40 years of solid profitability meant that what Dai called his 'war chest' of highly liquid assets was full. Whatever his other shortcomings, he was not personally an extravagant man, so cash had not been spent on flash cars and expensive holidays, or for that matter on UK tax – but that was another story! In addition, his brother Peter's son, David, not only had a degree in metallurgy, but he was also interested in the business. During his vacations home from university he had built up a good rapport with the workforce.

Then there were Dai's connections with the council. Though he, and they, had 'cleaned up their act', Dai was still a man of influence. Furthermore, the local Member of Parliament owed him a favour in return for all that Dai had done for him in the early days of his election campaign. Whether all this influence would work in helping him to relocate quickly, before all the problems were revealed, remained to be seen. But it was clear that some difficult decisions had to be made.

Questions
(50 marks; 60 minutes)

1   What sort of leader do you think Dai Evans is? Explain your
    answer.   (6 marks)

2   Identify two points where the law might have intervened in
    the work of Evans Brothers. Explain the possible effects of each
    piece of legal intervention.   (10 marks)

3   You have been brought into the firm as a consultant. Your first
    task is to undertake a SWOT analysis of the firm as it currently
    exists. Identify and explain two points under each heading.   (16 marks)

4   Outline three groups that could be said to be stakeholders in
    the Evans Brothers business.   (6 marks)

5   When Dai Evans is challenged about the ethics of business he
    argues that in the scrap metal business ethics are a luxury no
    one can afford. Discuss this position.   (12 marks)

POLLUTION PROBLEMS IN A CHEMICAL PLANT

A2
EXTERNAL
INFLUENCES

CONCEPTS NEEDED:

Company objectives, Trade unions, Social responsibilities, Leadership styles

Chemdex Chemicals is situated on Teesside, in the north-east of England. It employs 1,200 full-time workers – half the number of five years ago. Yet Chemdex is still the main local employer in an area where male unemployment is 11%. As with other local labour forces, the level of unionisation has fallen; just 41% of the workforce belong to a trade union. Chemdex produces weedkillers, pestkillers and chemical dyes for use in paint. Over recent years, fierce competition from Germany and from ICI has often pushed Chemdex into losses, as is shown by the graph.

The firm has recently launched a new, highly effective weedkiller (Weedex). Sales are building up rapidly, and the product is soon to be featured on BBC TV's *Gardeners' World*. The firm's management is already talking about the new product as the company's saviour.

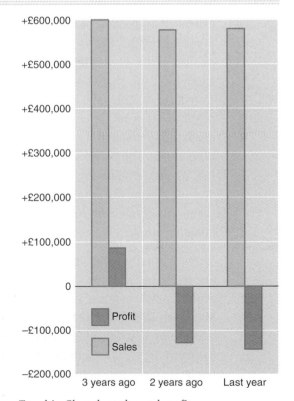

Trend in Chemdex sales and profit

Yet many in the factory are worried about the fumes given off in the production process. They frequently escape from the safety valves, leaving a fine blue powder everywhere in the factory, and even on the washing of the local houses. Following furious complaints from its members, the factory workers' union AGU has just held a meeting at which 18 operators have complained of blinding headaches, and seven say they have fainted when overcome by the air pollution.

AGU's membership also includes the maintenance mechanics, who tell the meeting that they believe the entire Weedex plant has been designed so poorly and constructed so shoddily that leaks are inevitable. The meeting votes that the shop stewards should discuss the situation with the management, and ask for an independent report on the nature of the blue powder.

The union's request that this issue be discussed at the Works Council is an irritant to a management that is wrapped up in the success of the Weedex launch. Latest forecasts show that in the coming year it should transform a £100,000 loss into a £400,000 profit. That would provide the funds for a desperately needed factory modernisation programme. The Works Manager is aware that the Weedex production equipment is leaky and unstable, but the Managing Director seems interested only in discussing ways of boosting output.

Frustration has led the Works Manager to ask the Chief Scientist at Chemdex to write a report on the chemical, and send a copy to the Managing Director. This has been completed and shows that the blue chemical is copper hydrocyanide. The concluding paragraph reads:

'*The quantities found in the atmosphere within the factory represent a serious, if long term, health hazard. As the situation is in direct contravention of the Health and Safety at Work Act, I strongly recommend the immediate adoption of lightweight oxygen masks for all factory workers in contact with Weedex.*'

At the Works Council, the Managing Director starts by saying to the employee representatives that the success of Weedex is vital, and that if its launch is disrupted and thereby falters, the whole weedkilling division will be closed, causing 400 job losses. He also declares that:

'*We are not willing to discuss the blue powder at all, as it is precisely the ingredient that our competitors would like to identify.*'

At the subsequent union meeting, there are many grumbles about the bullying tactics of the Managing Director, but the threat of redundancies is enough to weaken the workers' resolve. This would probably be where the matter rested were it not for a local journalist's enterprise in talking to local mothers and doctors. The local newspaper's headline 'Children Turning Blue!' is even picked up by the national media. As environmentally conscious supermarket stockists of Weedex start phoning for details, the Managing Director springs into action. The company puts out a press release saying that they are already implementing a 'green strategy' to make production 'even safer'.

Within a week, filtration devices costing £25,000 are fitted that halve the air pollution, and plans are under way for a new, safer production line to be built alongside the existing one.

Questions
(50 marks; 70 minutes)

1   How would you describe the leadership style of the firm's
        Managing Director?   **(7 marks)**

2   **a** Identify and explain the factors that led Chemdex to its
             apparent objective of short term profit maximisation.   **(9 marks)**
        b What conclusions can you draw from the Chemdex
             experience about the drawbacks of such an objective for
             companies in general?   **(10 marks)**

3   How strong a position does the AGU appear to be in at the
        plant? What constraints are affecting it?   **(12 marks)**

4   It is sometimes assumed that firms have a relatively simple
        choice between social responsibility and profit. Discuss the
        circumstances in which there can be conflicts between
        competing social responsibilities.   **(12 marks)**

AN ETHICAL DILEMMA

CONCEPTS NEEDED:

Profit, Business ethics, Social responsibilities, Government intervention

It was as if someone had spat in the Marketing Director's face. All round the mahogany boardroom table, the smartly dressed men sat stiffly, too shocked to move or speak. Teresa, the only woman present, gulped as she realised that her naive question had ground the meeting to a halt. She knew they were all highly sensitive on the subject, but it had seemed reasonable to ask:

'**D**id you see the World in Action programme last night?'

Of course, it had been a particularly ferocious attack on the tobacco industry, complete with stomach-wrenching pictures of smokers' diseased lungs, and legs amputated due to failing blood circulation. The programme had even aimed a barb at the man at the head of the table. It pointed out that the International Tobacco Company's Marketing Director had given public assurances that the firm's advertising was never aimed at young people, yet a leaked internal memo signed by him said:

'**M**otor racing sponsorship may be hard to justify on cost efficiency grounds, but it is the only way we can reach the teenage market.'

Teresa reflected that in the 20 or so meetings she had attended between International Tobacco Company (I.T. Co) and her advertising agency, the subject of health – let alone social responsibilities – had never been raised. Yet she had chatted with most of these men on their own over lunch, and knew them all to be caring parents who had thought deeply about the ethical dilemma of being responsible for advertising half the country's cigarettes.

One or two felt guilty about their situation, but most had rationalised it away by convincing themselves that their efforts were not persuading people to start smoking, only to get existing smokers to switch from one brand to another. Outside commentators might sneer at this idea, but they comforted themselves that research had never uncovered anyone who attributed their first cigarette to an advertisement.

Fortunately, the spell that had immobilised the meeting was broken by the arrival of tea. After the waitress had left, the advertising agency's Chairman was able to move on to the next item on the agenda: Project Plover. He presented data giving the background to this proposed new product (shown opposite).

Background research data for Project Plover

Recent market share trends for low tar brands		Views of smokers of low tar brands	
Last 6 months	22%	Would switch to lower tar if taste OK	52%
6–12 months ago	20.5%		
12–18 months ago	19%		
18–24 months ago	18%	Would switch for 40% less tar	59%
24–36 months ago	17%		

Source: Ex-factory sales figures   *Source: ANR Research*

Teresa sat there tensely as her Chairman ran through the presentation that she had written. She had spent four months on Project Plover (a codename used for security purposes), and dearly wanted the I.T. Co Marketing Director to approve the £200,000 needed for the final preparations before its launch as a new cigarette brand. Inwardly, she applauded her Chairman's clear explanation of the consumer proposition '40% less tar but no less taste than the leading low tar brand'; and his expert account of the middle class, female niche that this brand would fill in the market.

When he finished, it was the I.T. Co New Product Development Manager's turn. He explained that Plover was forecast to achieve a 1% share of the 5,000 million* pack annual cigarette market, with a gross profit margin of £120 per thousand packs (i.e. 12 pence per pack). Even with a launch advertising budget of £2.5 million, a handsome contribution should be generated. Nor would this be especially at the expense of other I.T. Co brands, as its competitors held 75% of the low tar market.

'So, what's your opinion, Bob?' asked the agency Chairman.

'Well ...' replied the Marketing Director, 'I'm worried at the longer term implications. We've already led nearly a quarter of the market down to low tar and low nicotine cigarettes. If we now encourage them to smoke even weaker cigarettes, are we not just helping them give up altogether? We have a responsibility to think of the company's future. I think we'd better shelve this project.'

Teresa blinked in amazement at what she had heard, and looked round the table to see who would challenge this statement. No one did. They moved on to the next agenda item – Snooker sponsorship.

*Apologies for the huge, but realistic, numbers. United Kingdom cigarette sales amount to 5,000 million packs times 20 per pack i.e. 100,000 million cigarettes per year.

Questions
(50 marks; 70 minutes)

1   Outline the ethical questions raised by the above account.   **(9 marks)**

2   **a** How profitable would Project Plover be to I.T. Co in its first
       year?   **(8 marks)**
    b What other reasons are there for the company to want to
       launch this product?   **(6 marks)**

3   Discuss the issues of responsibility that emerge from the text.   **(15 marks)**

4   What arguments might the cigarette industry put forward
    against a complete government ban on all cigarette
    advertising and promotion? Comment on these arguments.   **(12 marks)**

THE CHANGE IN GOVERNMENT

CONCEPTS NEEDED:

Cash flow, Economic policy, Government intervention, Pressure groups

'**N**othing's gone right since the Socialist Alliance got in,' said Mr Martin bitterly. Protex Limited had been very successful in the years prior to the election. Booming consumer demand for home security systems had enabled the firm to increase sales 50% by volume (100% by value) in the previous four years. This had made it appear economic to automate their production methods, as the costs of the new, high technology equipment could be spread over many units of output. Furthermore, the labour saving aspects of the

Protex Ltd cash flow

equipment not only helped to keep direct costs low, but also helped Protex to cope with the coincidental fall in the number of young people within the workforce.

The Finance Director had been the only one to question whether it was wise to borrow substantial sums to finance a mechanisation programme that would be unprofitable if demand fell. The other Directors made it clear that they were confident that the 15 years' continuous growth in the home security market was not likely to stop. Indeed, the Marketing Director had pointed out that the market had grown from £360 to £840 million over the previous four years. As the Board members took their seats at the start of the meeting, Mr Martin (the Managing Director) muttered:

'**W***ithin two days they'd pushed interest rates up to protect the pound. Then came that first budget, with its massive increase in income tax – that did for our top-priced, high margin range …*'

The Marketing Director took the story up:

'**E**ven worse was the decision to make every burglar alarm fitting firm apply for an operating licence. Half of them left the industry – they couldn't be bothered to go through the red tape to get their certificate; and of course those fitters were our customers.'

The Finance Director couldn't help wondering if there were other reasons they left the industry, but he said nothing. He wanted to get people on to the main item on the agenda – the cash flow crisis. He reminded everyone that they faced their poorest revenue period (December–February) with an overdraft just £20,000 below the limit set by the bank.

He presented the following figures:

After they had discussed ways in which the cash shortfall could be funded, conversation returned to the change in the political context of their business operation. The Production Controller warned that a new environmental pollution law would soon force them to invest in £80,000 of filtration equipment, ending their discharges of industrial paints and dyes into the river. Mr Martin exclaimed, 'The Socialists want to put us all out of business! How can we compete with the Japanese with the millstones they place round our necks?'

As they were leaving the boardroom, the Finance Director mentioned to Mr Martin that he had been glancing, that morning, at the Report and Accounts of Securimax (Protex's main United Kingdom rival).

'How are they doing?' asked Martin.

'Very well,' came the reply.

Winter quarter cash budget	
Forecast revenues	£540,000
Gross profit margin	30%
Salaries and overheads	£220,000
Interest payments	£82,000

Questions
(50 marks; 70 minutes)

1 Examine the factors that seem to have led to the marked decline in Protex's cash flow position since the election. **(10 marks)**

2 To what extent should the government be blamed for the problems Protex is grappling with? Or was Protex management responsible for errors of judgement? **(14 marks)**

3 **a** On the basis of its forecasts, how much more funding is Protex going to need in the coming quarter? **(8 marks)**
   b How might it attempt to finance this shortfall? **(6 marks)**

4 Businesses can try to influence the type and the policies of government in various ways. How do they do so and why? **(12 marks)**

THE BHOPAL TRAGEDY

A2
EXTERNAL
INFLUENCES

CONCEPTS NEEDED:

Communications, Multinationals, Laissez-faire v. intervention, Social responsibilities

On Monday 3 December 1984, a poisonous cloud of methyl isocyanate gas escaped from a storage tank at a pesticide plant in Bhopal, India. The factory was owned by one of the largest chemical producers in the world – the US firm Union Carbide. Eyewitnesses reported a mushroom cloud that escaped from the factory and descended on the town. The main effects of the gas were to cause serious damage to eyesight and to blood circulation by implanting cyanide into the blood's oxygen. Within days 1,200 people died and at least 10,000 were very seriously affected. It was the world's worst recorded industrial accident.

A major problem for the doctors was lack of knowledge of how to treat the chemical's effects. A pathologist working at Bhopal's main hospital said bitterly: 'Why hasn't Union Carbide come forward to tell us about the gas that's leaked and how to treat it? Is it not their moral duty? They have not come forward.' Doctors were disturbed by unexpected problems such as one child who died

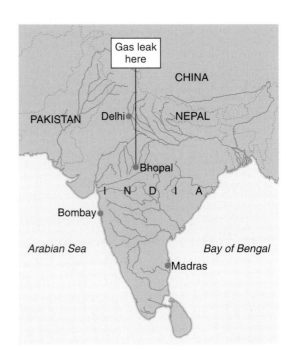

suddenly, two hours after having shown no previous ill effects. They were also swamped by the scale of the damage – more than 100,000 people needed treatment out of a total population of 800,000. Worst affected were those living in the slums that had built up around the factory.

The factory's owners emphasised immediately that the incident was 'unprecedented', and that the storage tank was equipped with sophisticated safety systems. However, Indian politicians asked whether safety standards in Third World nations were less strict than in the home countries of parent companies. They also criticised Western firms for selling India low technology plants that they then failed to keep up to date. Within a day of the accident, Union Carbide halted production of methyl isocyanate (MIC) at its United States plant, while awaiting the findings of an investigation into the causes of the disaster.

By Monday 10 December, the death toll had risen to 2,000 and Union Carbide was being sued for $12,500 million by American lawyers representing families affected. The lawyer argued, as did the Indian government, that Bhopal victims should receive the same, high compensation levels that American families would get. Union Carbide rejected this claim, and offered $1 million of humanitarian aid.

Soon it emerged that the company had no emergency procedures arranged with the local community. One of the plant's managers said:

> **'W**e did not know that such a small amount of gas had the capacity to destroy human lives to this extent. We thought our safety controls were adequate, so we did not do any community education.**'**

Even harder for the firm to explain away was that although the factory had started producing only five years before, it was not equipped with the computer controls used in the older US plant. So, for example, if gas leaked from a Bhopal storage tank, an employee had to spot it and then break the glass of a box that controlled a safety system;

in the United States, a computer would do this instantly and automatically. It also became clear that the Bhopal factory's safety record was very poor. Several gas leaks had occurred before, including one fatal incident. After that fatality, factory trade union officials had (in 1982) put posters up throughout Bhopal which said:

```
'Warning - Save Yourselves
         From Death.

The Lives Of Thousands Are
        In Danger.

The Factory Is Making Gas
But Does Not Use Safety
        Measures.'
```

The union officials now complained that their warnings had not been taken seriously enough by the press, the company or the State government. The press rejected that charge, however, stressing that they had written many critical articles including one headed:

> **'B**hopal on the brink of a volcano.**'**

The press turned to the responsibility of the Indian government. Why had safety inspectors been so lax and, above all, why had a shanty town been allowed to build up right next to the factory? It later became clear that the relevant authorities lacked the experience of this kind of Western technology to recognise the dangers involved. So, since they were happy to have jobs brought to a poor area, they left it up to Union Carbide.

American journalists were repeatedly surprised that the company's US spokesman knew nothing of these points. Then one Carbide official admitted that communications with the Indian operation

BHOPAL ON THE BRINK OF A VOLCANO

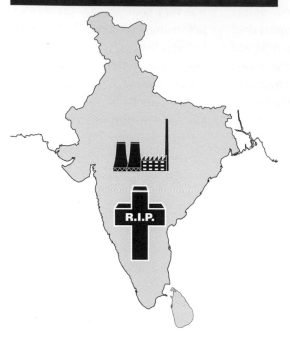

had virtually broken down. Nevertheless, Union Carbide's Chairman (Warren Anderson) continued to speak with pride about his company. He rejected suggestions that facilities at Bhopal were outdated and said the chemical industry's safety record was a 'wonder of the world'.

The short term effects of the tragedy upon the company appeared to be significant. The share price dropped sharply as investors worried about the firm's ability to pay the billions of dollars of compensation that were anticipated. The credit rating agency Standard and Poors lowered Carbide's credit rating, making it more expensive for the firm to borrow money. But by 17 January 1985, Mr Anderson was confident that 'the Bhopal tragedy would have little effect on the company's ability to conduct business'. He also felt that the firm was adequately

protected with insurance and had managed its cash flow well enough to 'put us in pretty good shape financially'.

By August the US MIC plant was in full operation and Carbide's shares had recovered to their pre-Bhopal level. For whereas the awful publicity of recent months would have hit the sales of a producer of consumer goods with a clear corporate identity, Carbide's products were bulk chemicals bought by other companies. So the sales turnover from its wide range of chemical products was barely affected.

On 20 March 1985, Mr Anderson presented the results of his company's inquiry into the tragedy. Its original cause was water getting into the underground tank of MIC, which sparked off a chain reaction. This would not have caused danger had not a refrigeration unit been inoperable for six months, and a gas escape safety flare been 'undergoing maintenance'.

What made world headlines, though, was the Chairman's innuendo that sabotage may have been responsible. This became the company's main defence over coming years, even though it failed to convince the Indian government. He also made it clear that he held the local management responsible for the alleged safety deficiencies. He said, 'Non compliance with safety procedures is a local issue.' By implication, he went on to blame the Indian government's policy of insisting that a high proportion of local management should be from the local community. Later that year, on 8 September, Carbide created a new post of Vice President in charge of community and employee health, safety and environment. His task was to coordinate the setting of corporate standards, and ensuring their effective implementation.

In the early months of 1985, bereaved or injured families were led to expect prompt settlement of generous compensation. Yet it took 18 months for Union Carbide to defeat the victims' attempt even to get the case tried in America. This was the crucial victory for the firm, as Carbide would have had to pay out more than the US firm the Manville Corporation, which had been instructed to pay $2.5 billion to 60,000 American victims of asbestos disease. Only in February 1989 was payment made to the victims in a 'full and final' settlement. Carbide's shares jumped $2 as the Indian Supreme Court awarded $470 million in compensation.

As *The Guardian* commented: 'The stock market registered its financial verdict on the gruesome tragedy.' The newspaper also reported that the death toll had risen to over 3,000 and that over 55,000 people remained chronically ill from lung disease, and permanent eye and stomach disorders. Union Carbide, with record 1988 profits of $720 million, made it clear to financial analysts that it would not be affected by the settlement, as it had already set aside more than $470 million from previous years' profits. For Union Carbide, the Bhopal tragedy was over.

Sources: Financial Times; The Guardian; The Times

Questions
(70 marks; 90 minutes)

1 Examine the problems of communication revealed in the text. **(12 marks)**

2 Discuss the difficulties of multinationals operating in Third World countries, from the point of view of the company and of the host government. **(15 marks)**

3 **a** Calculate the average dollar payment to the Bhopal victims compared with the asbestos sufferers. **(5 marks)**
   b Why may the courts have decided on such different levels of compensation? **(10 marks)**

4 Discuss how a free marketeer or laissez-faire thinker might justify his or her views in the face of a disaster such as this. **(14 marks)**

5 **a** Which different groups can be said to have responsibility for accidents like that at Bhopal? **(4 marks)**
   b Why do such groups seem so poor at living up to those responsibilities? **(10 marks)**

A CASE OF ELEMENTARY DECISION TREES

CONCEPTS NEEDED:

Decision trees

The scene is the drawing room at 221b Baker Street ...

'**M**y dear Holmes, what is it?'

'**W**atson, I must explain the facts to you. This slump in the stock market since the outbreak of the Boer War has left me penniless. I must seek my fortune.'

'**H**olmes, that's dreadful ... but perhaps this letter from Inspector Lestrade of Scotland Yard can help. He says that Moriarty's evil influence is spreading. An insurance company is offering 100,000 guineas to anyone who can catch him, and 50,000 guineas to anyone who leads the police to him. By Jove, they're even offering 10,000 guineas for genuine information on him, even if the bunglers at Scotland Yard fail to apprehend him.'

'**S**plendid, dear Watson, for my brother Mycroft has told me that Moriarty has travelled to Switzerland – near the Reichenbach Falls.'

'Then let us travel on the next boat train. It'll be my privilege to pay for us both.'

'Hold on a moment, Watson. If we visit Reichenbach, I would estimate our chances of finding him at no higher than 60%. If we do, we must decide whether to tackle him or bring in the police. On our own against Moriarty's thugs we have no better than a 40% chance of getting our man. The police have probably got a 60/40 chance of success.'

'Perhaps we should tell the police straight away, and let them go to Switzerland, then, Holmes.'

'Hm ... those idlers will take so long getting there that I suspect they've no better than a 3 in 10 chance of finding him and arresting him ... How much do you suppose the expedition will cost us, Watson?'

'About 200 guineas, I'd say, Holmes.'

Holmes drew his favourite Meerschaum pipe down from the mantelpiece, and a decision tree began to form in his mind ...

Questions
(20 marks; 30 minutes)

1   Draw the decision tree.   **(8 marks)**

2   Show your calculations in labelling the diagram, and indicate
    your decision, based on the expected value of each eventuality. **(8 marks)**

3   Outline the weaknesses of basing decisions entirely upon the
    calculation of expected values.   **(4 marks)**

WHITBREAD – THE BREWERY WITH NO BEER

A2
OBJECTIVES AND
STRATEGY

CONCEPTS NEEDED:

Vertical integration, Strategy, Takeovers, Ansoff's Matrix

The Whitbread family brewing business started in London in 1742. By the 1980s it was one of Britain's biggest and most successful. It had been quick to see the potential of continental lagers, bringing Heineken and Stella Artois to this country. By 1990, with 6,500 pubs and a 14% market share of beer sales, it was one of Britain's Big Three brewers.

As with the other major breweries, Whitbread's business strategy was based upon **vertical integration**. Whitbread owned hop farms in Kent, breweries throughout the country plus pubs, clubs, off-licences and restaurant chains to retail the beer to consumers. This provided the company with a degree of control over its business environment, and therefore secure, predictable profits. Three things changed all that:

1 Greater social mobility was undermining customer loyalty to the traditional 'local'. Younger people were more inclined to go to areas where a variety of pubs, bars, clubs and restaurants provided choice and variety. As the 1990s progressed, chains of modern bars and clubs such as All Bar One and J.D. Wetherspoons took advantage of these trends.

2 In 1989 a Monopolies Commission report into the beer market led the government to force breweries to sell off many of their pubs. Whitbread had to sell off 4,500.

3 The rise of supermarkets and hypermarkets was undermining the distribution strength of the brewery owned off-licence chains such as Victoria Wine and Threshers. The fearsome buying power of Tesco and Sainsbury's was undermining the profitability of beer sold off licence.

So when David Thomas was appointed Managing Director of Whitbread Inns in 1990, he was soon thinking about diversification. He already had an in-house model of how to proceed, as Whitbread's Beefeater chain, started in 1975, was expanding profitably. Its organic growth had already been built on by Whitbread's investment in Pizza Hut in 1982 and TGI Friday's in 1985.

In 1990 Whitbread raised £875 million by selling its wines and spirits business and its regional breweries. An attempt to buy Harvester restaurants failed, but in 1995 there were big strategic moves into health and hotels. In August 1995 David Lloyd Sports Clubs and Marriott Hotels were purchased. A year later Pizzaland and Pelican (which owned the Café Rouge and Café Dome chains) followed. When David Thomas was appointed Chief Executive of Whitbread plc in December 1996 the business press heaped praise on the firm for its diversification strategy. Further moves to strengthen the new arms of the company included the purchase of Swallow Hotels in November 1999. This doubled the size of the UK hotels division, leading the *Financial Times* to report: 'The deal looks sensible. It bolsters Whitbread's position in upmarket hotels – the bright spot in its portfolio – as well as offering **cost synergies**. In this respect Whitbread is surely being conservative in promising only £10 million of annual savings by 2002/2003.'

However, none of these diversification moves appeared to threaten the position of beer at the heart of the business. In May 1998 the company announced a £460 million investment in opening new pubs. A year later Whitbread began a long battle with Punch Taverns to buy the 3,500 pubs Allied Domecq had put up for sale. Whitbread admitted defeat only when its bid was referred by the government to the Competition Commission.

Whitbread's defeat seemed to force it to rethink its corporate strategy. In early 2000 the company sold off all its breweries and then its stake in the off-licence chain First Quench. Most decisively of all, in October 2000, it put its entire 3,000-strong pub division up for sale. After 250 years in the beer business, Whitbread was pulling out altogether. Company Chairman Sir John Banham said: 'We have a very attractive set of businesses going forward and we want to devote all our attention to that. We will not be able to do that and do justice to our pubs and bars.'

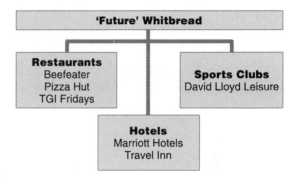

The 'Future Whitbread' would focus on three divisions: restaurants, hotels and sports clubs. In each of the three areas the company owned brands with a distinctive niche and a national reputation. This should provide the value added the company wanted. In addition, all three divisions were operating in growth sectors of the leisure market. Some analysts questioned the strength of the brands, with *The Guardian* reporting comments such as a 'mish-mash of mediocre brands'. Generally, though, the City was pleased to see the decisive move towards a more clearly focused company. Without question, David Thomas had been responsible for a complete reshaping of the company. Whitbread the business would no longer have Whitbread beers or Whitbread pubs. After 258 years, the brand was on its deathbed, but the company might be about to enjoy a rebirth.

Sources: Whitbread Annual Reports; *Financial Times*

Appendix A: Whitbread divisional performance 1997–2000

		1996/7	1997/8	1998/9	1999/2000
Brewing	Turnover	£999m	£996m	£1,056m	£1,116m
	Trading profit	£40m	£45m	£52m	£47m
Pubs	Turnover	£890m	£962m	£964m	£1,016m
	Trading profit	£210m	£233m	£221m	£238m
Restaurants	Turnover	£573m	£731m	£693m	£734m
	Trading profit	£58m	£70m	£57m	£57m
Hotels	Turnover	£192m	£195m	£223m	£288m
	Trading profit	£34m	£37m	£48m	£54m
Sports & Health	Turnover	£47m	£63m	£78m	£104m
	Trading profit	£15m	£19m	£19m	£23m
Other	Turnover	£326m	£251m	(£73m)	(£307m)
(+inter-company trade)	Trading profit	(£54m)	(£23m)	(£96m)	(£163m)
Total	Turnover	£3,027m	£3,198m	£2,941m	£2,951m
	Trading profit	£303m	£381m	£301m	£256m

(Source: Extel/Sequencer 2000)

Questions
(80 marks; 90 minutes)

1   **a** Explain the meaning of 'vertical integration'.   **(3 marks)**

    b Draw and label a diagram showing the vertical integration
described in the second paragraph.   **(5 marks)**

2   **a** Examine the corporate plan pursued by David Thomas.   **(9 marks)**

    b Outline two strategic decisions taken by the company in
pursuit of its plan.   **(9 marks)**

3   **a** Explain what is meant by 'cost synergies'.   **(3 marks)**

    b Consider whether Mr Thomas was right to be cautious
about the cost synergies available from a horizontal
takeover.   **(12 marks)**

4   **a** Plot each of the following of Whitbread's strategic moves
on an Ansoff's Matrix:

      i the acquisition of the UK Pizza Hut business in 1982

     ii the acquisition of David Lloyd Sports Clubs in 1995

    iii the £460 million investment in new pubs in 1998.   **(9 marks)**

    b Discuss the value of Ansoff's Matrix in analysing the risks
and rewards involved in Whitbread's main strategic decisions
over the period covered by the case.   **(15 marks)**

5   Use the data provided in Appendix A plus any supporting
material from the case to consider whether Whitbread was
wise to withdraw from beer in order to focus on the three
divisions referred to as 'Future Whitbread'.   **(15 marks)**

HARD CASH FROM SOFTWARE

A2
OBJECTIVES AND
STRATEGY

CONCEPTS NEEDED:

Impact of a change in size, Takeovers, Retrenchment

In the mid 1980s two teenagers, Richard and David Darling, moved on from playing computer games to writing them. Early experiments with imitation Space Invader games progressed to designing more sophisticated software. Originally done for their own amusement, they decided to save up the money to advertise their products through a half page in *Popular Computing Weekly*. Under the name Galactic Software, they offered 14 games. A £70 advertisement yielded £4,000 of orders. Further advertisements kept sales rising and rising. After completing their exams they went into business full time.

In 1986 they formed a company, Codemasters Ltd. Early successes such as BMX Simulator for the Commodore 64 were followed by Micro Machines for the Sega Megadrive. More recently, Colin McRae Rally and TOCA Touring Cars for the Sony Playstation have pushed the business to become a major force internationally. Both of the latter titles sold more than three million

units. A report on the games market published by the European Leisure Software Publishers' Association in Spring 2000 stated that Codemasters creates 'hit titles with more frequency than perhaps any other company in the world'.

After the 1986 start-up, Richard and David built up from a mail order business to a software supplier through normal distribution channels such as HMV and other retailers. They also built up a workforce in Leamington Spa, and later in development studios in California. By 1999 there were 250 staff. A year later the number reached 400, even though the games industry as a whole was suffering from delays to the launch of the Sony PlayStation 2. In its 1998/1999 financial year a profit of £25 million was made on turnover of just £69 million. In the same period, the better known Eidos lost £27 million on a turnover of £195 million. Codemasters duly came second in the *Sunday Times* Top 100 fastest growing private companies in Britain.

Given this fantastic success, financial advisers started to suggest that the company should float on the stock market. Games can cost over £2 million to develop and require marketing spending of much more. So it could be helpful to have a substantial injection of share capital from a stock market quotation. Yet the Darlings could see major drawbacks in moving from their private company status. A quick look at the share price for Eidos gives a clear idea of how changeable can be the views of investors towards software companies. Tomb Raider's Lara Croft became a stock market favourite, then villain, all within the space of a year.

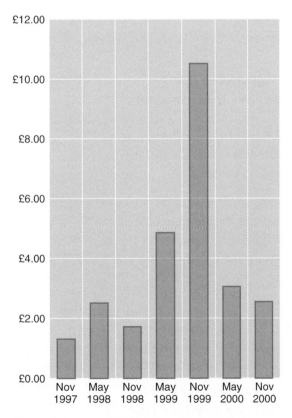

Ups and downs in Eidos share price 1997–2000

Codemasters would rather keep away from such a rollercoaster.

To David Darling, the key issue is confidentiality. He says:

'*When you consider it, by listing you are almost giving away your commercial secrets. You often have to tell (City) analysts your underlying strategies and that information helps competitors.*'

Codemasters' Managing Director Nick Wheelwright is more concerned about the evidence he sees of short termism in the City of London. He says:

'*If a game is not up to standard we will put it out six months later than planned. Very reputable games companies are being hit unreasonably whenever they make such a judgement. The City seems to see the delay in the release of a game as a bad thing – but it can often mean it will be even better and will become a bigger hit than predicted.*'

Despite scepticism from the City about the ability of the firm to grow further without floating, Codemasters' Chairman is convinced that 'as long as we keep doing the same as we have always done – making good games, controlling our finances and not getting into debt – there's no reason we can't be a world beater without floating'. If companies as buoyant as Codemasters cannot see the value of a stock market listing, perhaps it is time for City analysts to rethink their attitude to creative, modern businesses – and to short termism.

Sources: FAME; *Financial Times*

Appendix A: Extracts from Codemasters Group Ltd accounts 1997–1999

	05/98–06/99	05/97–04/98	05/96–04/97
Turnover £m	68,968	20,265	10,752
Pre-tax profit £m	25,322	7,193	2,112
Net tangible assets £m	15,800	8,355	4,566
Return on Capital	137.34%	85.99%	46.21%
Employees	195	115	62
Sales UK £m	26,852	9,070	5,141
Sales for export £m	42,117	11,194	5,611

Questions
(50 marks; 60 minutes)

1 From its origins with £4,000 of sales turnover, Codemasters grew to nearly £70 million of turnover by 1999. Consider the problems it may have encountered as a result of such rapid growth. **(12 marks)**

2 Discuss whether the business should change from being a private to a public company, if it wants to achieve the aim of being a 'world beater'. **(14 marks)**

3 By September 2000, the shares of rival software companies such as Rage Software plc had fallen so low as to make it possible for Codemasters to make a takeover bid. Outline the possible difficulties for Codemasters of buying a rival software business. **(10 marks)**

4 Excellent though Codemasters' growth record has been, software companies tend to suffer from occasional major downturns. To what extent might a period of retrenchment be helpful to Codemasters in the long term? **(14 marks)**

THE SUPER-JUMBO

A2
EXTERNAL
INFLUENCES,
OBJECTIVES AND
STRATEGY

CONCEPTS NEEDED:

Government intervention, External costs and benefits, Environment, European Union

Imagine a long distance flight on a plane with a bar area, sleeper cabins and generous leg room. That is the promise of the Airbus A380, already known as the Superjumbo. This double decker plane was given the go-ahead in December 2000 and is expected to be in service in 2006/7. The decision to go ahead was difficult for the European producers of Airbus, given the ferocious competition from the world's biggest aircraft producer Boeing, plus the huge scale of the investment. At £7,200 million, the A380 is the most costly new product launch ever. But then it will create one of the world's most expensive products. Each Superjumbo will carry a £140 million price tag.

The American Boeing company dominated world aircraft production for over half a century. When the proposal first arose to create a European rival, Boeing was openly sceptical. Given the difficulties of running a business as complex as aircraft manufacture, how could there be success from a group of separate businesses in separate countries? At the time, the British were also unconvinced. So when French and German pioneers, backed by government finance, began Airbus Industrie in 1970, there was no British presence. Only in 1979, after the commercial success of the first two Airbus planes, did British Aerospace become a full partner, with a 20% stake. Ever since then, British workers have built the wings for all the Airbus aircraft. At the time, several British newspapers condemned British Aerospace for entering what they saw as a woolly partnership that could never succeed in the long term against Boeing.

Nevertheless, Airbus Industrie continued to develop a range of technologically advanced planes that steadily won over European, then Asian, then American airlines. By the late 1990s Airbus had developed a product range that more than matched Boeing in every sector apart from 'Jumbos'. In 1999 and 2000 Boeing and Airbus argued about who was the world leader, but most independent observers believed that the Europeans had overtaken the US company for the first time. Flushed with this success, Airbus announced that it would proceed to develop a new generation of planes with 49% more floor space and 35% more seats than a Boeing 747 jumbo jet. This would mean entering a sector worth 25% of the market value of the entire world market for passenger aircraft – a sector estimated by Airbus to be worth a mind numbing £200 billion between 2000 and 2020.

The difficulty in making an investment such as this is the uncertainty that results from the timescale involved. The Boeing 747 had a 30 year monopoly of the market for very large passenger planes, so the economics of the Airbus A380 may hinge on a similarly long period. If so, the chances of accurate forecasting are close to zero. Proceeding, then, has to be a matter of calculation, hope and careful consideration of the consequences of failure. For the partners in the Airbus project, the risk was eased slightly by European government backed low interest rate loans of £1.8 billion, covering one third of the capital outlay.

Boeing responded by announcing the development of a 'stretched' 747 that could seat 520 people on long haul flights and with extra room for sleeper cabins. The American firm openly questioned the financial viability of designing and building an all-new aircraft, implying that Airbus would suffer cost and time overruns that would affect customers. Boeing also stressed two key arguments: commonality and 5% lower passenger costs per mile. Commonality was their term for the security that putting Boeing Stretched 747s into service would involve minimal change for the airlines. Pilot controls, maintenance programmes, baggage handling systems and air crew operations would be changed little from the present. Therefore only minor retraining would be needed, and it would be easy to operate new 747s alongside older ones. The Airbus A380, by comparison, would involve huge changes. A further important argument in favour of Boeing was that it

could bring its planes into service by 2005, a full two years before the A380.

During 2000 Boeing and Airbus argued their cases with each of the world's major long haul operators. Early breakthroughs would be vital. If one or two major airlines opted for the all-new Airbus A380, others might feel they could not afford to be left behind.

The Airbus case for the A380 rested on several points:

- passenger comfort, with wider seats, each with separate armrests

- higher profit potential for the airlines, despite a slightly higher break-even load factor; the greater profit potential coming from extra seats (see diagram); extra price potential as a result of the value added by extra passenger comfort; and also design ingenuity into speeding up passenger entry and exit, which will allow the planes to be put back into service more quickly

- more environmentally friendly, as the A380 is built with new, lighter metals that allow passenger miles to be flown more economically; Airbus also argued that more passengers per plane means fewer take-offs and landings, thereby reducing noise and air pollution near to cities.

The Airbus case clearly proved attractive, as Singapore Airlines, Air France and Qantas opted for the new European plane. Then Virgin Atlantic pitched in with a £2.6 billion order for six A380 planes plus an option on six more. On 15 December 2000, Virgin announced that it had abandoned plans to purchase the Boeing plane. A few days later Airbus announced that with 50 firm orders (to none for Boeing) the A380 would definitely go ahead.

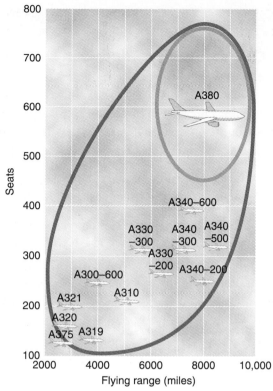

Source: Airbus Industrie

widely among the manufacturing sector. Furthermore, aircraft manufacturing has two unusually attractive features:

1 It is in a sector growing at 8% a year (whereas the car markets of western Europe and America are saturated).

2 It is very high value added manufacture, so the exchange rate of the pound against other currencies has relatively little impact upon demand or profitability.

On hearing of the Virgin order, the British media focused upon Richard Branson's promise of 'a bedroom for passengers' and a 'giant flying cruise ship'. The wider story went relatively unreported, however: that European cooperation backed initially by government finance had led to an effective challenge and then commercial triumph against the mighty Boeing. This paved the way for the A380 development that would generate over 145,000 high quality jobs in Europe. No single British, German or French company could have succeeded on its own. None would have dared to try. Yet in the same month, opinion polls showed the British as more hostile than ever to Europe and its single currency.

In early 2001, Boeing announced that it would not proceed with its stretched 747. The way was clear for the Airbus A380.

Sources: The Observer; Financial Times

The announcement coincided with a very difficult week for British manufacturing. Vauxhall had announced the loss of 2,000 jobs due to the closure of its car manufacturing plant at Luton. Therefore the 30,000 UK jobs forecast from the A380 project were more than welcome. Although their main focus would be on Bristol and Chester, the knock-on effects upon suppliers of machinery, computers and components would spread the work more

Questions
(80 marks; 90 minutes)

1 Examine three ways the British economy may benefit from the development and manufacture of the Airbus A380. **(12 marks)**

2 Governments are often criticised for risking taxpayers' money in grants to industry. To what extent can the Airbus case be taken as proof that government aid to industry *is* worthwhile? **(14 marks)**

3 **a** Outline the external costs and benefits that may result from operating an airline. **(8 marks)**

   b Consider why airlines such as Virgin or British Airways might be interested in the environmental impact of the planes they buy. **(12 marks)**

4 **a** Explain why companies or countries may need to work together in markets as huge as world airplane construction. **(8 marks)**

   b Consider why this issue is important when considering whether Britain should participate fully in the European Union. **(10 marks)**

5 All new product launches are risky. Discuss the factors you consider most likely to create difficulties for the Airbus A380 project in the coming years. **(16 marks)**

THE OIL CRISIS

A2
EXTERNAL
INFLUENCES,
OBJECTIVES AND
STRATEGY

CONCEPTS NEEDED:

Inflation, Company objectives, Shortage of resources, Diversification

Looking back, it was hard to believe that no one in the firm had seen the warning signs. The Chairman of Shell reminded everyone recently that he had made a public statement three years ago that there would be an oil supply shortage in the foreseeable future. Datona Plastics was not the only firm to be caught unprepared for the doubling of oil prices within the last eight months, yet few other firms were in such an awkward position.

Datona made high grade plastic mouldings, such as car control panels, car seats, and the casings for computer keyboards and monitors. Half its output went to the motor industry, and much of the rest to consumer appliance and electronics businesses. These markets had been booming while oil and petrol prices and general inflation were low, but had been hard hit during recent months. Rising prices had hit people's real incomes; many responded by postponing the replacement of items such as cars, carpets, and home computers.

Datona's special problem was that not only were its sales slumping, but also its costs were spiralling upwards. The plastic pellets that it bought from BP and ESSO were direct products of oil refining, and had therefore doubled in price. As shown below, this had brought about a big change in the composition of the firm's costs, as well as increasing their per unit total.

Whereas its car assembly customers could look for suppliers of substitute materials such

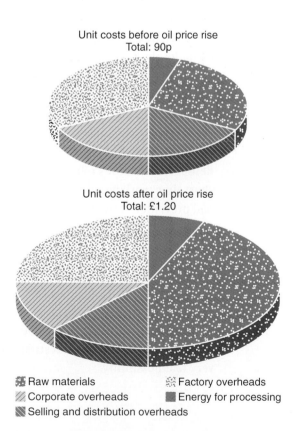

Unit costs before oil price rise
Total: 90p

Unit costs after oil price rise
Total: £1.20

🦴 Raw materials   ⬚ Factory overheads
▨ Corporate overheads   ■ Energy for processing
▧ Selling and distribution overheads

as leather seats or wood casings (which would add value to the products anyway), Datona was equipped only to handle plastics. Just 12 months ago a leading City journalist had showered praise on the firm's 'sharply focused, clear-sighted management … wisely refusing all temptation to diversify away from its area of core competence.' Then its share price had been 285 pence – up from 80 pence four years before. Now it stood at 160 pence, and even that was partly because the market had not yet appreciated just how hard it had been hit by the oil price rise. As *The Sunday Times* had pointed out the previous week, several of Datona's Directors had sold large portions of their shareholdings over recent months.

During the early weeks of the decline in demand, the managers had decided to continue to produce at normal output levels; they believed that the manufacturers were just trimming back stock levels, and would therefore push demand back up within a week or so. By the time it was clear that this was a misreading of the marketplace Datona had excessive stock levels and a troublesome cash flow position. Ever since, it had been trying to cut stocks back to their normal level of six weeks' worth of sales. However, the Human Resources Director's reluctance to put staff on short time working, plus ever falling demand, had prevented it from succeeding.

Another twist to the tale had emerged recently. With inflation over the past six months at an annual rate of 6%, the workforce was pushing for an 8% pay rise. The unions rejected outright the firm's case that the *annual* Retail Prices Index stood at 5%, but only 3% could be afforded. A strike appeared a very real possibility.

So the monthly Board meeting took place in very tense circumstances. Opinions split between two positions: one group agreed with the Financial Director's analysis that as there was a danger of making an operating loss of £4.2 million over the coming six months, one of the firm's three factories must be closed down and sold off; the others sided with the Marketing Director who worried that the oil price might slip back if the OPEC cartel members were to break ranks, leaving Datona unable to meet reviving demand from its two remaining plants.

The firm's choice of strategy was to hinge, therefore, on the Directors' hunch about future actions by governments and markets over which they had no control or even influence. As discussion began to get heated, the Chairman asked the Financial Director whether the situation posed a significant threat to the firm's survival. All were stunned at the reply:

> '*If we continue with the current level of overheads, any further slippage in demand will push us into the hands of the Receiver within the year. Even at current levels of demand our operating losses combined with our poor cash flow will set us back five years. I believe it is our responsibility to our shareholders and the majority of our workforce to cut back without delay.*'

The Marketing Director stayed silent as the others slid over to the Financial Director's side. She reflected that in good times the marketing department dominates, but in times of crisis power lies with the purse strings.

Questions
(60 marks; 80 minutes)

1 State the term given to:
  a household items such as cars, carpets and home computers
  b inflation sparked off by rising input prices
  c share dealing based upon knowledge not yet available publicly. **(6 marks)**

2 a Explain why, in Datona's circumstances, it proved unwise to refuse 'all temptation to diversify'? **(8 marks)**
  b The journalist's opinion was based upon the many cases of unsuccessful diversification. Why do firms struggle so often when they move away from their area of core competence? **(12 marks)**

3 Comment upon the negotiating positions adopted by labour and management within Datona's collective bargaining process. Would you see the Financial Director's policy of cutbacks as part of that process? **(10 marks)**

4 Explain the meaning of the Marketing Director's statement about the oil price. Why would this worry the marketing department especially? **(9 marks)**

5 If the oil price sticks at its higher level, evaluate two strategies Datona might consider for the longer term. Which of the two would you recommend and why? **(15 marks)**

RAILTRACK PLC – A CULTURE OF COMPLACENCY?

A2
EXTERNAL
INFLUENCES,
OBJECTIVES AND
STRATEGY

CONCEPTS NEEDED:

Ethics, Social responsibilities, Privatisation, Social audits

On 21 July 2000 Railtrack was fined £200,000 for an accident in which a man was decapitated. It happened when a businessman travelling home from a party leaned out of a train window. Accident investigators found scaffolding just four inches from the train instead of the legal minimum of 22 inches. The mistake by a contractor was not spotted by an overworked Railtrack project manager. It gave a warning of what was soon to hit the company.

Railtrack plc was formed in 1994 as the first stage in the Conservative government's plan to privatise British Rail. The old, nationalised railway had been run as a single business, responsible for track, rolling stock and passenger services. Now it was being divided up, both to make it easier to sell off in bite-sized chunks and in order to create an element of competition between the different parts of the rail network. Railtrack was to look after the track, signalling, scheduling and the main line stations. It would earn its revenue by charging operating companies for the right to use the track.

In early 1995 Prime Minister John Major announced the go-ahead of privatisation to transform the railways from a national joke to 'the envy of the world'. The *Financial Times* noted: 'As with most privatisations, there will be great scope to increase efficiency.'

The Conservatives' chosen method was to split British Rail into four parts:

- passenger train operating companies (25)
- train owners, who would lease the engines and carriages to the operators (three)
- track operations (through Railtrack)
- track renewal and maintenance companies (13)

Although Railtrack would be a monopoly, the other elements in the railway would theoretically be in competition with each other. This would foster competition which was considered to be a key force in maximising efficiency, innovation and investment.

In March 1995 Sir Bob Reid, Chairman of British Rail, said he was opposed to the government's privatisation method, specifically hiving off the track and signalling operations into a separate company, Railtrack. He warned that this might cause problems of coordination and accountability. The *Financial Times* reported him as saying:

> **'T**he break-up of the railways will impose a deadening layer of bureaucracy, and the creation of so many separate businesses will make it harder to provide a good service.**'**

Others made more specific points about the risks to safety in the government's proposals. In August 1995 a safety adviser to Railtrack warned of a possible 'major disaster some very short time in the future' because of inadequate track maintenance work. The report highlighted problems in a relationship between Railtrack and outside contractors that was 'neither clear nor available'. A Labour party transport spokesman said that the report 'highlighted the depth of disarray in Railtrack. They are unsure of who is even in charge of private contractors working on the line.' Labour concluded that the underlying problem was a result of rail privatisation that had broken up 'unified management control of the rail network' and put cost cutting before safety.

In September 1995 the *Financial Times* wrote a glowing article focused on the 'marketing innovations' in the newly created railway operating divisions. New logos, smart new staff uniforms and new corporate colours were cited. So, too, were special offers such as Scotrail's £5 ticket allowing pensioners to travel anywhere within Scotland. 'The lid has been lifted off marketing,' said one commentator. A *Financial Times* leading article pressed the case for privatisation with many references to efficiency but without mentioning safety. It was as if smart uniforms outweighed the safety concerns.

On 3 January 1996 the privatisation of Railtrack was confirmed and in May the company was floated on the stock market. The launch price of 390p valued the business at £1.93 billion – well below the value of the property assets Railtrack was inheriting from British Rail. Within two years the shares trebled in price.

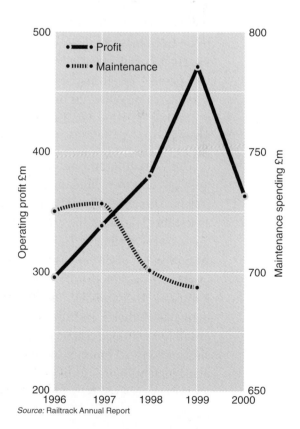

Source: Railtrack Annual Report

As the graph shows, the following years saw no increase in maintenance spending on Railtrack's infrastructure, despite sharply rising profitability. Staff levels fell and there were many expressions of concern from the trade unions and independent inspectors about safety standards. Then, in 1999, came tragedy at Paddington as a head-on collision led to a fire in which 31 people died.

When the public inquiry was held in summer 2000, Railtrack Chief Executive Gerald Corbett admitted that he knew of serious signalling problems before the crash occurred. The bereaved familes accused Railtrack of putting profit before safety. Corbett told the inquiry: 'I cannot recall any example where I've rejected a safety proposal on the basis of cost.' The QC representing the bereaved families suggested this might be because costly projects were 'crushed' before they reached Mr Corbett's desk. It emerged that in the five years to 1998 signals had been passed at danger 48 times within two miles of Paddington Station. The driver of the train that passed the red signal – causing the crash – had been qualified for only two weeks and, according to the families' QC, had had inadequate training.

The Paddington public inquiry also pointed to more fundamental, underlying issues. One was the failure of successive governments to back the case for investing in the fail-safe Automatic Train Protection (ATP) system used elsewhere in Europe. No less important was the culture of complacency at Railtrack. The families' lawyer went on to blame 'Railtrack's institutional inertia and obsession with performance. This disaster is, above all else, a story of an abject failure of management.'

The inquiry kept going through the summer and autumn but was then punctuated by another rail tragedy. On 17 October 2000 a broken rail led to a derailment of a train travelling at 115 mph at Hatfield, Hertfordshire. Four people died and 33 were injured. The following day it emerged that Railtrack had discovered weaknesses in the five year old stretch of track in January, but although some work had been carried out, the remaining work was not thought a high priority. Railtrack admitted that there were a further 100 sites where track problems were comparable.

Gerald Corbett offered his resignation, but it was refused. In the days that followed, Railtrack imposed 30% speed limits on hundreds of sections of Inter-City track. The company went on a public relations offensive, emphasising its commitment to safety. A massive programme of rail renewal was undertaken rapidly over weekends. For a few weeks the press accepted that the more the disruption the stronger the evidence that safety was being taken seriously. Yet the National Union of Railwayworkers was able to show that 6,000 track maintenance workers had lost their jobs since Railtrack took over from British Rail. And many argued that a safety culture had never been part of Railtrack as it had been part of the nationalised railways.

The following weeks saw misery for rail passengers as delays doubled or trebled journey times. Even car drivers were affected as people switched from rail travel. As Railtrack started to warn of delays continuing until Easter 2001, Gerald Corbett was replaced as Chief Executive. He left with a £1 million payoff and was replaced by two men with only

13 months' rail industry experience between them. *The Times* wrote quite warmly about Mr Corbett, but acknowledged that many 'held him to blame for a corporate culture which put profits above safety, shareholder rewards above public service and commercial efficiency above railway experience.' What the newspaper failed to mention was the role played by the underlying problems set up at the time of the privatisation. The political culture of the time had assumed that competition and the profit motive would take care of safety.

The final chapter in the Railtrack story began in September 2001, when the government announced that it would no longer provide the company with financial support.

Sources: Financial Times, The Guardian and *The Times* 1995–2000

Appendix A: Selected data from Railtrack Report and Accounts 1996–2000

Year ending March 31:	1996	1997	1998	1999	2000
Sales turnover (£m)	2,300	2,437	2,467	2,573	2,547
Operating profit (£m)	296	339	380	471	363
Infrastructure maintenance (£m)	725	732	702	694	*
Directors' remuneration (£000)	1,180	1,910	2,167	2,046	*
Total staff employed	11,358	11,298	10,700	10,704	*

*Not available in comparable form

Questions
(80 marks; 90 minutes)

1 Outline the evidence within the case that Railtrack 'put profits above safety'. **(8 marks)**

2 The Conservative government was determined to privatise Railtrack in order to increase the efficiency of Britain's rail services.

  a Why, in theory, should privatisation improve efficiency? **(8 marks)**

  b Why may it have failed to achieve this in the case of the railways? **(8 marks)**

3 Responsibility relies upon clear lines of accountability.

  a What was the problem in this case with accountability for rail safety? **(6 marks)**

  b Outline what changes might be needed in the rail industry to correct this problem. **(9 marks)**

4 'Business ethics are embedded in the corporate culture.' Discuss this view in relation to Railtrack's approach to safety. **(15 marks)**

5 To what extent might social auditing have helped prevent Railtrack's difficulties in 2000? **(12 marks)**

6 Is it inevitable that the profit motive conflicts with ethical considerations such as passenger safety? **(14 marks)**

THE 3 IN 1 WASHING MACHINE

AS INTEGRATED CASE

CONCEPTS NEEDED:

Break even, Cash flow, Advertising, Product life cycle

It was Jane's idea that had started it. She had been so fed up with her Mum's moaning that she snapped: 'You won't be happy till there's a machine that washes, dries, and irons all the clothes automatically.' When her boyfriend heard about it, he started messing about with electronics; 10 months later the 'Washerman' 3 in 1 washing machine was a full, working prototype.

Now came the big decision; should they sell the idea to a big company, or try to manufacture it themselves? All Tim was sure of was that he should patent the idea as soon as possible.

They decided to visit a bank manager for advice. Before going, they tried to work out what kind of sums were involved. Much of the costs would come from bought-in components, so they felt fairly certain of the following estimates:

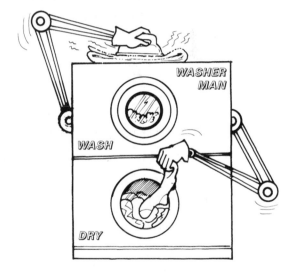

components	£280 per unit
materials	£60 per unit
factory labour	£10 per unit

(They had argued about whether labour was a fixed or a variable cost, but Jane's view prevailed – that as they intended to pay their workers per unit produced, they must treat factory labour as a variable cost.)

They were less certain of the fixed costs, and so decided to work on both optimistic and pessimistic figures.

rent and rates	£6,000–12,000 per month
staff salaries	£14,000–24,000 per month
other overheads	£10,000–14,000 per month

After further arguing, they agreed that they could charge £500 per machine, and should sell their total output of 300 machines per month. Armed with this information, they went to the bank.

The manager worked out the best and worst profit position based upon their information, and frowned. He then said:

'*You really need to do a lot more work before I can help. Have you thought about the likely length of life cycle of the Washerman? After all, your forecast of overheads assumes that the machinery you buy will have useful life of five years. But what if the product fades away after three? And what about a cash flow forecast? Surely you realise the importance of that.*'

By the end of the meeting, though, the bank manager was becoming increasingly impressed with Tim's explanation of the mechanics and performance of the 3 in 1. So Jane and Tim went away feeling optimistic that the bank would help, once they had given their financial and marketing planning some more careful thought.

Questions
(50 marks; 60 minutes)

1   **a**   What is meant by the term patent?   **(3 marks)**

     b   If they wished to stop anyone else from using the brand name 'Washerman', what should they obtain?   **(1 mark)**

2   What profit could be expected (both optimistic and pessimistic) if the forecasts made are correct?   **(8 marks)**

3   Explain three ways in which a break-even chart could be of use to them.   **(6 marks)**

4   Discuss the factors that would influence their decisions on an advertising strategy to ensure consumer acceptance of the 3 in 1.   **(15 marks)**

5   On the assumption that the product works well, how might Jane and Tim set about forecasting the probable length of the life cycle of the 3 in 1? (Try to come up with specific ideas, i.e. just 'market research' will not do.)   **(9 marks)**

6   Outline two reasons why a cash flow forecast would be of value in this situation.   **(8 marks)**

FORD'S MODEL T – THE BIRTH OF MODERN INDUSTRY

AS INTEGRATED CASE

CONCEPTS NEEDED:

Scientific management, Demand, Division of labour

In the early 1900s, production of cars was mainly done by skilled workers who crafted the car with the aid of quite simple machinery. Henry Ford's small car factory followed this pattern, until demand for his newest model (the Model T) forced him to look for ways of speeding up output.

Ford's 12 to 15 young engineers were given the freedom to test the performance of new machine tools against their existing methods. If they could prove the superiority of their new system, the factory layout would be changed in whichever way would allow output to be expanded most rapidly.

They soon found that the easiest way to increase output per worker was by getting parts moving automatically from one production stage to another. At first this was done with downward sloping chutes, then later with conveyor belts. When cost saving measures were introduced, Ford passed these on as price cuts to his customers. As demand increased further, they found it possible to subdivide different units of work into smaller and smaller operations. At first, unskilled workers were used to produce these parts repeatedly; then the engineers set about devising machinery that would simplify the work even further.

By 1910, Ford's success had enabled him to afford to construct a massive new factory at Highland Park. By 1913, many of the main components were being constructed on assembly lines. In late 1913, experiments were carried out on a moving line for the car chassis. This proved highly successful. By June 1914, a chain-driven line (as is still used in

many car factories) had cut assembly time from 12 hours to 93 minutes. Within a year, Ford had introduced moving assembly lines throughout the plant.

Yet the ever increasing mechanisation of the plant made it a progressively more unpleasant place to work. The constant pressure to keep up with the pace of the line, plus the appalling noise and dust levels, resulted in Ford's labour turnover reaching 380%. A 13% pay rise (to $2.34 per day) had no impact on the problem, so in January 1914 Ford created world headlines by adopting the unprecedentedly high figure of $5 per day (more than many American and British workers earned per week).

The five-dollar-a-day wage ensured that **Fordism** became widely discussed and admired by managements, workers and consumers throughout Europe; and Ford became a folk hero in America. He had shown that mass production could enable high wages to be paid, yet consumer prices cut (see Appendix A). The fact that Ford offered no choice of colour or model design was not seen as a disadvantage at a time when people were thrilled to be able to afford their first car. At their height, Ford's Highland Park and the new, massive River Rouge plants produced two million Model Ts in one year – giving Ford 50% of the US car market in the early 1920s. It was only later in that decade that customers began to switch to the wider range of models provided by General Motors. Model T production ended in 1927, by which time Ford had produced over 15 million.

Appendix A: Model T pricing and sales 1909–1916

Year	Retail price	Sales
1909	$950	12,292
1910	$780	19,293
1911	$690	40,402
1912	$600	78,611
1913	$550	182,809
1914	$490	260,720
1915	$440	355,276
1916	$360	577,036

Questions
(40 marks; 50 minutes)

1 Explain your understanding of the term Fordism (in bold print in the text). **(3 marks)**

2 **a** Draw a demand schedule that plots price against quantity for Ford's Model T. **(12 marks)**

   b Outline three factors that might have been operating to distort the relationship between price and demand during this period. **(9 marks)**

3 What terms are usually used to convey the meaning:
   a output per worker **(2 marks)**
   b subdividing different units of work into smaller and smaller operations? **(2 marks)**

4 To what extent does the passage show evidence of the influence of F.W. Taylor's views on 'Scientific management'? **(12 marks)**

THE WIND
OF CHANGE

A2
INTEGRATED
CASE

CONCEPTS NEEDED:

Human resource management, Change management, Technological change, Just-in-time

Devinder looked out of his office window at the wind farm on the far horizon. Round and round went the propellers, slowly beating a rhythm, but not, apparently, doing anything. They seemed to move at the same pace as Jim, the company's storeman, who was at that moment trudging across the yard, the inevitable cigarette in his mouth. Not a happy comparison, Devinder thought. The wind machines worked in harness with nature, and kept going 24 hours a day if conditions were right. Jim seemed to know only conflict, and as for working, 24 minutes was probably about right.

Devinder couldn't understand it. His father, the firm's founder, had always spoken fondly of Jim, about the storeman's encyclopaedic knowledge of the stock and his willingness to adapt. Of course, Devinder accepted that Jim's job had changed beyond recognition and that, as a result, Jim probably resented the current position. The reasons for this resentment were obvious. First of all, just-in-time delivery meant that stock levels were much lower than they had been in the past, and second, the introduction of computerisation meant that Jim's knowledge

of the stock was no longer of such importance. Devinder had only to switch on his computer to find out that kind of information.

But Jim wasn't the only problem facing Devinder. His whole workforce seemed to be breaking up. He couldn't understand what was wrong. After all, he'd taken his father's business in an entirely new direction, from old to new technology; he'd found markets and obtained sales, both in the UK and abroad, and he'd achieved it without making one person redundant. Yet no one seemed happy. Inevitably, when Devinder's dad retired, some of the longest serving staff went too, but it hadn't just been some, over the past two years or so they'd almost all gone. Except for Sheila in personnel, poor old Jim was practically the last one, and even he was retiring in three weeks. Devinder had just agreed to the advertisement for a new storeman a day or so ago.

Worryingly, it wasn't just the 'old guard'. Younger people, those in their 20s and 30s, were also leaving. With unemployment high locally, Sheila had been able to replace them without too much difficulty, but even these recruits weren't staying long. Devinder was concerned about the lack of long term expertise and experience in the company.

Devinder's thoughts were interrupted by a knock on the door. In walked Anne Haynes, an old university friend of his, who had spent her career in human resource management (HRM) with a large multinational. He had telephoned her in desperation two weeks earlier, and sent her details of staff organisation, recruitment and turnover, a move that Sheila in personnel clearly resented.

Three hours later, Devinder felt as though he'd been run over, or perhaps tied to one of the wind generators' sails and sent spinning round and round! He'd also offered Anne a job as head of HRM, which she had accepted, subject to certain conditions. These were, first, that the Personnel Department be renamed the HRM Department and that staff should be seen as a major strategic resource. Second, that Sheila be retrained or encouraged to retire. Third, that in-house training schemes should be established, and liaison with local colleges started immediately with the objective of introducing up to date courses relevant to the firm's new situation. As Anne put it: 'You've just focused on sales, new investment and profits; your staff have had little by way of training and no sense of involvement. Is it any wonder that they don't want to work for you?' Fortunately, Devinder was big enough to accept the criticism and start working to improve the situation.

Questions
(60 marks; 70 minutes)

1 Explain the business significance of
   a just-in-time production   **(5 marks)**
   b new technology   **(5 marks)**

2 Analyse the likely short and long term effects on Devinder's business of a fall in unemployment locally.   **(8 marks)**

3 Use the text as a starting point to discuss why many commentators believe that successful change is about people first and technology second.   **(12 marks)**

4 Outline two mistakes you think Devinder has made in managing his staff.   **(6 marks)**

5 To what extent may there be significance in altering the name of the Personnel Department to 'Human Resource Management'?   **(10 marks)**

6 Consider the possible benefits to the firm of adopting Anne Haynes's proposals.   **(14 marks)**

81 THE PRINCE AND THE TURNSTILE

A2
INTEGRATED
CASE

CONCEPTS NEEDED:

Direct and indirect costs, Depreciation, Profit, Raising finance

When made redundant, 25 year old Jim Tilley was left with £5,000 and a fierce determination to be his own boss. As a fanatical supporter of Blyth Spartans Football Club, he had become used to helping out by maintaining and repairing their turnstiles. Now he would set up Tilley Turnstile Services and try to make a living out of his hobby.

His first step was to get 1,000 brochures printed that explained the two main services: repair and maintenance. These he mailed out to the professional and leading amateur football clubs, plus other venues such as cricket clubs and racecourses. The week after completing the mailing was the worst of his life. He had no responses at all.

Then a letter arrived from Kilmarnock inviting him to come up and give a quote for a pre-season overhaul of their 16 turnstiles. He was up in Scotland within three hours; by the end of the afternoon he had the contract. For £400 the club had its turnstiles made good and on arriving home three days later, Jim worked out that he had made £200 as pay/profit.

The next four weeks were crazily busy, as club after club invited Jim to work for them. He priced each job along the same lines as his first, working out all the direct costs, then

adding 100%. With money flowing in, he bought a van and rented a factory unit on an industrial estate.

Then in late August the phones went dead as the pre-season work dried up. Eventually jobs came through from clubs that needed repair work to broken turnstiles, but the turnover was pretty low. Jim realised that he needed longer term work to fill the gaps. He decided to move into the manufacture of turnstiles for new sports stadia or the replacement market.

First, however, he would need extra finance. Discussions with his local banks got nowhere, but a television programme led him to contact the Prince's Youth Business Trust. Jim was allocated an adviser who helped him construct a business plan as the basis for a loan application. The Trust itself lent £4,000 on a low interest rate and this commitment encouraged Barclays to lend the same amount.

Most of the £8,000 of new capital went into the machinery needed to make the turnstile structure. Jim planned to subcontract the production of many of the components, but he wanted full production control over the most critical parts. The Prince's Trust adviser helped to set up a software package to enable Jim to calculate the data in the table below on unit production costs.

The adviser queried the rise in unit labour costs for 5+ units, but accepted the explanation that Jim would have to employ extra workers. These he expected to be less efficient than himself due to their lack of product familiarity and their lesser incentive to make the business successful.

The decision was made to price the turnstiles at 50% above total direct costs. Jim reasoned that his £2,000 per month of ongoing overheads had to be covered by the existing repair and maintenance business, so there was no point in counting them twice. The only specific turnstile overhead was £200 per month of interest and depreciation on the new machinery.

A new mailing to the same list of clubs plus a press feature in *Sports Management* magazine led to two orders. One, from the Greenacre Cricket Club, was for four turnstiles and the other was for 12 turnstiles from Ayr racecourse. Fortunately the delivery dates were staggered, with Greenacre wanting the turnstiles installed within three months and Ayr within six months.

Turnstile production costs per unit

	Production run			
	1	2–4	5–9	10+
Bought-in components	£485	£455	£360	£320
Raw materials	£145	£125	£90	£80
Labour	£330	£330	£450	£480
Other direct costs	£100	£90	£80	£70

Even though the four turnstiles were Jim's first ever production run, the Greenacre job went remarkably smoothly. The only hiccup was over cash flow, as his suppliers demanded early payment whereas the Cricket Club proved to be very slow at paying. Although Barclays helped by providing a £5,000 overdraft, the charges and interest costs involved took £500 off the profit on the job.

For the Ayr contract, Jim knew he would have to hire a welder and a fitter. This proved very time consuming, as 40 people responded to the small advertisement he placed in the local paper. Even after two days of interviews he did not feel confident that he had picked the right people. The job had to be started, though, so it seemed silly to waste any more time. Two men were hired on the understanding that the job would cease when the contract was completed.

On the day they started, both workers were keen to learn about the job. By the end of their first week, however, Jim kept noticing how different they were. The fitter worked enthusiastically, helping in all sorts of ways as well as getting on with his work. Some of his suggestions for increasing efficiency were very astute. The welder, however, took frequent breaks and was never willing to do anything other than weld. The quality of the work was fine, but his attitude was infuriating.

As the weeks went by, Jim became ever more aware that the job was slipping behind schedule. Then vandalism at Cardiff F.C. forced Jim to spend a week in Wales. On his return, the fitter was spitting with rage at the welder's laziness and off-hand manner. Jim was torn between the desire to sack the welder and the knowledge of the time it would take to replace him. He stumbled on without making a decision, living with conflict in his workplace until the Ayr job was finally completed, five weeks late.

The Ayr officials were so upset by the delay that they refused to pay in full; they deducted 5% from the bill as compensation. Jim squawked, but was too desperate to get paid to argue. The delay had pushed up his costs and sent him up to the overdraft ceiling. For a fortnight he was unsure of survival, but eventually the payment came that solved the cash shortage.

After that experience, Jim was far more careful with his recruitment procedure, always employing the same fitter whenever possible. In the second year, work flowed in more consistently, giving rise to the possibility of making a permanent appointment. Tilley Turnstile Services was on its way.

Appendix A: Extracts from the business plan

Sales turnover to date		Forecast monthly turnover (excluding turnstile manufacture)
July	£1,400	October–June (average) £4,500
August	£15,000	
September	£3,100	

Questions
(50 marks; 70 minutes)

1 Outline Jim's main strengths and weaknesses as a manager of a small firm. **(10 marks)**

2 Calculate the salary/profit Jim could expect to receive in his first year of trading. State clearly any assumptions you have made. **(11 marks)**

3 **a** What might explain the differing attitudes to work of the fitter and the welder? **(6 marks)**
   b How might Jim have handled the situation better? **(8 marks)**

4 Organisations such as the Prince's Trust exist to help small firms start up and develop. Use this case as the starting point to consider the main problems faced by new small firms. **(15 marks)**

82

THE SURVIVAL GAME

A2
INTEGRATED
CASE

CONCEPTS NEEDED:

Location, Marketing mix, Profit

The Survival Game was first played in June 1981 in the woods of New Hampshire, USA. Two teams – each armed with paint pellet guns – attempt to infiltrate each other's base camp, capture their flag and return it to their own base. It proved to be a huge success and by 1988 it had become at $150 million industry.

Survival Game UK Limited was formed in 1984 to establish this new sport in Britain. Its owners identified two markets: weekend leisure for sporty types and a weekday business market training course in teamwork.

In 1985 the company achieved 2,500 customers. Word of mouth plus television coverage pushed demand up rapidly to 60,000 players by 1988. This sales explosion was accommodated by Survival Game UK setting up three of its own sites plus 21 franchised outlets. Each site covers over 20 acres of partly wooded terrain, and is usually rented from a large landowner or local authority.

Allan Burrows is an enthusiastic Survival Game player, whose £15,000 redundancy payout has tempted him to become the 22nd franchisee. He has been having to make a 100 mile round trip to travel to the Norwich site, and so sees potential in developing one in Ipswich. A phone call to the firm's London offices reveals the following information:

1 Franchise fee – £10,000 for an eight year contract to manage the sole Survival Game UK site in Suffolk. Included would be all the equipment needed to start, including 50 'Splatmaster' pistols and 12,000 Splatballs (filled with washable orange paint).

2 Training and promotion – full training is given to all franchisees, not only in the running of the game but also in accounting and publicity techniques.

3 Back-up services – including supplies, national marketing and public relations.

4 Financial projection (assuming 40 players for 75 days in the year, i.e. 3,000 customers) – as follows:

Sales revenue	
Game fee	£48,000
Paint pellets	£30,000
Other revenue	£10,000
Total sales	£88,000
Cost of sales	
Paint pellets	£20,000
Other costs	£5,000
Total direct costs	£25,000
Overheads	
Site rent	£3,750
Wages	£6,500
Other overheads	£19,750
Total overheads	£30,000
Pre-tax profit	£33,000

Allan was impressed, and decided to contact a local landowner to see if a suitable site could be rented per day. There proved to be a 30 acre wooded site available at a daily rate of £80. He also wanted to consider catering facilities before committing himself. Allan knew that he and his friends found food the only disappointment about their trips to Norwich. After a morning's action one wanted a substantial and enjoyable meal. So Allan negotiated with a local caterer to provide a hearty, barbecued meal for £8 per head. He felt he should charge his customers no more than £5 for this, so he had to build this loss into his profit projections. Apart from the fact that high local labour costs would add 50% to the wage bill, Allan was happy about the rest of Survival Game UK's forecasts.

A fellow game-player sounded a note of caution, however. He said that Survival Game magazine had been carrying advertisements offering a complete set of 'Splatmaster' guns and equipment for just £1,200. As he said: 'Anyone could start up in this business now.' Furthermore, he knew the editor of the magazine, and had learned that its circulation had levelled off after its sharp rise in recent years. Allan phoned Survival Game UK about these points and was reassured to hear that they attributed the magazine's sales hiccup to its editorial weaknesses, not to flat demand for the game itself. In fact Survival Game UK's managing director said that:

'*In the first six months of this year there have been 10% more game players than in the same period last year. So business is booming.*'

Questions
(50 marks; 60 minutes)

1 Allan appears to be willing to accept the first site he finds. Discuss the factors he should consider when deciding on the location of his Survival site. **(10 marks)**

2 Evaluate how Allan's marketing to the weekend leisure market might differ from that towards the business market. **(12 marks)**

3 **a** Calculate the annual pre-tax profit Allan could expect if he went ahead with the Survival Game UK operation. **(8 marks)**
   b How could he try to increase this level of profitability? **(5 marks)**

4 Discuss the factors Allan should consider in deciding whether to buy the Survival Game UK franchise, or set up an independent Survival outlet. **(15 marks)**

33 A SUMMER FANTASY

A2
INTEGRATED
CASE

CONCEPTS NEEDED:

Investment appraisal, Problems of start-ups, Research, Company aims

It all started when she was eight. A family trip to Siena introduced Dionne to the wonders of an Italian ice cream parlour. She had never forgotten the sheer delight at the amazing array of colours, flavours and combinations. It had always nagged at her, and now it seemed time. Her eight years in advertising had been great, but she knew she was losing her enthusiasm. She had £38,000 in cash and shares, a flat worth nearly £200,000 and only £40,000 of mortgage commitments. So it seemed quite possible to generate £150,000 as an initial investment on a serious, 'destination' ice cream parlour. The sort that would have people travelling from all over London to see what the fuss was about.

Her intention was to site 'Ice Cream Fantasia' not far from the River Thames in trendy Battersea. She had her eye on a site fronting on to a major traffic crossroads, but backing on to Battersea Park. She envisaged a large conservatory and patio facing the park and a huge glass shop front facing the crossroads to attract custom.

Inside would be three zones: Italy, America and Britain. The Italian zone would be run by an ice cream maestro she knew from a year spent in Rome. He could make 40 different flavours of Italian style ice creams and water ices. The American zone would sell the full range of Ben & Jerry's varieties, while the British section would sell homemade dairy ices, produced on site, behind glass, but in full view of the customers. There would be a total of over 100 flavours available at any one time, by scoop or ice-packed in special pint containers. In addition she planned to devise a huge array of sundaes, milkshakes and even cocktails, plus coffees and capuccinos.

Dionne took her holiday at a huge trade exhibition called Euro Ice-world 2001 in Hanover, Germany. There she was able to discuss her equipment requirements and start to get an idea about costs. The prices came as a serious shock. Equipping 'Fantasia' would cost over £200,000. Dionne already knew that an eight year lease would cost £120,000 and she expected to spend £200,000 on the building plus fixtures and fittings. So the total investment would exceed half a million pounds.

Clearly, proceeding further would require outside investors. And they would need unbiased market research findings to give them confidence. Fortunately, Dionne's work contacts enabled her to get Gallup Poll to produce a low cost survey in which 500 Londoners were shown a card describing the proposition and the site. 40% said they would 'definitely visit', including 60% of those who lived within four miles of Battersea. (More detailed results are shown below.) As more than one million people live within a four mile radius, this was promising. An interesting idea emerging from the research was enthusiasm for Fantasia as a children's party destination. So Dionne decided to plan for a special room that could be for kids in the daytime, and hired out for drinks parties in the evening.

Several weeks of careful calculations about running costs left Dionne in a position to start trying to sell her idea to potential venture capital investors. Based upon her calculations, she forecast that a total investment of £600,000 would pay back in two years and make an average rate of return of 40% per year for the eight years of the lease. No wonder she approached the first potential investor with a great deal of confidence.

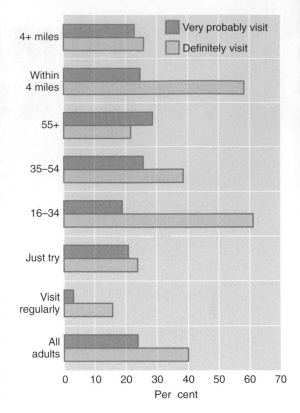

Fantasia research results

Research findings: Gallup poll, May 2001

	All adults	Visit regularly	Just try	16–34	35–54	55+	Within 4 miles	4+ miles
Definitely visit	40%	16%	24%	62%	39%	22%	59%	26%
Very probably visit	24%	3%	21%	19%	26%	29%	25%	23%
May visit	11%	1%	10%	10%	11%	12%	11%	11%
Probably won't visit	14%	0%	14%	2%	14%	20%	1%	23%
Definitely won't visit	11%	0%	11%	7%	10%	17%	4%	17%

The investor spent a long time grilling Dionne over her cash flow forecast (see Appendix A) but eventually was satisfied. The only additional data he required was a sensitivity analysis. This yielded the following:

	Sales 20% higher than expected	Sales as forecast	Sales 20% lower than expected
Pay-back	1.25 years	*see Q4*	4.25 years
ARR	62.5%	*below*	17.5%

Having considered the evidence he decided to offer to invest £400,000 for a 49.5% share stake, as long as a High Street bank was prepared to provide a £100,000 overdraft to help finance working capital. Happily for Dionne, the Coop Bank proved very helpful and she was able to get started on the huge task of transforming a paper plan into a business success.

Appendix A: Net cash flows forecast for Fantasia ice cream parlour

	Cash in	Cash out	Net cash
NOW	–	£600,000	−£600,000
Year 1	£1,800,000	£1,600,000	+£200,000
Year 2	£2,200,000	£1,800,000	+£400,000
Years 3–8	£2,000,000 p.a.	£1,700,000 p.a.	+£300,000 p.a.

Questions
(60 marks; 70 minutes)

1 Assess which aim you consider to have been the most important to Dionne during her business start-up. **(10 marks)**

2 Outline the types of primary research Dionne might have conducted during the early stages of her business start-up. **(8 marks)**

3 Consider how effectively Dionne addressed the practical problems of business start-ups. **(14 marks)**

4 Calculate Dionne's pay-back and average rate of return, based upon Appendix A. **(12 marks)**

5 **a** Explain the meaning of the term 'venture capital'. **(4 marks)**
   b During her first year of operation, assess which financial factors may prove difficult for Dionne. **(12 marks)**

84 FACTORY SAFETY

CONCEPTS NEEDED:

Communication, Break even, Piece rate

'**N**ot another accident! That's the eighth this week, and the day shift hasn't had a single one.' As Production Manager of PowerMo Lawnmowers, Mike was responsible not only for safety but also for output, and he knew each production line accident lost him an average of 60 units. He was a great believer in delegation, so he left the Night Shift Manager to get on with things. Though, as Mike admitted to himself, he had not seen much of him lately, so they ought to meet to discuss the situation. The night shift would not be in until five o'clock, so Mike spent the morning digging out figures on the accident rate by shift over the past year. He passed them to his management trainee for comment, who turned them into the bar chart shown.

Meanwhile, Mike consulted his six day-shift foremen about the monthly variations in safety. One explained:

'**W**ell, *you're always going to get peaks before holiday times when you're on piece work, aren't you? The lads are aiming to earn a good 20% more in July and December than they do regularly. And, if you work 20% faster on those grinding machines, it's not surprising that you get sloppy.*'

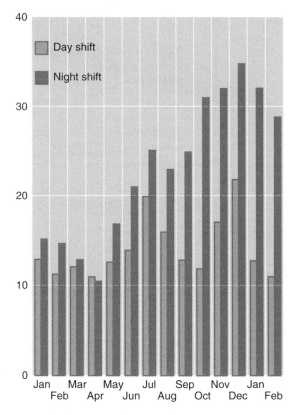

Accidents per 1000 workers per week

All agreed that there seemed no reason for the long term accident rate to be rising, and that all seemed well for the coming spring sales peak.

A quick check on the night shift's productivity figures revealed no improvement since last May, so there was evidently some other cause. Instead of talking to his Night Shift Manager that afternoon, Mike decided to call in unannounced that evening. It occurred to him that he had not actually been there at night since just after the Manager's appointment last May.

The afternoon's monthly management meeting proved sticky. The Sales Manager presented a report on customer feedback, which showed dissatisfaction with product quality and with delivery reliability over the past six months. Mike defended his department stoutly, blaming the 'second rate materials and components bought in by Purchasing' (whose manager was away that day). Yet he found it harder to fend off the implied criticism from the Financial Controller:

'I *cannot understand how we have let the reject rate rise 50% in the last year. If it's due to faulty components, why are they not checked before wasting labour time on them? This has put our variable costs up to £1.40 per unit instead of the budgeted £1.32, which has cut our contribution per unit by 8 pence to 32 pence. So now our break-even point has risen to 100,000 units.*'

Mike's evening visit proved illuminating. During the day, the factory was a hive of purposeful activity. Now, he observed men shouting out conversation, even jokes, above the din. They were working on dangerous machinery, and supposed to be producing products to exact specifications, yet concentration levels seemed low. Mike looked in vain for the Night Shift Manager or his foreman, until he found them in the office. He kept calm enough to find out that neither man knew of any problems. Both assumed that the safety, productivity and wastage figures were quite satisfactory; they had heard nothing to the contrary.

The next day, the trainee completed the misery of Mike's week. He had heard that the shop stewards for the night shift had asked for an urgent meeting with Mike's boss.

Questions
(50 marks; 70 minutes)

1 **a** What indications are there that PowerMo's internal communications are poor? **(5 marks)**

    b Outline the main problems this could cause the firm. **(8 marks)**

2 Draw a fully labelled break-even chart to show the planned and the actual financial position of the firm. Note that the firm's maximum capacity is 150,000 units. **(10 marks)**

3 Discuss the likely advantages and disadvantages to PowerMo of using a piece rate payment system. **(12 marks)**

4 Use the evidence provided as a basis for discussing the general importance to business of monitoring factory safety. **(15 marks)**

THE BODY SHOP INTERNATIONAL

A2
INTEGRATED
CASE

CONCEPTS NEEDED:

Ratios, Social responsibilities, Mission statement, Flotation

When Anita Roddick launched her first The Body Shop in a small street in Brighton in 1976, she devised a publicity stunt. A phone call to the local paper led to headlines alleging an attempt by a neighbouring funeral parlour to block the shop and its name. That flair for publicity was to remain a theme throughout the following dazzling years of growth.

Anita and her husband Gordon had hit on a commercial rarity – a trendy concept with staying power. In 1976 'green' still meant a

colour, not an environmental label, but there were already notable movements against animal experimentation and towards healthy, natural products. The Roddicks' success was to encapsulate this into a genuine niche in the retail market: a shop providing a range of natural cosmetics and toiletries that had not been tested on animals and that came in refillable, recyclable containers. Bright window displays and prominent locations ensured high sales without advertising. As the biggest costs in producing most cosmetics were the packaging and the advertising, The Body Shop was able to enjoy very high profit margins.

With the Brighton shop proving an instant success, the Roddicks decided to expand by selling franchises. This meant that the capital for expansion came from the franchisees, rather than The Body Shop. Consequently the business could expand rapidly, allowing the brand name to be established nationally before competitors arrived. It also ensured that the shops were run by enthusiasts with a clear incentive to achieve sales success.

By 1981, 22 outlets had been established in Britain and 17 overseas. Company profits of only £31,000 reflected the fact that Anita and Gordon were still teaching themselves how to handle a successful business. Finding suppliers to make their ever widening range of products, screening franchise applicants and organising distribution had all to be **delegated to new, salaried managers**. It also took the Roddicks some time to realise just how high they could push the prices of their unique, highly fashionable products.

In 1984 The Body Shop floated on the stock market, backed by the £1 million profit made that year. Twelve months later, the Roddicks' shareholdings were worth over £50 million. The flotation provided capital for further expansion and gave the business a stronger public profile. Gordon explained that:

> '**W**e were attracted by the advantages of a high profile, especially because of our High Street image. It also improved our credibility. We became contenders for prime retailing positions with people who would have shown us the door a year before.'

The company's continued growth moved increasingly towards overseas markets. By 1986 The Body Shop was Britain's biggest retail exporter by far. Its **unique niche** made it better able to succeed overseas than companies such as Marks & Spencer. Yet the Roddicks also showed great sense in waiting until their formula had worked in countries such as France and Canada before tackling the huge US market in 1988. Retailers as varied as Sock Shop and Sainsbury's had struggled in America; The Body Shop entered the US market with caution.

The late 1980s proved phenomenally successful for the business. Anita Roddick became famous internationally as a critic of conventional business and as a tireless campaigner for environmental and Third World causes. As concern mounted about the impact upon the ozone layer of the destruction of the Brazilian rainforests, Anita acted. Under the slogan 'Trade not aid' she set about creating a range of rainforest based cosmetics, such as a cleansing cream containing Brazil nut oil. Creating a demand for raw materials from the forests would, she hoped, give the Brazilian government and landowners an incentive to keep the forests intact.

Within Britain, Anita's social zeal found outlet in the establishment of a soap factory in Easterhouse, Glasgow. Its origins were in a visit made by the Roddicks in 1988. A community leader pointed out that while The Body Shop was helping less developed countries, it was ignoring 'Britain's own Third World': the inner cities. As the company needed extra supplies of soap, it decided to set up a factory in Glasgow rather than in the affluent area surrounding the firm's Sussex headquarters. It opened in April 1989 with 29 employees. The Body Shop received widespread publicity for going, in Mrs Roddick's words, 'where angels fear to tread'. A sceptical reporter from the *Financial Times* found locals who were irritated by 'her patronising attitude'; but no one could doubt that the company had a magical way of combining social and environmental initiatives with self-publicity and therefore profitability.

Anita Roddick had become a household name for her selfless campaigning, and at the same time the value of the family shareholding had risen to £200 million by 1989. The media's enthusiasm for The Body Shop meant overlooking the contradiction between the firm's ethical stance and its extraordinarily high profitability. In 1989 its return on capital was 60% – more than three times the level of profitability of its rivals. The reason was simple: it had pushed prices up to take advantage of its niche market positioning.

The early 1990s recession caused the first cracks to appear. In America, a me-too retailer called Bath and Body Works was providing stiff competition. In Britain, falling demand for premium priced products plus competition from Boots left sales flagging. After years of spectacular growth, profits slipped in 1992/93 and continued to waver during the rest of the 1990s. Anita Roddick was still as active as ever, promoting her new social and environmental audits, but the public seemed less interested. Store and product revamps had less and less effect. The Body Shop was starting to be seen as just another High Street multiple.

In 1998, with profits under severe pressure, the Roddicks took the advice of many in the City, and brought in a new Chief Executive. Patrick Gournay, from Danone Foods, would manage the business in as profit conscious a manner as every other retailer. Three hundred Head Office staff lost their jobs, two The Body

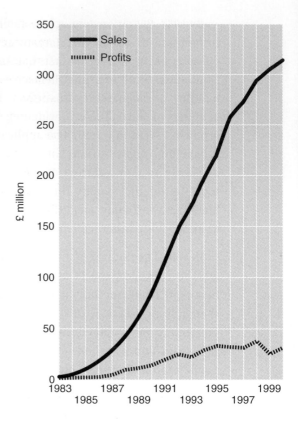

The Body Shop financial history 1983–2000

Shop factories at Littlehampton were put up for sale, and there was soon a question mark over the future of the Easterhouse Soapworks. The Roddicks, with a highly influential 25% of the shares, stood back and let idealism be

Appendix A: The Body Shop growth 1983–2000

	1983	1985	1990	1995	2000
Sales turnover (£m)	2,100	9,400	84,500	220,000	313,000
Pre-tax profit (£000)	202	1,929	14,508	33,500	31,500
No. of outlets	101	168	455	1210	1730

Source: The Body Shop plc annual reports

swept aside. With the annual accounts starting to talk more about cost cutting and 'efficient supply chain development' than about **ethical trading**, it was becoming hard to take seriously the stated The Body Shop mission:

'**T**o tirelessly work to narrow the gap between principle and practice, whilst making fun, passion and care part of our daily lives.'

Sources: The Body Shop prospectus and annual reports; *Financial Times; The Guardian; Investor's Chronicle*

Questions
(80 marks; 90 minutes)

1 Outline the business significance of the following phrases (in bold print in the text):
   a delegated to new, salaried managers   **(5 marks)**
   b unique niche   **(5 marks)**
   c ethical trading   **(5 marks)**

2 To what extent was Anita Roddick's flair for publicity the key to the success of the business?   **(12 marks)**

3 Use the evidence within the case to consider whether the Roddicks' ethical stance was based upon morality or the desire for favourable public relations.   **(12 marks)**

4 **a** Use Appendix A to calculate the profit margin made by The Body Shop for each of the years stated.   **(9 marks)**
   b Examine two possible explanations for the results you have produced.   **(10 marks)**

5 The Body Shop mission statement was written by Anita Roddick in the 1980s. Discuss the impact it may have on Patrick Gournay's work as the new, profit focused Chief Executive.   **(10 marks)**

6 At various times, Anita Roddick has questioned whether she and her husband were right to float The Body Shop on the stock market. Evaluate the case for and against flotation for a business such as this.   **(12 marks)**

86 CHESSING-TON WORLD OF ADVENTURES

A2 INTEGRATED CASE

CONCEPTS NEEDED:

Internal and external constraints, Business strategy, Budgeting, Macro economy

Running a business is never easy. Imagine, though, trying to run a business that closes down every autumn and restarts every spring; where daily customer numbers vary between 800 and 18,000; and where customers want to do the same things at the same time, but resent queuing. At 12.30 the catering outlets can be heaving while the souvenir shops are dead. Towards the end of the day the souvenir shops can be packed. And every day a burst of sunshine can push ice cream sales up 500%, while a rain shower sends people scurrying to buy rainproof 'ponchos'. Welcome to Chessington World of Adventures, one of Britain's top five theme parks.

It was once the rather sleepy Chessington Zoo, but developed dramatically during the 1980s and 1990s, adding a series of thrill rides such as 'The Vampire Ride' and 'Nemesis'. Now it is part of the group that owns Madame Tussauds, Alton Towers and many other leisure attractions. Despite the expertise implied by this, the unique business features of a theme park make Chessington an exceptionally difficult test of good management. This case focuses on the retail side of the business, especially the 'merchandise' – clothing and souvenir shops.

For salaried, full-time managers the year starts soon after the annual closure at the end of October. Immediately meetings are held to discuss the main conclusions from the year just ended, to build improvements into the plans for next spring. The site itself may be in for major changes, such as a new ride. In spring 2000 the new feature was a children's area – Beanoland. This entailed new shops and new catering facilities – with many of the products featuring *Beano* comic characters. Even if no changes are planned for the attractions, new ranges of merchandise and new types of food may be required to keep abreast of changing tastes or fashions.

Well before the start of the season the team leaders responsible for the 10 retail outlets walk through each unit with the product manager responsible for buying strategy. This enables the strategist to learn what worked well in the previous season and to discuss new ideas for the year ahead. Late autumn is the time for discussions with suppliers about product lines and prices, so that samples can be designed and bulk stock produced before the park reopens in March.

The retail team leaders have many other things to prepare at this time of the year. Alan Bowyer, retail team leader with responsibility for five outlets, has concluded: 'Training – you can't really get enough of it.' Chessington has a full two-day induction programme for all new staff, but Alan wishes he could do more during the season. This is partly for practical commercial reasons, including the value to the business of 'upselling', such as 'Do you need batteries with that?' It is also because many of the staff are so young (typically 16 or 17) that well planned training can generate huge benefits, whether in customer service or in the willingness of staff to return next year.

For Alan there are several key performance indicators to enable him to assess how successful his personnel policies have been. The key short term one is the drop-out rate between recruitment time (February and March) and the end of Easter – the first period of serious business. In spring 2000 the drop-out rate was 20–25 per cent. This sounds bad, but it has been as high as 40 per cent in the past. Chessington recruits young people because of the image it presents to customers, but the downside is that many prove unreliable in this, their first job, and some cannot cope with part-time work as well as school/college commitments.

The second performance indicator is the rate of returning in the following season. About half the staff are invited back the following year. Not all agree, so about one third of the season's staff have experience from the previous year. Many will be made

supervisors and have a key role in training and managing the newcomers, even though many supervisors will themselves be no more than 17 or 18 years old. In 2000 the rate of returning was unusually low, so the season had begun with a particularly inexperienced crew. Alan, after six years at Chessington, knows that 'people who work here see it as a laugh – a summer laugh'. Yet visitors expect professional service, so the key is to persuade the young staff to 'buy in' to the concept of the park as a business. Daily briefing sessions are held to keep staff informed and discuss problems, but also to provide an opportunity to discuss social arrangements. Usually the season starts with staff paying little attention to business issues such as budgets and whether targets are being beaten or missed, but as the months pass some begin to take more interest in the business. Reflecting back on the 2000 season, Alan is determined to spend the next few months preparing training packages for next year's staff. He feels 'a real sense of pride in looking at how they developed this year', but is keen to do even better next time.

The 2000 season proved very difficult. Actual attendance levels of 1.4 million were sharply down on the 1.65 million budget. The budget had been set cautiously because of the expected competition from the Millennium Dome. This did have an impact, because despite its problems the Dome's 6 million visitors made it Europe's second biggest paying visitor attraction during 2000. No less important, though, were the Euro 2000 football tournament in June/July and the dreadful weather that set in during the late summer and autumn. The weather not only affected demand, it also affected the ability to supply. Chessington's huge overspill car park has a grass surface and was frequently unusable during the season. So even on days when the sun peeped through, the park had to turn away visitors.

Impressively, the park's management made sure that the retail budgets were adjusted to allow for these factors beyond anyone's control. Instead of focusing upon the sales revenue budget, the key target became revenue per head. Budgeted at £1.23 per visitor, the actual achievement for merchandise (non-food) sales was £1.25. As the figure had been £1.12 in 1999, this represented impressive growth. Within those figures, dramatic changes occurred. At the start of the season 35,000 rainproof ponchos were ordered, each branded with the Chessington logo. These were sold out by early September (before the *really* bad weather started!), losing potential sales of perhaps 10,000 at £3.50, i.e. £35,000. Needless to say, sales of ice cream were down sharply.

Although the retail managers were caught out by the poncho experience, it encouraged them to continue with what was already a significant new strategy. Financial Coordinator Justin Stevington explains: 'Previously the buying focus was buying cheaply. Buyers went out to China and bought in bulk for the whole season. Now we negotiate to get smaller quantities more frequently ... There's also a move towards better quality items branded with our logo.' The lost profit opportunity stemming from bulk buying the ponchos reinforced the need to negotiate flexible delivery deals with suppliers.

And what next for Chessington? The most important strategic change is the decision to reposition the park from its recent marketing focus upon the teenage and young adult market (as embodied in the 'Vampire Ride'). In the future Chessington will target families. Thorpe Park (a theme park sited just 10 miles away and owned by the same group) will concentrate on the teenage sector. This change will require a steady shift in the product, bringing in new rides such as Beanoland.

Source: Visits and interviews

Questions
(80 marks; 90 minutes)

1 Examine the business significance of:

   a Buying in bulk   **(5 marks)**

   b Factors beyond anyone's control   **(5 marks)**

2 **a** Outline the key internal and external factors that led to Chessington's revenue proving to be below budget in 2000.   **(12 marks)**

   b To what extent was the shortfall the fault of management?   **(10 marks)**

3 Alan Bowyer is officially responsible for the success of five retail outlets, but also feels a sense of responsibility for the development of his staff. To what extent may there be a conflict between these two aims?   **(15 marks)**

4 **a** Outline two significant economic trends in Britain during the past six months.   **(6 marks)**

   b Examine the likely effect of each of these trends upon trading at Chessington World of Adventures. Discuss which of the two is likely to have the greater effect.   **(15 marks)**

5 As the nearby Thorpe Park has the same owner as Chessington, there appears to be little direct competition. The only competition comes from indirect sources such as days at the seaside or – in 2000 – a day at the Dome. Discuss the implications for business strategy at Chessington of there being no direct competitors.   **(12 marks)**

FAT SAM'S FRANCHISE

A2 INTEGRATED CASE

CONCEPTS NEEDED:

Break even, Contribution, Profit, Marketing Model

Fat Sam's Pasta Joint was a highly successful restaurant in Soho, London. It offered

'All the pasta you can eat for £2.95**'**

This good value was combined with lively, bright design and atmosphere to make Fat Sam's a hugely popular place for young people. Fat Sam's owners realised that the same concept could work in many other locations, but they did not have sufficient capital to develop a large chain of restaurants themselves. So they appointed a Franchise Manager, who was set the objective of developing Fat Sam's into a hundred-strong chain.

The new manager decided on the following terms for anyone who wished to become a franchisee:

1 A £5,000 fee to be paid on signing a five-year Franchise Agreement;

2 Fat Sam's to be paid 8% of the franchisee's sales turnover (including 3% to be used for advertising).

In return, Fat Sam's would provide assistance on siting, interior design and shop fittings, menu and provision supplies, and financial management advice. A franchisee would hardly need a chef, as all sauces could be supplied directly by Fat Sam's.

Although the company advertised their franchises in the magazine *Franchise World*, the first person to apply was a waitress working in the Soho branch. Gill had no business experience, but she was sure she understood how to create the fun atmosphere needed for success, and was willing to take out a £100,000 second mortgage on her house to fulfil a lifetime dream of being her own boss.

She already knew that Fat Sam's took an average of £7 revenue per customer, with variable costs per head of £1.80 for food and 50 pence for drink. Even a novice entrepreneur could appreciate that a mark-up of over 200% presented a promising prospect.

Within a week, the Franchise Agreement had been approved by Gill's solicitor and was signed. She was sure that a good site existed in the centre of the town nearest her house (Colchester) and as it had no competing pasta restaurant, Fat Sam's agreed with her choice. Fat Sam's calculated that the site would take five months to be fully decorated, fitted and therefore become operational. The start-up costs were estimated at £100,000 (including the franchise fee).

Within a few weeks, Gill was becoming increasingly worried by the dithering of the Franchise Manager who was supposed to be helping her. Progress was slow, and many of the interior fittings were being supplied at what Gill thought were outrageous prices. Yet as the suppliers were the only ones who could supply her with fittings in the correct Fat Sam's colours and designs, she was stuck. After seven months, her money had run out, and the opening was still not in sight. She borrowed £25,000 more from her family, and two months later the outlet was finished.

Having spent out all £125,000 she was desperate to start trading, in order to bring in some cash. It came like a thunderbolt to hear from the Franchise Manager that he had still not managed to obtain the licence needed to serve alcoholic drinks, but she could not wait. Fat Sam's Pasta Joint opened in Colchester without any advertising, and with signs up apologising for the fact that only the soft drinks on the menu could be served. In such circumstances, it was quite pleasing that 800 customers were served in the first week – only 200 down on her forecast. Of course, the extra start-up expenditure meant higher interest charges on her borrowings, so her fixed costs were higher than originally planned, at £2,898 per week.

Sadly, the poor start meant that Gill's restaurant was rarely full, which undermined the bustling atmosphere she knew she needed. So not even the arrival of the drinks licence (one month after starting) stopped a relentless decline in the Colchester outlet's revenue. A friend worked out the following chart to show her how her customer base was moving towards the break-even level.

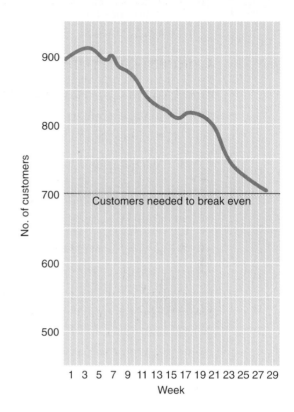

Sales graph for Colchester outlet – four period weekly moving average

Forty weeks after she started trading, Gill's bank manager persuaded her to give up. Her bitterness towards Fat Sam's and its Franchise Manager turned into rage as she was forced to sell her house. The price it fetched was enough to repay all her debts, but she was left homeless and virtually penniless.

Source: discussion with the real Gill

Questions
(50 marks; 70 minutes)

1 What does the text demonstrate about the weakness of taking out a franchise when starting your own business? **(10 marks)**

2 Before the delays occurred, Gill had budgeted for weekly fixed costs of £2,500 and an average of 1,000 customers per week. Assuming a 50 week year:
  a What profit would she have made in the first year? **(6 marks)**
  b How long would it have taken her to repay her £100,000 loan? **(6 marks)**

3 Much Business Studies theory revolves around the idea of scientific decision making. What does this mean, and how might the adoption of a framework such as the Marketing Model have helped Gill avoid the difficulties she encountered? **(12 marks)**

4 **a** How does the sales graph on page 253 differ from a break-even chart? **(10 marks)**
  b Prove that the break-even number of customers is 700. **(6 marks)**

MARLBORO AND MARKET POWER

A2
INTEGRATED
CASE

CONCEPTS NEEDED:

Company objectives, Marketing strategy, Price elasticity, Profit, Social responsibilities

Within seconds of the announcement, its shares had plunged in value by $13.5 billion, and those of its rivals by even more. The whole US stock market suffered its biggest one day fall for over a year. Within days newspapers were questioning the billion dollar value placed upon brands throughout the world. The cause was the decision by Philip Morris, the world's most profitable cigarette company, to slash the price of the world's most valuable brand – Marlboro cigarettes. The American media soon dubbed 2 April 1993 as 'Marlboro Friday'.

The price cut of a full 20% applied only to the American market, but since Marlboro accounted for over 100 billion of the 500 billion cigarettes sold per year in the USA, the profit implications were huge. Philip Morris acted to try to reverse the erosion of Marlboro's US market share, from 25.8% in

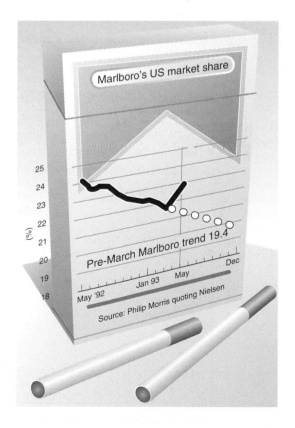

Marlboro's US market share

Pre-March Marlboro trend 19.4

Source: Philip Morris quoting Nielsen

1991 to 24.5% in 1992. Recession-hit consumers were switching to cheaper branded cigarettes and to own label varieties with no brand image. Discount cigarettes had grown from a 7% market share in 1985 to 19% by 1990 and up to 36% in 1992. Philip Morris, the industry's price leader with its best selling Marlboro brand, felt it had to respond. As a Wall Street analyst put it:

> **'T**his is not a new price war. It's the latest blast in a price war which has already been going on. Philip Morris has come down with both feet on the market. It's going to destroy the discount brands.**'**

> (Roy Burry, Kidder Peabody,
> *Financial Times*, 5 April 1993)

William Campbell, the Tobacco President of Philip Morris, laid himself open to potentially fierce criticism for a decision that was expected to cut 1993 and 1994 profits by over $2 billion dollars per annum. The image building of the brand had been so successful that by the 1980s Marlboro outsold its nearest rival more than four times. With annual marketing spending of over $100 million in the USA Marlboro had been able to impose a series of price increases that rival brands had to follow. Otherwise their image might have become devalued.

Leading brands in 1991 (by volume)	
Marlboro	25.8%
Winston	7.5%
Salem	5.4%
Newport	4.7%

Source: Tobacco Reporter/Euromonitor

Between 1980 and 1991, the price of 20 Marlboro trebled while prices generally (and government taxes) only doubled. This created an opportunity for the companies whose minor brands had been squeezed by the Marlboro marketing machine. For although Philip Morris had pushed the price of the main brands up to $2.20 by early 1993, the economics of cigarette production pointed to lower rather than higher prices. Raw tobacco prices were falling in real terms, and modern machinery could produce 15,000 cigarettes per minute – more than twice the speed and productivity of a decade before. It was now possible to manufacture and distribute a pack of 20 cigarettes for 30 cents. Even with 40 cents of tax and a retail mark-up of 20%, a profit could be made by selling at one half of Marlboro's price.

As Philip Morris pushed prices up, small producers were able to offer supermarket chains an own label product that could sell below the **psychological price barrier** of $1 per pack. As discount sales shot ahead during the 1980s, the large manufacturers moved into the cut price market. The second largest manufacturer, RJ Reynolds, made a key move in 1987 when it set up the Forsyth Tobacco Company to make a $1 house brand of cigarettes for the huge K-Mart store chain. The cigarettes were made at the same factories that produced the $2.20 Winston and Salem brands. RJ Reynolds hoped that the use of the invented company name 'Forsyth' would minimise the **cannibalisation** of their own brands. Its success, however, merely forced Philip Morris to pursue the same discount market.

By early 1993, the cigarette market had split into three price segments. The established brands at $2.20, second ranking brands at $1.50, and discount or own label products at $0.99. When it cut the price of Marlboro, Philip Morris also tried to merge the two bottom segments into one. Philip Morris pushed the prices of its mid range brands down to around $1.30, and raised its cheapest products towards that same figure. The tobacco giant wanted to change the market's structure as indicated below.

Within a month RJ Reynolds announced that it was following Marlboro's lead. It cut the price of its Winston brand. By September it was forecasting that its 1993 US tobacco operating profits would be 43% lower than the previous year – a fall of $900 million.

Philip Morris, meanwhile, was putting a brave face on its announcement of a 53% fall in US tobacco profits for the three months to June. It declared that its price cut had been successful, reversing an eight month decline in Marlboro's market share. From a low of 21.5% in March, Marlboro's share was said to have risen to 24% in July. This would do little to restore the brand's short term profitability, but that was not the point of the strategy. William Campbell was attempting to regain the initiative in the American cigarette market, to ensure the long term success of Marlboro and Philip Morris.

Although the Marlboro move made sense strategically, it led analysts to question the **brand valuations** that many companies were placing on their balance sheets. If the world's most valuable brand could not hold its desired price premium, could it be that consumers had learned to see beyond the packaging and the image to the product inside? In which case should companies such as Guinness drop the brand valuations from their balance sheets?

Whereas the financial analysts were worried, marketing professionals showed less concern. They felt consumers were still fully prepared to pay a price premium for a reputable brand, but that Marlboro had pushed that premium too far. Their only doubt was that Philip Morris may have overreacted to a problem made worse by recession. If the market share of discount brands stabilised at 35–40% of the market, Marlboro could still have traded very profitably at $2.20. No one doubted, however, that Marlboro's action was one of the boldest decisions in marketing history.

Sources: Financial Times; The Independent; Wall Street Journal.

Price segments pre-April 1993		Segments post-April 1993
$2.20	Established brands	
$1.80		Established brands
$1.50	Second-rank brands	
$1.20		Second-rank and discount products
$1.00	Discount products	

Questions
(60 marks; 80 minutes)

1 Explain the meaning of the following terms (in bold print in the text):
psychological price barrier
cannibalisation
brand valuation **(9 marks)**

2 What appeared to be the price elasticity of Marlboro cigarettes in 1993? **(7 marks)**

3 **a** What profit could a manufacturer make per pack from a discount brand selling at 99 cents? **(7 marks)**
   b What would be its annual profit if it achieved a 1% market share? **(7 marks)**

4 To what extent was Marlboro Friday the result of a change in Philip Morris's corporate objectives? **(15 marks)**

5 American doctors worried that the Marlboro price cut might lead to an increase in the demand for cigarettes and therefore in the health problems caused by smoking. Should the managers of Philip Morris concern themselves about this, or is this purely a matter for the government's health department? **(15 marks)**

LET'S HAVE A PARTY

A2
INTEGRATED
CASE

CONCEPTS NEEDED:

Communications, Autonomous work groups, Extrapolation, Marketing strategy, Stock turnover, Debtor days, Location, Critical path analysis

Despite all the dot.com disasters, Letshaveaparty.com was booming. The business idea had been simple enough – a website providing a one-stop shop for the drinks, food and many other items needed for a party. The customer would pick from the online shopping list, pay by credit card and get a home delivery, including all the heavy and bulky items involved. Extras such as low cost hire of glasses, tables, disco lights and even an MC were all possible online.

Debbie and Chas started the business in their home town of Belfast, soon spreading their service throughout Northern Ireland. Then came the huge leap of opening up operations within the M25, an area with eight times the population. In many ways this brave leap was a huge success. Debbie became a darling of the London media and her picture in the papers plus all the radio and TV interviews provided publicity worth millions of pounds. Helped by this, sales turnover raced ahead. Already there was newspaper talk of a stock market flotation valuing the company at £250 million.

Behind Letshaveaparty's shiny public face, however, there were very real problems.

Dramatic growth in turnover was placing huge strains on the management, the staff and the finances. An immediate issue was the latest cash flow forecast, which projected a cash shortfall of just under £900,000 in the lead up to the busy Christmas period. Chas felt confident that better working capital control could solve most of this problem. He was determined to avoid bringing in outside shareholders, even if it meant telling Debbie that her ambitious marketing plans would have to be put on hold.

The warehouse they had leased in South London was already too small for the huge level of business. They had known this was likely for some weeks, but neither Debbie nor Chas found the time to look for a new site. Perhaps rightly, Chas was more focused on solving their underlying problems by bringing in a new layer of senior management, just below Board Director level. He had always taken responsibility for staff, so was keen to make decisions quickly on structure and then personnel. He was aware of staff concerns about poor communications and a deteriorating level of participation in decision making. Most understood that Debbie and

Chas were too busy for lengthy democratic procedures, but still disliked what they took to be irrational, top-down decisions. A much quoted example was Debbie's announcement on *Sky News* that they would soon be offering to collect customers' rubbish at the end of a party, to recycle all the cans, bottles and paper. The phone lines were jammed with inquiries, but the staff knew nothing about it. Chas wanted the new senior managers to take responsibility for employee participation, perhaps through autonomous work groups.

Debbie, who was in charge of operations as well as marketing, was more concerned about the need for a new warehouse. 'With Christmas looming, we're going to be overwhelmed if we can't increase our supply levels. We need a new depot in north London, close to the M25.' Chas agreed, but wanted to carry out a full investment appraisal before proceeding with any site. He thought this should be linked to a careful forecast of future sales. He had produced a graph showing sales

to date, but couldn't pin Debbie down to agree how to extrapolate the sales forward. By his calculations, an extra warehouse would break even only if overall sales beat the £30 million mark by the end of 2002.

At their weekly Board meeting, Debbie was in buoyant mood after Letshaveaparty.com had been named the official supplier of party goods to Barclays Bank. This would provide sales of higher profit margin products such as wine and continental cheeses. It was especially satisfying for her because it was the first triumph within her new marketing strategy of targeting prosperous business users. Nevertheless, as she sat down she could see that Chas was unhappy. 'How long a credit period have you offered them?' he asked. 'They insisted on 60 days,' responded Debbie. 'Come on Chas,' she continued, 'I know you're worried about cash flow, but we have to grab opportunities such as this. Higher margin business is bound to benefit us in the long run.'

Appendix A: Growth of Letshaveaparty.com

	1999	2000	2001
Sales turnover	£1,150,000	£4,300,000	£18,200,000
Staff total at end of year	8	38	152
Labour turnover (% per year)	0%	16%	22%

Appendix B: Full accounts for Letshaveaparty.com, year to 30 September 2001

Profit and loss account year to 30/9/01		Balance sheet as at 30/9/01	
	£000		£000
Turnover	**18,200**	**Fixed assets**	**1,200**
Cost of sales	14,000	Stock	2,800
Gross profit	**4,200**	Debtors	700
Overheads	3,550	Cash	45
Depreciation	240	Creditors	3,900
Operating profit	**410**	**Net current assets**	**(355)**
Interest	40	**ASSETS EMPLOYED**	**845**
Pre-tax profit	**370**	Loans	400
		Share capital	20
		Reserves	425
		CAPITAL EMPLOYED	**845**

Questions
(80 marks; 90 minutes)

1 **a** How might Letshaveaparty.com benefit from the
introduction of autonomous work groups? **(8 marks)**

b Assess whether it is inevitable that communications suffer
as a business grows bigger. **(12 marks)**

2 **a** Plot the annual sales turnover figures on graph paper, then
extrapolate the annual sales figures forward, and thereby
estimate the sales figure for 2002. Show your workings on the
graph and state your estimated figure. **(8 marks)**

b Discuss whether the company should open a depot in
north London, or whether it should find an alternative
strategy for using its existing warehouse more effectively. **(12 marks)**

3 **a** Calculate the stock turnover and debtor days for
Letshaveaparty.com. **(8 marks)**

b Consider whether the cash shortfall of £900,000 should be
tackled by cutting stocks and debtors. **(12 marks)**

4 **a** Debbie's new marketing strategy will place a greater
premium on quality and reliability of service and delivery.
How might critical path analysis assist in this? **(8 marks)**

b Like most entrepreneurs, Debbie is excellent at making
marketing decisions on the basis of hunch. If
Letshaveaparty.com becomes an established, publicly quoted
company, she will have to use more scientific methods such
as the Marketing Model. Assess whether this is likely to help
or hinder the business. **(12 marks)**

SOLARTILE: A MINI-MULTINATIONAL

CONCEPTS NEEDED:

Raising finance, Multinationals, Profit

James was the Engineering Director of a heating company when the idea hit him. Why not make roof tiles with a solar panel coating, so that energy saving in the home becomes easy to install? Then, whenever new houses are built or householders are replacing their roof, people could choose an energy saving alternative. James experimented in his workshed at home, and eventually devised the solar tiles, plus an energy collection and storage system that could easily be plumbed into a hot water or central heating tank. Then he patented the idea, and registered SolarTile as a trademark.

Raising the finance to establish production was not too difficult, because his engineering contacts enabled him to identify suppliers of every single component. Therefore his only requirement was for a small assembly plant which could be rented inexpensively. Thirty thousand pounds of his own money plus a £15,000 bank loan was enough to provide the working capital he needed.

The key figure in the start-up, however, was probably James's wife Nicola. She proved to have a flair for PR (public relations). She sent stylishly packaged SolarTiles to the producers of TV programmes such as *Tomorrow's World*, and generated a remarkable amount of free publicity. Production had just been geared up to meet the resulting high demand when the Saudi Arabian Revolution sparked off the third oil crisis. With the trebling oil and gas prices, James's innovation was suddenly pushed into the international spotlight. Demand from Germany, Holland, and Austria was only outweighed by that from America and Canada.

From the start the business had been highly profitable, so reserves of £60,000 had been built up – half of which was in cash. James felt he needed £100,000, however, to increase production capacity to the level of demand, so he turned to a merchant bank for venture capital. He negotiated a finance package of £55,000 of loan capital and £15,000 of share capital. Giving up one third of his control of the firm was a blow, but he was very keen to seize the market opportunity.

Should they expand output in the United Kingdom, though, or establish production overseas? Reasons of management control suggested staying at home, but transport costs made a multinational structure attractive. An average-sized UK house cost the customer £6,000 to roof using the SolarTile method. This comprised £3,000 of materials, £1,000 of assembly and overheads, £250 of delivery costs, £1,000 of installation cost, with the remainder being profit. A few phone calls to freight companies revealed that each complete system would cost £400 to transport to Chicago (a logical site bordering Canada and the United States).

James was also aware that although he could control production more easily in the United Kingdom, successful marketing, distribution, and installation of the systems would need good local management. When he made his profit calculations, he reasoned that increasing capacity in America or Britain would create similar extra factory overheads, and was therefore not a key factor.

A £20,000 market research analysis of the potential North American market convinced James that he would not be able to pass the extra £400 transport cost on to the customers. Therefore he decided to set up an assembly plant in Chicago. He knew that even if local

Breaking into the US

component suppliers could not be found, shipping the (mainly small) components from the United Kingdom would not be very expensive.

For the next four weeks, James interviewed potential managers, and was delighted to recruit an impressive 35 year old as Managing Director. To ensure his loyalty and commitment, the Managing Director was given a 10% stake in SolarTile US Inc., as well as an $80,000 salary. Together, they worked out revenue and cost forecasts based on the research prediction of 2,000 sales a month. Within eight weeks, the Managing Director had identified a suitable site, and appointed a Production and a Sales Manager. Just 10 weeks later, the first complete system came off the US assembly line.

To minimise costs, and to make it easier to set up quickly in the United States, many of the high value, low bulk components were ordered from SolarTile's British suppliers. This enabled lower unit prices to be negotiated, which helped James's profit margins in the United Kingdom. With two of the components, he found that the higher output levels made it cost efficient to buy automated machinery to produce them within their UK factory, so they carried out the production themselves.

After six months, the US operation began to break even, and its fat order book made high profits look inevitable. Yet four months later, when visiting the Chicago plant, James was shocked to see the chaotic factory organisation. It emerged that the Production Manager had proved weak and disorganised, but that firing him three weeks before had revealed his popularity among his workforce – 12 out of the 15 workers had walked out. By the time the staffing problem was ironed out, SolarTile US Inc. had lost $250,000.

The British parent was nearly dragged under by the drain on its financial resources but, having survived, went on to become highly profitable. The decision to set up in the United States rather than export from the United Kingdom was fully vindicated when,

two years later, America decided to place a 15% tariff on all manufactured exports from Europe. Other assembly sites were also set up in Germany and Singapore.

A new accountant showed James how he could take advantage of his multinational organisation to minimise his company's tax bills. The tax rate on company profits in Germany is much higher than in America, so SolarTile UK began charging higher component prices to Deutsche SolarTile and lower ones to SolarTile US Inc. In that way, the higher costs being absorbed by the German subsidiary ensured lower (apparent) profits. The accountant was able, in this way, to transfer £200,000 of SolarTile's profit from Germany to the United States, and thereby paid the 20% US tax rate instead of Germany's 40% rate. James was a bit worried about the legality of this financial juggling, but the accountant assured him: 'It's a common tax avoidance practice ... called transfer pricing. It's perfectly legal.'

Questions
(60 marks; 80 minutes)

1 What were the main elements in James's success in financing SolarTile in its early years? **(10 marks)**

2 **a** At the time he was deciding whether or not to establish production in the United States, what would James have forecast to be the effect on profit of transporting complete systems from the United Kingdom? Show your workings clearly. **(8 marks)**

    b Consider the assumption James made about factory overheads. How might this assumption have affected the accuracy of the profit estimates? **(6 marks)**

3 Outline the main benefits SolarTile gained from its multinational expansion. **(8 marks)**

4 **a** Should transfer pricing be 'perfectly legal'? **(6 marks)**

    b Why is it more likely that a group of countries (such as the European Union) would ban this practice than that any individual country would? **(8 marks)**

5 Entrepreneurs need a good idea, the ability to get the best out of others, and a lot of luck. Discuss this statement in the light of the SolarTile example. **(14 marks)**

CHOCOLATE SOLDIERS – THE ROWNTREE TAKEOVER

A2 INTEGRATED CASE

CONCEPTS NEEDED:

Takeovers, Opportunity cost, European single market, Brand names

At 8.30 a.m. on 13 April 1988, the Swiss chocolate group Suchard launched a 'dawn raid' on the shares of Rowntree. In a 35 minute buying spree it bought £160 million of Rowntree's shares in the London stock market – 14.9% of the British firm's share capital. This was achieved by offering shareholders 630 pence for shares worth 475 pence the previous day. Suchard made it clear that its objective was to build a 25% stake in Rowntree; few doubted that it would soon be used to launch a full takeover bid.

Rowntree's Chairman said: 'Suchard may need Rowntree, but Rowntree does not need Suchard.' Although he was clearly shocked at the threat to the York firm's 130 year history, the Chairman seemed confident that he could fight off a competitor of a similar size to Rowntree itself. As he proclaimed:

'**R**owntree, the largest confectionery business in the United Kingdom, has one

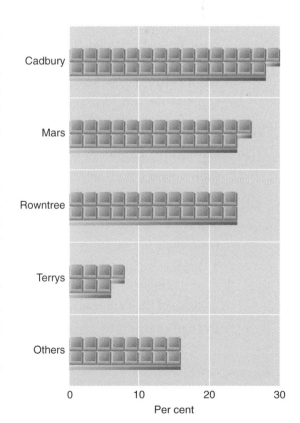

Market share by volume of goods sold (The Sunday Times *17 April 1988*)

*of the best **portfolios** of brand names in the world ... Kit Kat, Smarties, and After Eight have taken years of investment.*'

Two weeks passed before the real hammer blow – a full takeover bid at 890 pence cash from the huge Nestlé group (the world's biggest food company). This valued Rowntree at £2.1 billion.

The Swiss giant made it clear that it was not willing to allow Suchard to gain such a strong position in the European chocolate market. A City analyst maintained that:

'**N**estlé cannot afford to allow Rowntree to fall to Suchard. Rowntree is a dead duck.'

The latter view came from examination of Nestlé's balance sheet. This showed that the Swiss multinational had bank deposits worth £2.7 billion. So it could swallow Rowntree from, in effect, its petty cash. With sales and profits more than 500% higher than either Rowntree or Suchard, Nestlé could not be stopped in the marketplace. So action switched to the only other forum for determining the outcome – the government and its Monopolies and Mergers Commission (now renamed the Competition Commission).

For Rowntree's management there appeared to be three possible ways of persuading the government to intervene:

1 On the grounds that the merger would be anti-competitive, given Nestlé's substantial share of the European chocolate market.

2 That as Swiss laws enabled its companies to protect themselves from being taken over, it would be unfair to allow a Swiss predator to buy up a British firm.

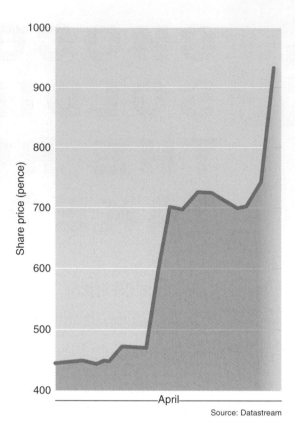

Source: Datastream

3 That Rowntree's unusual position of being a major British company based in the north meant that keeping it independent was important for regional policy.

Rowntree's problem with the first possibility can be seen in the table opposite. Neither Nestlé's 3% nor Suchard's 2% of the UK chocolate market would add sufficient to Rowntree's market share to match that of Cadbury's. Many politicians suggested that with the strengthening single European market, the proper consideration should be European market shares, but the British government rejected this view.

European chocolate confectionery market shares

	UK	Austria	Belgium	France	Italy	Netherlands	Switzerland	W.Germany	Total
				(% by sales value)					
Mars	24	4	6	11	1	23	9	22	17
Suchard	2	73	82	13	–	–	17	15	13
Rowntree	26	–	2	17	–	13	–	3	11
Ferrero	2	–	5	6	34	–	–	16	10
Cadbury	30	–	–	8	–	–	–	–	9
Nestlé	3	5	3	10	5	–	17	8	9

Source: Henderson Crosthwaite (*Financial Times* 27 April 1988)

Rowntree chose to present an upbeat image as a caring employer, a solidly northern firm, and the developer of world markets for such British products as After Eights and the Lion bar. The latter became an important part of Rowntree's defence. For, despite its weak performance in Britain, the Lion bar had become a notable success in the rest of Europe. Rowntree's management was keen to get across the notion that the sleepy Swiss producers of solid chocolate bars were desperate to buy a firm with proven skills in the marketing of the growing chocolate 'count-lines' sector (single, hand held bars such as Mars, Flake and Lion).

The battle of the brand names

Rowntree	Nestlé	Suchard
Kit Kat	Nescafé	Toblerone
Quality Street	Carnation	Milka
Aero	Crosse & Blackwell	Côte D'Or
Black Magic	Findus	
Rolo	L'Oréal	
After Eight	Chambourcy	
Smarties	Libby's	
Yorkie	Milky Bar	

Suchard's Chairman was quite open about the attractions of Rowntree:

'**R**owntree is an excellent company with a fascinating range of brands. Brands are the most important thing.'

Behind the scenes, Rowntree carried out extensive lobbying of MPs, Ministers, and the employers' organisation, the Confederation of British Industry (CBI). Public relations schemes were devised to promote the idea: 'Hands Off Rowntree'. In early May the CBI recommended that the takeover be referred by the government to the Monopolies and Mergers Commission. That would ensure the suspension of the bid for many months while its likely impact was investigated. This source of pressure on the government was silenced, however, when the CBI gave in to Nestlé's public threat to cancel its membership.

The Rowntree unions were also active in supporting the existing management. For the Rowntree family had established at the turn of the 20th century a pattern of **paternalism** that led to the early introduction of a shorter working week, a pension scheme, and good working conditions. Recent managements had tended to maintain these traditions, so the workforce were especially loyal to the company.

By mid May, over two hundred MPs had signed motions of support for Rowntree. They were thwarted, though, by the government's desire to be seen to be welcoming to foreign firms, in the hope of attracting investment into extra production here. On 25 May, Lord Young announced that the Department of Trade would not be recommending that the bid be investigated. Although the Labour Party's Bryan Gould described this as a 'betrayal of British industry', many commentators accepted the government's stance that:

'**I**ntervention by public authorities in lawful commercial transactions should be kept to a minimum since ... decisions of private decision makers in competitive markets result in the most desirable outcomes for the economy as a whole.'

The following day Suchard challenged Nestlé with a £2.32 billion counterbid at 950 pence a share. This may well have been no more than a ploy to push Nestlé into paying more for Rowntree shares. For Suchard already held over a £100 million profit on the shares it had bought for 630 pence just six weeks before. It convinced Rowntree's largest union that the end was near, however, for on 1 June its Executive urged the management to end its opposition to the bids, and to start negotiating with both of the Swiss firms. The union believed it essential that the new owners should view their Rowntree division with favour, not hostility.

The battle ended, as expected, with a knockout blow by Nestlé. On 23 June Nestlé offered 1075 pence (£2.55 billion), which Suchard accepted was more than it could afford. Having accumulated a 29.9% stake in Rowntree, Suchard could sell its shares to Nestlé at a profit of more than £200 million. Nestlé announced that it had given assurances that York would continue to be the centre of Rowntree activity, and that the firm's employment policy and practices would be respected. Nevertheless, the Swiss would not give any job guarantees to Rowntree's 13,000 UK workers. Within a few days Nestlé had won the acceptance of the Rowntree Board and shareholders.

Following Nestlé's success, two issues continued to be hotly debated:

1 Is it right to allow successful, profitable, well managed firms like Rowntree to be taken over unless the bidder can demonstrate some clear social or economic benefit?

2 Do company accounts give sufficient weight to the enormous value of the 'goodwill' represented by the value of brand names? For one of the reasons that Rowntree was 'a dead duck' was because the Swiss rivals were able to offer Rowntree shareholders such a large premium over the pre-bid value of the shares.

Sources: Financial Times; The Guardian; The Independent; The Observer; The Sunday Times

Questions
(80 marks; 90 minutes)

1 Explain the meaning of the following words (in bold print in the text):
dawn raid
portfolio
paternalism **(9 marks)**

2 On 13 April, many shareholders sold out to Suchard at 630 pence per share. What percentage profit had they made overnight? What was the opportunity cost of their decision? **(8 marks)**

3 Use the table of figures on European market shares to discuss the attractions of Rowntree for the two Swiss firms. **(10 marks)**

4 Why may the establishment of the single European market in 1992 have influenced the bidders' desire to buy Rowntree? **(10 marks)**

5 Nestlé was in a position to fund the purchase of Rowntree with cash. How else might one finance the takeover of another firm? Outline the implications of these alternative methods. **(12 marks)**

6 Rowntree management and unions carried out a united, extensive programme of pressure group activity. Why was it unsuccessful in this case? **(6 marks)**

7 Nestlé paid over £1.5 billion more than the value of Rowntree's physical assets in order to acquire its brands. Why are brand names so valuable? **(10 marks)**

8 Examine the implications for firms generally of one of the two issues that remained unanswered after the takeover was completed. **(15 marks)**

TOILET ROLLS TO MOBILE PHONES – THE NOKIA STORY

CONCEPTS NEEDED:

Ansoff's Matrix, Research and development, Market v. asset led marketing, Communications

In 1991 the economy of Finland was hit by a sharp recession. Even a manufacturer of essentials such as toilet paper and tyres struggled to survive. The company was Nokia, and that year it lost £65 million and nearly went under. Despite its 130 year history, Nokia could have been bought on Finland's stock market for just £50 million. Nine years later Nokia's stock market value amounted to £65,000 million. £100 of shares purchased in September 1991 would have turned into £325,000 by September 2000, making it one of the most profitable investments of all time.

The evolution of Nokia from toilet rolls to mobile phones began before 1991. The company had started investing research and development funds into wire-free phones in the 1970s. The attraction was the geography and climate of Finland, with its arctic winters and widely spread population. By 1980 there were over 23,000 wire-free phones in Finland, though they were big and bulky – far from mobile. In 1984 Nokia's Managing Director Kari Kairamo asked a young banker to help turn the conglomerate into an electronics business. The banker – Jorma Ollila – considered this aim to be challenging but possible, so he accepted.

The term mobile phone was introduced in 1987, when Nokia produced the Cityman – the world's first mobile. In fact it weighed nearly a kilogram, and was far from portable. Its sales were far too modest to cover the research and development costs.

In July 1991 Nokia showed its ambition by launching the first GSM (Global System for Mobile) phone. The adoption of this technology as the standard operating system for European mobile phones did a lot to cement Nokia's later huge success. Despite the company's innovations, Nokia relentlessly lost money in its electronics division. By 1991 the losses made by other sections of the company forced the Board to act. They appointed Ollila as the new Managing Director and told him to turn the company round, if necessary by selling off or closing down the phone business. The six months after Ollila's appointment in January 1992 seemed to confirm the Board's advice. The phone business went down and down.

However Ollila had no doubts about the long term future of the mobile phone business. In mid 1992 he surprised everyone by getting the Board to agree to put all Nokia's traditional businesses up for sale. To provide the finance to develop Nokia electronics, the paper, rubber and tyre divisions were sold off. It was now all or nothing.

Fortunately for Ollila, the home market for mobile phones entered a boom period, as Finns responded enthusiastically to Nokia's development of smaller, smarter digital phones. Text messages, intended for business use such as conveying sales figures, became a means of conversation between friends and lovers. At the time, the US giant Motorola was the world leader in mobile phones, but Nokia's insight was to realise that phones could be fun. Attractive design, miniaturisation and the brainwave of interchangeable front panels meant that Nokia was bringing to mobile phones what Swatch had brought to the market for watches. Big corporations were still buying from Motorola, but on the street the word was Nokia.

Apart from a slight setback in 1996, the following years saw fantastic growth in Nokia sales, first in Europe, then in the United States. By February 2000 the *Wall Street Journal* was identifying Nokia as the world's number one mobile phone maker and Europe's most valuable company. Its stock market valuation was 213 billion euros (translating into over £125 billion). American commentators found it incredible that any world leader in electronics could come from outside the USA or Japan, let alone from tiny Finland.

According to Chairman Ollila the company outpaced competitors such as Ericsson because it managed to launch new models continuously, reducing its new product lead time to half that for certain rivals. He is also

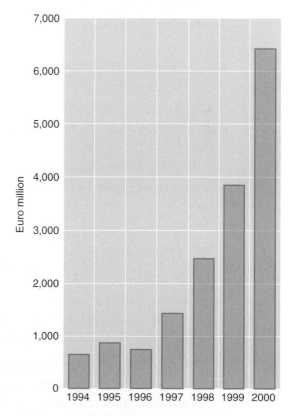

Nokia annual operating profit

clear that Nokia's marketing strategy proved superior. The strategy was to present phones as fun, stylish consumer products, not as toys for techies.

In spring 2000, the developing issue was mobile phone Internet access. Typically, Nokia's WAP phone was among the earliest to hit the market, but the evidence was not yet clear that the public wanted the technology.

Despite slow sales of WAP phones, Nokia's sales continued to power ahead. Sales revenue and profits in the six months to June 2000 were up 62% and 65% respectively. A slowdown would eventually come, but already Nokia had achieved Kari Kairamo's aims to an extraordinary extent.

Sources: Financial Times: 'The Business'; The Observer

*Appendix A: Nokia share price 1 September 1991–2000 (in US dollars)**

1991	1992	1993	1994	1995	1996	1997	1998	1999	2000
0.05	0.03	0.14	0.36	3.18	2.00	4.48	7.78	19.20	52.32

*because of rights and scrip issues, these figures *understate* the growth in the value of Nokia shares!

Questions
(60 marks; 70 minutes)

1 Use Ansoff's Matrix to analyse Nokia's successful move into mobile phones. Support your answer with a diagram. **(12 marks)**

2 **a** Explain the differences between research and development (R&D) and market research. **(6 marks)**
 b Why may Nokia's investment in R&D have proved so successful for the company? **(12 marks)**

3 Discuss whether Nokia's successful positioning of its brand as the technology and style leader should be seen as an example of market led or asset led marketing. **(14 marks)**

4 To what extent are mobile phones with Internet access likely to resolve the communications problems suffered by many large firms? **(16 marks)**

MONEY FROM THE TAP

A2
INTEGRATED
CASE

CONCEPTS NEEDED:

Decision trees, Contribution, Profit

After three years of highly profitable growth, decisions were needed on the future of Dalesmere. Its sole product was Dalesmere Natural Mineral Water, which it had marketed as the first home delivery, 'luxury' water. It had been sold at a price premium over the market leader (Perrier), and on a shamelessly snobbish message:

'The exclusive product for exclusive people**'**

Extensive direct mail advertising in the South-east, plus sampling stands at London's commuter railway stations, proved a successful way of getting custom. The idea of door to door delivery in glass bottles that Dalesmere would collect and recycle fitted well with the 'green' mood of the times. Most important of all, however, were the circumstances of the year in which Dalesmere happened to be launched. Not only was the summer exceptionally hot, but also there were countless stories in the media about the poor quality of British drinking water.

Now, with £500,000 on bank deposit, Dalesmere could afford to consider its next

move carefully. A management consultancy had been commissioned to conduct a SWOT analysis, summarised below.

Dalesmere SWOT Analysis
Summary of main findings and conclusions

Strengths:

1 Exclusive image, especially among the 20,000 regular users.

2 Reputation for reliable service, and an environmentally sound product (hence the high repeat purchase average of 10 bottles 25 times per annum).

3 High profitability due to very high margins (*price 79 pence minus bottling and distribution cost 19 pence*).

4 90% of custom in the South-east.

Weaknesses:

1 High promotional cost of getting new customers (currently £50 per head).

2 Sales declining.

3 Poor image among non-customers.

Opportunities:

1 To use the exclusive image among users, plus the distribution network to market other upmarket products.

2 To invest £500,000 in corporate television advertising in the South-east, to improve the image among non-users.

Threats:

1 Competition in the home delivery market from three cheaper rivals, plus the recent announcement of milkman delivery of Perrier.

2 That improvements to water quality, led by the European Union, may cut demand for bottled waters generally.

Within the main body of the report, possible approaches to the new product strategy were set out. Dalesmere's core

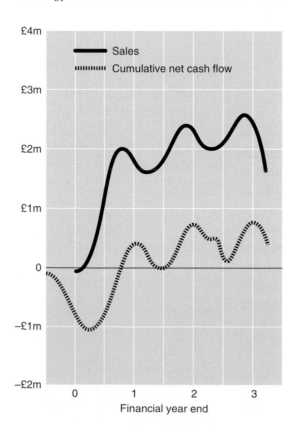

competence lay in its management of its upmarket customer list and its established delivery service. So the new products should be ones that wealthy people would find inconvenient to obtain or to carry home. Group discussions among regular customers examined the rival attractions of offering a delivery service in:

a whole hams and farmhouse cheeses

b a range of Dalesmere soft drinks and juices

c a range of organic wines and beers.

Both **a** and **c** were very well received, though it emerged that most were likely to purchase **a** on special occasions only. So option **c** became the favourite.

The choice facing Dalesmere was clarified to proceeding either with the television advertising, or with the 'line extension' – organic wines and beers. Its advertising agency estimated that the £500,000 campaign should boost sales by one of the following possibilities (depending upon the response of competitors):

- 0.2 probability of a 40% rise in customers and sales
- 0.5 probability of a 20% rise in customers and sales
- 0.3 probability of a 10% rise in customers and sales.

The management consultants estimated that the organic wines and beers would cost £500,000 to set up, and would have a 60% chance of providing sales of £2,000,000 at a profit margin of 40%; plus a 40% chance of half that sales level, though at the same margin.

The management consultants decided to prepare a decision tree based upon this information, and use it as the basis of a final strategy meeting with the Dalesmere directors.

Questions
(50 marks; 70 minutes)

1   What conclusions can you draw from the graph shown?   **(8 marks)**

2   Construct the management consultants' tree diagram.   **(8 marks)**

3   Calculate the expected values of each decision based upon
    forecast contribution over the first year; show them and the
    decisions they point to on your diagram.   **(12 marks)**

4   Discuss how useful a decision tree is in circumstances such
    as these.   **(10 marks)**

5   Taking into account all the information available, explain
    which of the options you would choose, and why.   **(12 marks)**

GOOD MANAGE-MENT PRACTICE IN RETAILING

CONCEPTS NEEDED:

Balance sheet, Ratios, Scientific decisions, Payback, Economies of scale

Marie started in the shop at nine years old, helping to fill shelves and occasionally serving customers. Later, she helped her mother deal with the buying side and with the accounts. So by the time she was 20, her knowledge of the grocery trade was good enough for her parents to feel happy to hand the business over. Marie arranged a mortgage on the shop flat and premises to provide the capital to buy them a Devon cottage, and then, one day, found herself on her own.

She had taken over a medium sized, independent grocery shop of 2000 square metres. Its weekly sales turnover was £24,000 at a gross profit margin of 15 per cent. This was sufficient to cover the £1,000 wage bill and £1,800 of other fixed costs, yet still leave a healthy profit. Marie had no intention,

however, of allowing the business just to tick over. She wanted to prove that she could build it up into the biggest independent grocery chain in Derbyshire. To do this would require either a programme of store openings, or buying out rival owners. Whichever way she eventually chose, she knew that the starting point was raising finance.

Having already undertaken a large mortgage on the shop, she had neither the **collateral** nor the capital structure to borrow any more. For the business's shareholders' funds were outweighed 2–1 by borrowings. She had no wish to bring new shareholders in, so the only option was to generate capital from the business itself. Could she squeeze cash out of her assets? Not from the premises or van; and as she offered no credit to customers, there was no kitty of **debtors**. So stocks were the only asset that might have some potential. Yet her parents had boasted when they handed the shop over that stock was being turned over fortnightly, so it was hard to imagine that much wastage existed there. If stock reductions had limited potential, that left profits as the sole remaining source.

Marie decided to undertake a detailed analysis of the **profitability** of the different sections of the store, to find out what to do next. She spent three weeks measuring up the shop and sifting through the stock books to produce the breakdown shown below.

Before rushing to draw conclusions from this analysis, Marie decided to spend a fortnight chatting to customers about their usage of, and attitudes towards, the shop. They emphasised that convenience was the key – best achieved by offering a wide enough range of goods to ensure that they would not have to travel the six km to the nearest large supermarket.

Then she embarked on her new strategy. Fresh foods would be expanded by installing in-store bakery equipment. This would not only give more space over to a section that appeared to deserve it, but would also make the store smell inviting and wholesome. Confectionery would be expanded by means of a high quality Pick-and-Mix counter, and by increasing the range of children's lines. It would be supplemented by installing two new counters that would each – she felt – attract more passing trade (and therefore confectionery impulse purchasing): newspapers, magazines and a video library. All these items would, between them, require 45 square metres of floor space. Ten could come from converting a small office, while the remainder would have to come from the other departments.

The conversion cost £12,000 but soon

Weekly turnover and profit analysis

Product	Turnover £	Gross profit £	% of total gross profit	% of sq. m.
Fresh food	2,800	580	16.5	14.0
Frozen food	1,500	200	5.5	4.5
Other food	6,500	820	22.5	33.0
Confectionery	3,800	810	22.5	8.5
Tobacco	2,400	200	5.5	4.0
Household items	3,500	590	16.5	23.0
Alcoholic drink	3,500	400	11.0	13.0
Total	24,000	3,600	100.0	100.0

proved a great success. Turnover rose to £30,000 per week and margins expanded to 17%. This meant a payback period of eight weeks – an astonishingly short time – and a greatly improved profit level thereafter. Marie followed this up by extending the video library into full children's and pop music ranges. For the first time, she advertised this development in the local paper, and featured an 'Opening Day Offer – 50p For Any Title'. Just as she hoped, video and confectionery sales grew still higher, reaching £35,000 a week. At this level of trading, £250 of extra staff costs were necessary, but profit was still buoyant at £2,900 per week.

Within six months, the firm's bank balance was high enough to enable Marie to obtain a second outlet. Several weeks of careful looking revealed two interesting opportunities. One was shop premises in a new private housing estate on the outskirts of Mansfield. The other was a thriving grocery and delicatessen in the centre of Chesterfield. The latter was much nearer to her original shop, so ease of transport and delivery persuaded her to concentrate on it. She was certain that the next step in improving the profitability of her first store lay in direct purchasing from the manufacturer.

This would entail dropping the business's long association with Spar, but buying direct would boost margins by three per cent. The minimum delivery size imposed by the manufacturers would mean that all deliveries would go to the one site, and would then have to be shuttled from one to the other by a full-time delivery driver. It would also make it likely that higher average stock levels would have to be held. So Marie planned to install a computerised stock control system – efficient enough to counteract the upward pressure on stock levels. She realised that all these apparently high costs would be covered comfortably by the 3% margin improvement on her forecast revenue of £50,000 per week.

In the event, her purchase of the Chesterfield branch provided Marie with another benefit. The store manageress had many useful ideas on improving customer service, such as training staff to keep an eye on the check-outs and to open up an extra till if there was ever more than one customer waiting.

Five years later it was the manageress who was the Human Resource Director of Derbyshire Supermarkets, a chain of 14 stores employing over 400 people. Marie, the Managing Director of the county's largest independent grocery chain, was starting to set her sights on national horizons.

Questions
(80 marks; 90 minutes)

1 Explain the meaning of the following terms (in bold print in the text):
collateral
debtors
profitability **(9 marks)**

2 **a** Prior to the expansion, what were the firm's approximate gearing and stock turnover ratios? **(6 marks)**

b Outline why Marie felt that she had to finance expansion primarily from profit. **(9 marks)**

3 To what extent did Marie's management approach fit a scientific decision making model? **(15 marks)**

4 Demonstrate that:
a The payback period was eight weeks. **(7 marks)**
b 'Profit was still buoyant at £2,900 per week.' **(7 marks)**

5 Discuss which departments the desired floor space should be taken from. **(12 marks)**

6 Outline the main benefits Marie's business seemed to derive from its horizontal expansion. What pitfalls might it meet as it expands still further? **(15 marks)**

SONY'S MARKETING PHENOMENON

CONCEPTS NEEDED:

Strategy v. tactics, Diversification, Monopoly, Government intervention, Internet

The late 1980s were hugely successful for the Sony Corporation. It boasted the must-have Sony Walkman, Discman, Trinitron TV and many, many other top sellers in the consumer electronics market. The Japanese companies Sega and Nintendo dominated the quite separate and much smaller markets for games consoles and software. This market was hugely profitable, but there was no reason to suppose that there was room for a new rival. In 1991 Nintendo was the most profitable company in Japan. Its profits per employee were $250,000 compared with $17,000 at Sony.

Yet in that year, Sony chose to tackle Sega and Nintendo head-on. Its vehicle, the PlayStation, was a 32-bit console, giving it twice the performance of the 16-bit products sold by Sega and Nintendo. Staff at Sony's European headquarters in Surrey showed little interest when the product arrived from Japan in September 1995. Chris Deering, hired to set up the European division of Sony Computer Entertainment in 1995, said he had

'thought it would be successful, but sales over the last five years have been two or three times bigger than my wildest dreams on day one'. In fact, with sales of over 30 million units in Europe, the PlayStation became a multi-billion pound phenomenon.

Sony's development of the PlayStation owed a great deal to its strong understanding of CD and CD-ROM technology. This gave it a lead over Nintendo and Sega. With first-mover advantage in developing the new generation, more powerful 32-bit machines, Sony was able to break the stranglehold of its two rivals. This could have been expected to be a short lived advantage, given Nintendo's powerful name and grip on the two most successful console games of all time: *Super-Mario Brothers* and *Tetris*. *Super-Mario* alone had grossed more than the cinema's greatest ever box office successes, such as *ET* and *Star Wars*.

Sony's plan was not to devise better games than Nintendo. It chose to invite independent software companies from around the world to develop games compatible with PlayStation technology. Sony would provide the computer codes, the technical support and its well known sales, marketing and distributional flair. The software houses would provide the great games. This proved a master stroke. For games players the thrill of mastering a new game can quickly turn to boredom through familiarity. A constant stream of innovative new product launches keeps the console alive. Between 1995 and 1998 a flood of new games became available – and most were launched first on the PlayStation. Sega and Nintendo found themselves unable to resist Sony's success. By 1999 Sony had an astonishing 80 per cent of the European market for games consoles. For Nintendo, the Pokémon craze proved a financial saviour. Sega, though, plunged into four years of huge trading losses. By August 2000 Sega was forecasting losses of over $200 million in 2000/2001, even though it had managed to bring out the technologically advanced Sega Dreamcast a year before the eagerly awaited PlayStation 2. In early 2001 Sega withdrew from hardware production completely.

Despite the vast worldwide sales value of PlayStations (nearly £10,000 million), the key to making money in this market is software, not hardware. In Deering's words: 'The business model of console gaming is not to be profitable from hardware sales – most often it just about breaks even.' The intention is to run the hardware almost as a loss leader to stimulate sales of the highly profitable complementary games software. Software sales have some key benefits compared with hardware:

- much higher profit margins
- more stable, less seasonal sales

- sales based upon the total number of machines sold (the cumulative total) rather than on current sales of the machines.

The importance of the latter point became very clear in 2000, when the industry awaited the launch of PlayStation 2. Hardware sales dried up, but UK sales of PlayStation software (games) actually rose 17% to 19.2 million in January–September 2000 compared with the same period in 1999.

The financial impact of PlayStation on Sony was extraordinary. During a period of economic depression in Japan, profits from electrical and electronic goods were becoming ever harder to come by. By 1999 Sony was making a return of only 4% on the

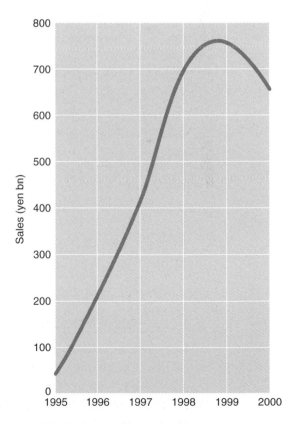

Sony PlayStation sales revenues

capital employed in its world class electronics division. The games division, in the same year, made a return of 72%!

Despite the huge success of PlayStation, there was no doubt that it had reached maturity by 1999. PlayStation 2 was much needed. Launched in March 2000 in Japan, PlayStation 2 managed sales of over 1.4 million units (valued at about £280 million) in that month alone. Yet despite capital spending of over £700 million to build the microchip capacity for the new product, Sony proved unable to keep up with the huge level of demand. The product's autumn 2000 launch in America and Europe had to be scaled down drastically because Japan was absorbing most of the available product supply. Sony remained confident that customers would be patient and that PlayStation 2 would outsell its predecessor. What was unquestionable, though, was that the diversification into the games sector of the electronics industry had proved a brilliant strategy for Sony. Not even Microsoft's announcement of its brand new rival X Box could dent Sony's confidence in the future of its moneyspinner.

Sources: Sony annual reports; *Game Over* by D. Sheff, Hodder & Stoughton 1993; *Financial Times*

PlayStation sales by volume since launch in December 1994

Financial year ending 31 March	PlayStation 1		PlayStation 2	
	Hardware	Software	Hardware	Software
1995	1.0m	2m		
1996	4.5m	29m		
1997	9.0m	63m		
1998	18.3m	142m		
1999	21.6m	194m		
2000	18.5m	200m	1.4m	2.9m
2001 (forecast)	12.0m	160m	10.0m	45.0m

Source: Sony annual accounts, plus trade estimates

Questions
(60 marks; 80 minutes)

1 Examine whether Sony's original development of PlayStation should be considered a strategic or a tactical decision. **(8 marks)**

2 a Why might governments be concerned that 'by 1999 Sony had an astonishing 80% of the European market for games consoles'? **(10 marks)**

b Discuss whether government should intervene to break up such a strong monopoly position. **(12 marks)**

3 Use Ansoff's Matrix to evaluate Sony's development and launch of PlayStation in 1994. **(10 marks)**

4 Use the websites of the *Financial Times* (www.ft.com) and/or *The Guardian* (www.guardianunlimited.co.uk) to research the latest information on PlayStation 2's sales performance.

a Describe its sales performance, using criteria such as sales volume, market share and market size. **(8 marks)**

b Evaluate the performance of PlayStation 2 compared with the data provided in this case study about PlayStation 1. **(12 marks)**

96 INTEREST RATES AND THE GROWING BUSINESS

CONCEPTS NEEDED:

Cash flow, Interest rates, Value of the pound, External constraints

Having worked for six years as a design engineer, it seemed natural for Sean Parker to want to start up his own business. His customer contacts gave him an idea of the opportunities that existed and his skills enabled him to create an appropriate economic product. So when he met two brothers who, between them, had financial and production expertise, he sounded them out. The brothers, Tim and Aylott Batchelor, were very keen, so T.A.S. Limited was born.

They chose to specialise in the design and manufacture of machines for printing packaging labels. This was because the enormous range of packaging materials used in modern business means that a very wide range of printing machines is needed; as a result, it is hard for established firms to mass produce cheaply enough to prevent new firms getting established.

Having started with £60,000 of equity and £40,000 of fixed rate loan capital, within two

years T.A.S. Ltd had sales of £540,000 at a 10% net profit margin. With fast rising demand, it was a constant struggle to find the extra resources needed: the finance, the managers, the labour, and the factory floor space. It was a relief when, in April, Aylott negotiated a £100,000 bank loan; sufficient to finance the whole of next year's plans. The terms of the loan seemed reasonable (4% over bank base rates) as it meant paying just 11 per cent.

When the Bank of England pushed interest rates up 2% in the following month, the trio thought nothing of it. Yet worries about inflation forced the Bank to keep pushing rates up until, five months later, rates stood at 14%. This soon applied pressure to the firm's cash flow, as customers stalled paying their bills, while suppliers chased harder for payment. Back in April, the length of credit time taken by customers was much the same as the length given to suppliers – 45 days. Now customers were stalling until

60 days, while deliveries were being cut off if payment was not made within 30 days. This meant a large cash drain from a sales level that had reached £600,000 per annum.

In the months that followed, T.A.S. received further shocks. The first was a marked downturn in signed orders. Customers still talked about placing them, but the uncertainty over the effects of the high interest rates meant that they kept putting off a commitment. With orders sliding down towards an annual level of £450,000 by February, Sean decided to fly out to a Trade Fair in Munich, to try to generate some export business. Looking round competitors' stands, he was perturbed to see that their prices were lower than his, when converted into sterling. This, he realised, was because the pound had risen 8% against other currencies since the increase in UK interest rates. He returned home without a single order.

Then, in March, came two fierce setbacks. The first was the loss of two major customers to a German supplier. Months of design work were wasted as the Germans were able not only to undercut T.A.S. prices by 3%, but also to offer longer credit terms. For in Germany the 6% rate of interest meant that offering three months' credit would cost just 1.5% off the profit margin. It became horribly clear that sales would be down towards the £300,000 mark by May. The second blow was the failure of a key supplier – forced into liquidation by the difficult economic position. Although not as drastic as the liquidation of a customer, Sean had been used to a close

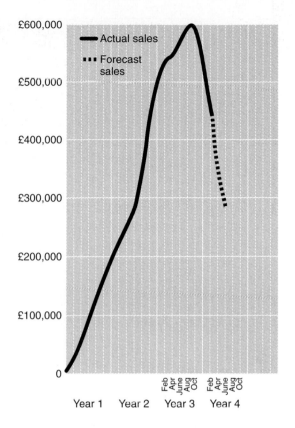

working relationship with this firm, and its engineers had often come up with design ideas that helped to keep production costs down.

On 30 May – 13 months after the first increase – the Bank of England pushed interest rates down by 1%. Journalists began to forecast that rates would be below 10% by the autumn. Too late, unfortunately, for Tim, Aylott and Sean. In mid May they had decided to go into voluntary liquidation; dissolving the company before losses wiped out their original share capital.

Questions
(50 marks; 60 minutes)

1 **a** Calculate the 'large cash drain' suffered by T.A.S. after
interest rates had risen. Assume 30-day months.   **(8 marks)**

   b Explain why the firm's suppliers and customers responded
as they did to the higher interest rates.   **(8 marks)**

2 In Germany, the Reconstruction Credit Bank provides
£4.5 billion of cheap finance for small firms. The funds are at
a fixed rate set several points below the standard commercial
rate.

   a To what extent would such a scheme have helped T.A.S. in
the situation outlined above?   **(10 marks)**

   b Why should small firms receive such favourable treatment
from government backed schemes?   **(9 marks)**

3 With the benefit of hindsight, discuss how T.A.S. should have
responded to the interest rate increases.   **(15 marks)**

FASHION
GOES WEST

A2
INTEGRATED
CASE

CONCEPTS NEEDED:

Cash flow, Elasticity, Balance sheets, Investment appraisal, Economic
policy

'The Americans are crying out for clothes
like these,' said Hazell, the fashion
journalist. Lucy and Ted looked pleased, but
not totally convinced. They still remembered
the £40,000 they lost when they tried to
market products in the United States
last time. Those losses had almost forced
their company into **receivership**. Ted,
who was responsible for production and
finance, recalled this episode with particular
horror.

Hazell saw their scepticism and so went
into further detail. 'Nothing has hit the young
scene over there since punk. High fashion
womenswear is worth £850 million in the
United States, and any new craze can easily
pick up 1% of that.'

Lucy explained that the real problem was
financing such a venture. 'At present,' she
said, 'our monthly cash inflow is balanced by
outflows, and we've only got £50,000 on
deposit at the bank.' Lucy then jotted down
some estimates:

Start-up costs:

   £100,000 (incurred in month one)

Running costs:

   Cost of stock - £16,000 per month
   Transport costs - £4 per item
   (Both these costs would affect the
   month before sale)

U.S. overheads - £10,000 per month

'From day one we'd start incurring those
overheads,' said Lucy, 'but I think we would
only start selling clothes from the start of
month four. So even if we managed sales of
1,000 garments a month at £40 each, it'd take
us over a year to get back into the black. And
that is assuming we can get away without
giving our customers any credit.'

Ted decided to look more closely at the US
fashion market. He found a distribution
pattern dominated by big, staid firms.

He wondered if New York would be a good starting point, and so checked on the regional sales pattern. He found that although New Yorkers are only 8% of all Americans, they buy 12% of all new fashion wear. A research report stated: 'Fashion clothing in New York is price inelastic, but has an income elasticity as high as four.'

As the weeks went by, Hazell convinced Lucy that they should try America. This was potentially decisive, as Lucy owned 51% of the company's shares to Ted's 49%. She used this lever to persuade Ted that they must have a go.

Ted prepared a business plan, including a cash flow forecast and a thorough investment appraisal, which they took to their accountant. Having looked at the balance sheet (see Appendix A), the accountant expressed concern: 'Borrowing all the extra funds would put you in a very difficult position if the United States move fails. Can you increase the equity capital?' Neither Lucy nor Ted wished to.

Taking this **constraint** into account, the accountant modified Ted's business plan to make it seem as professional as possible to the bank. When Ted and Lucy went there, they were delighted to find the manager happy

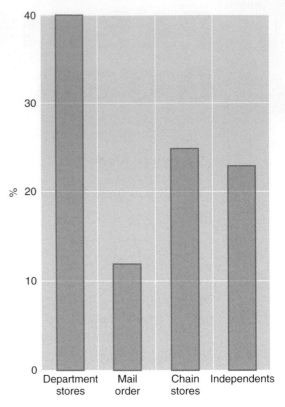

Share of fashion wear for 16–24 year old women (total US market)

about the financial side, though he seemed concerned about the protectionist climate in America since the US trade deficit was so high. Happily, within a few days a loan was agreed and the expansion could begin.

Appendix A: Balance sheet (as of yesterday)

	£000	£000
Fixed assets		
Machinery[1]	45	
Property	95	140
Current assets		
Stocks[2]	40	
Debtors	10	
Cash	50	
Current liabilities		
Creditors	65	
Overdraft	10	
Net current assets		25
Assets employed		165
Shareholders' funds		
Share capital	50	
Reserves	60	110
Long term loans	55	55
Capital employed		165

Notes: (1) Assuming 10 year straight line depreciation.
      (2) Including £20,000 of stock written down by 10% for being over 12 months old.

Appendix B: Discount factors

At 10%:		
end of year 1	–	0.91
end of year 2	–	0.83
end of year 3	–	0.75

Questions
(80 marks; 90 minutes)

1   Explain the meaning of the following terms (in bold print in
    the text):
    receivership
    overheads
    constraint   (9 marks)

2   **a** Set out a cash flow forecast for the first six months,
        assuming Lucy and Ted start their American expansion
        today.   (10 marks)
    b What aspects of this forecast would you feel lay the firm
        open to the greatest risks? Explain why.   (8 marks)

3   From the information given, outline where you would
    recommend the firm should concentrate its distribution
    effort. Detail the further data you would want to find out to
    check that recommendation thoroughly.   (10 marks)

4   Explain the meaning and implication of fashion clothing
    being 'price inelastic, but with an income elasticity as high
    as four'.   (6 marks)

5   On the assumption that the firm's US venture lasts three
    years, and that interest rates are 10%, assist Ted by carrying
    out a 'thorough investment appraisal' of the project. (The
    information in Appendix B may help.)   (12 marks)

6   Identify the elements of a balance sheet that may have
    caused the accountant concern, and suggest the positive
    aspects of the balance sheet that might have convinced the
    bank manager.   (10 marks)

7   Discuss the pressures and problems that are likely to affect
    the firm managerially as a result of the expansion plan.   (15 marks)

OVER-TRADING IN JEWELLERY

A2
INTEGRATED
CASE

CONCEPTS NEEDED:

Small firms, Cash flow, Profit, Variances, Sources of finance, Marketing strategy

Claire had always loved jewellery and with the help of her grandfather could make rings and earrings before the age of 13. By the time she reached sixth form, her production sideline was generating a useful income from her fellow students. After a year's foundation course at art college, Claire decided to turn full-time.

Although she could produce all types of jewellery, Claire's favourite items were rings and necklaces. She had experimented with high quality silver gemstone rings, but found these hard to sell. So she decided to concentrate on costume jewellery, using the flexibility of her one woman business to respond quickly to changing fashions and musical tastes. When Take That became the group girls screamed for, Claire's were the TT rings and Robbie Williams chains.

Even though her business had been growing fast, she was in no way prepared for what hit her when Blade arrived. The Blade twins' blond hair and good looks made them

stars even without their great dancing and singing. Claire had chanced upon them just before their first number one record, when it was still possible to meet them without bribing the bodyguards. They had loved her suggestion of sword-shaped 'Blade' earrings and a neckchain. She designed and made them just in time for their first appearance on *Top Of The Pops*. As their single and album raced to number one, Blade's management signed a deal with Claire to provide the jewellery for sale as official merchandise on their hastily arranged British tour.

Occasionally in the past, Claire had needed to bring an old friend in to help meet a large order. Never before had she hired unknown staff to work with her in the small workshop. Overnight, everything had to change. The initial order for Blade earrings and chains was for 40,000 of each – within three weeks. This was as much as she had produced in the whole of the previous year. Thank goodness, she told herself, that I negotiated such a profitable deal.

Each item would be bought by Blade Management Incorporated (BMI) for £1.25, but the materials cost was only 10p and she had always costed her labour time at 25p per unit. Other unit costs usually came to no more than 5p, so there was plenty of contribution for covering the overheads plus the fixed cost of designing and making the mould in which the jewellery was produced.

Through her tutor at art college, Claire quickly brought in three new workers. None had experience, but all they would need to do was pour powdered gunmetal into the moulding machine, take the finished rings out, then give them a vigorous polish. More of a constraint was the lack of machine capacity and physical space. After setting up her new staff at their posts, Claire scurried round commercial estate agents trying to find bigger premises. Within two days she found an adequately sized unit in a smart business park nearby. At £1,500 per month rent and rates, it was more expensive than she wanted, but impatience led her to accept it.

In those two days, several problems had occurred in the workshop. The student workers had no idea what to do. For some time they carried on producing rings they knew to be sub-standard (all of which were later scrapped), then decided to wait for Claire's return.

Even with her greatest endeavours, it was 10 days before the new workshop was operational, with its two new moulding machines – each costing £10,000. The machinery suppliers had given her two months' credit, but the materials for the 80,000 units had to be obtained with cash that Claire did not have. Fortunately the bank manager proved very helpful, extending the business overdraft to £10,000 without even asking to see her books (the loan was secured, however, on her parents' house).

The contract was completed only after Claire had switched to two-shift production at the new factory unit. This required higher pay for the night-shift workers and the recruitment of her old friend as the night supervisor. To find the funds to pay the wages, she had to go cap in hand to BMI for a 20% interim payment. Claire was, again, fortunate to get cooperation. Without it, lack of funds would have meant no wages and therefore no workforce.

When, three weeks late, she delivered the full order, she found BMI desperate for still more product. They paid her immediately and asked for a further 60,000 rings and 40,000 necklaces within two weeks. This caused still more feverish work, with each shift extended to 10 hours and with weekend working as well. Again cash proved terribly tight, as the bill for the machines became due.

A visit to the bank manager led to a full discussion of how she was handling the finances and administration of the business. The manager was horrified to realise that Claire was operating without budgets or a cash flow forecast. He insisted that she should take time out from the production process to work out exactly what her cash inflows and outflows had been since the start of the Blade boom, and then forecast the coming three months. He also wanted a full calculation of the actual profit generated by the first contract. Only then would he consider a loan or an overdraft extension. The bank manager said sternly: 'You are suffering the symptoms of overtrading: expanding too rapidly from a low capital base and with an inadequate management structure.' He recommended that Claire should hire a small firms consultant to come in for a couple of days and make recommendations on how to proceed.

Although her diversion into accounting held the completion of the job back by five days, it probably saved her business and her parents' home. It persuaded her to take on an office manager who would handle the administration and the finances, while she focused upon design, production and sales. Blade's success proved far more long lasting than anyone had imagined, and when, three years later, the twins' popularity faded after a failed film production, Claire's business was well enough diversified to cope.

Appendix A: Actual production costs on first Blade contract

Wages and salaries	£48,000
Materials	£12,800
Other direct costs	£3,000
Fixed costs	£1,200
Overheads	£14,000

Questions
(60 marks; 80 minutes)

1 Examine two factors that make small firms such as Claire's more flexible than large companies. **(8 marks)**

2 a What profit was made on the first Blade order? **(5 marks)**

b Calculate the variances from the costs Claire expected for labour and materials. For what reasons did these cost overruns occur? **(10 marks)**

c Given the profit made on the order, why did Claire run into such severe cash flow problems? **(10 marks)**

3 Outline the internal and external sources of finance that Claire's company made use of. **(9 marks)**

4 Write a report to Claire, as her small firms consultant, making detailed recommendations for action under the following headings:

4.1 Financial controls
4.2 Personnel and management structure
4.3 Marketing strategy **(18 marks)**

99 XEROX – FROM RICHES TO RAGS

CONCEPTS NEEDED:

Diversification, Quality, Motivation

In Britain we call it photocopying. In America it's known as Xeroxing. Just as the once mighty Hoover gave its name to the task of vacuuming, so did the Xerox Corporation to the task of photocopying. Between the 1950s and the 1980s Xerox grew into one of America's richest and most powerful multinationals. Yet by early 2001, it was on its knees, with its stock market valuation of $8 billion dwarfed by debts of over $18 billion, and with the company itself admitting that it was not wholly confident of its **liquidity position**.

The first severe hiccup faced by Xerox coincided with the 1980 recession. Japanese firms such as Canon and Ricoh brought out smaller, lighter, cheaper yet more reliable photocopiers. As Xerox saw its market share dwindling, it fought back with a massive programme of quality improvement. Much of the TQM (Total Quality Management)

movement in America and Europe was based on the work done by Xerox. It was a huge and successful attempt to catch up with Japanese standards for quality and reliability. It helped halt the market share slide, as large companies kept faith with Xerox. Yet Canon kept launching new machines aimed at niches that were small in percentage terms, but generated sufficiently large sales worldwide to be profitable. Xerox had succeeded in meeting its objective of matching Japanese quality standards, but was that a sufficient objective in itself?

Strategically, Xerox faced the same problem suffered by IBM in the computer market, with the rise of the PC (personal computer). IBM's huge profits relied on large companies leasing large, powerful computers at high monthly charges, but with the IBM promise of peace of mind. If anything went wrong, an IBM engineer would arrive within an hour to fix the problem. Similarly, big Xerox machines were serviced by engineers who would rush along if any problem occurred. Now, at the very time PCs were appearing on people's desks and making firms less willing to lease IBM's expensive mainframe computers, Xerox customers were buying small Canon photocopiers for every office. The one or two giant Xerox machines in a central Xeroxing department were looking vulnerable.

The comparison with IBM is all the more striking given Xerox's extraordinary links with the whole development of computing and the Internet. In 1969, the company set up the Xerox Palo Alto Research Centre (PARC). Brilliant computer scientists were hired, given a large budget and an open brief. Within four years they had come up with an extraordinary list of the technologies that were to prove world beaters in the years to come: high resolution computer screens; the graphical interface (used by Apple and by Microsoft Windows); the laser printer; and local area networking. In April 1974 a PARC employee switched on the 'Alto', the first computer that was like a modern PC or Apple. By October PARC had invented the first user friendly word processing software (the origins of Microsoft Word).

And what happened to all these inventions? Nothing. Xerox executives could not see how to market this technology. Their focus upon big business customers and upon copying meant they were too short sighted to see the potential among small firms or within ordinary households. They showed what the business guru Theodore Levitt called **marketing myopia**. It took a Bill Gates to come up with the vision of 'a PC on every desk'.

When struggling to interest senior Xerox executives in their inventions, the PARC staff showed what they had done to two brilliant young computer scientists they knew: Steve Jobs and Bill Gates. When Jobs heard that there were no plans to develop the products, he 'borrowed' some of the key ideas and built them into his famous Apple Macintosh computer. Bill Gates, of course, managed an even greater success, eventually becoming the world's richest man on the back of Microsoft Windows, Microsoft Office and much else.

Despite these tales of what might have been, a business with the wealth and the reputation of Xerox should not have let things slip so badly in its core market. The problem for Xerox in 2000 and 2001 was that it had made a serious distribution and marketing error. In the 1980s and 1990s Canon and others had continued to chip away at the Xerox market share worldwide. Despite this, Xerox stayed profitable because many big businesses continued to lease the company's top-of-the-range photocopiers. Yet by 1998 Xerox decided it could no longer rely on direct sales of leased copiers. It would have to take on Canon within the distribution method pioneered by the Japanese – selling photocopiers through wholesalers and retailers, and outsourcing maintenance and repair servicing. This cuts out the huge overhead costs of a large direct sales force and a large team of salaried repair engineers.

However logical this strategy might have seemed, the consequences proved disastrous. The company had given up its only significant protection against the competitors – the reassuring peace of mind that comes from personal service and strong after sales service. Furthermore, it had neither the product range nor the sales staff to sell successfully into a new area: the wholesale and retail trade. Xerox found sales volumes, selling prices and customer confidence sliding simultaneously. An announcement of 15,000 redundancies in August 2000 reinforced the impression of a business with nowhere to go but downwards. It would take miracle workers as bright as those at PARC to find ways for Xerox to rebuild itself.

Source: Financial Times

Questions
(65 marks; 75 minutes)

1 Explain the business significance of the following terms:
   a liquidity position
   b marketing myopia **(10 marks)**

2 Xerox was in a position to diversify away from photocopying.
   a Examine how Xerox might have benefited from successful diversification. **(10 marks)**
   b Outline two possible reasons why it failed to diversify successfully. **(8 marks)**

3 In the early 1980s, Xerox responded to Japanese competition by focusing on quality improvements. Discuss whether this was the right strategy in the short and long term. **(14 marks)**

4 In its PARC division, Xerox set up a research centre that came up with an extraordinary series of major inventions. How might this centre have been managed and organised to lead to such motivation and inspiration from staff? **(8 marks)**

5 The business guru Tom Peters urges firms to 'stick to the knitting'. By this he means sticking to what you know, i.e. focus on your core business. To what extent can the Xerox experience be said to be proof that Peters is right? **(15 marks)**

DE LOREAN CARS – 'FROM COW PASTURE TO PRODUCTION'

A2
INTEGRATED
CASE

CONCEPTS NEEDED:

Productivity, Elasticity, Value of the pound, External constraints, Government intervention

On 3 August 1978, Mr John De Lorean announced agreement with the Labour government on a financing package for the establishment of a new sports car factory in Belfast. De Lorean, an American former Vice-president of General Motors (the world's largest car producer), was to invest £20 million, with government funded bodies such as the Northern Ireland Development Agency (NIDA) putting in £45 million. NIDA would have an equity stake worth £15 million, and would also provide grants and loans.

Sceptics pointed out that the Irish government had already turned the scheme down, believing it to be too risky. Their doubts hinged on the sales forecasts being put forward for an untried product, and on

technological factors. De Lorean's prototype called for construction methods never before used in the motor industry.

Mr Roy Mason, the Northern Ireland Secretary of State, was understandably jubilant, however. It had long been his belief that the sectarian violence in Northern Ireland was connected with the high unemployment. Indeed violence and economic underdevelopment seemed to form a vicious circle. Now he could announce a factory to be sited next to one of Belfast's largest Catholic housing estates, where male unemployment stood at 35%. Its projected employment of 2,000 people could help break through that circle.

De Lorean announced that:

'We aim to move from cow pasture to production within eighteen months.**'**

Some regarded his choice of this 'greenfield' site as risky, because the lack of local car production meant that his workforce would be completely inexperienced. De Lorean countered this by stressing the potential benefits of a workforce with no traditional restrictive practices.

The car, to be designed by the Italian Giugiaro, would have a body shell of glass fibre reinforced plastic, bonded to a stainless steel outer skin. Although technologically novel (and therefore potentially troublesome) it conformed to an essential element in De Lorean's marketing proposition. He was famous in the United States as the man who quit General Motors, and then exposed that company's practice of 'built-in obsolescence', i.e. they used materials and components with a relatively short life span, so that customers would need to replace their car regularly. De Lorean had long promoted the notion of an 'ethical' car that would last 15 years, not five. He claimed that this new car would be completely rustproof, and therefore the body could last for ever. It was to be marketed in the United States alone, as that was where De Lorean's standing meant that dealers were prepared to invest in the project. And at an anticipated $14,000 it would be priced below General Motor's Corvette – the biggest selling sports car in the United States. Hence the expectation of sales of 30,000 cars a year.

By August 1980, 'technical problems' had caused sufficient delays for De Lorean to have to warn his US dealers that the car's launch would be put back from November to early 1981. It also meant that extra funds were needed, which the firm managed to get from the (by now, Conservative) government.

On 21 January 1981, De Lorean drove one of the first finished production cars off the assembly line. He announced that a batch of 700 cars would be delivered to US dealers in April. Cars were said to be coming off the line at a rate of three per day, rising to 30 per day by the end of the following month. The US dealers' worries about the supply delays were compounded by the company's ever escalating view of the car's price tag. In August 1980, De Lorean declared that his pricing strategy was that the car should sell for just under $20,000 – about the same as the Corvette. Now, in January 1981, he was speaking of 'the mid $20,000s', i.e. around 20% more than the US produced rival. A major Kansas City car dealer said that the price was pressing up against the threshold at which consumer resistance could be expected: 'If it goes above $24,000 we have a problem.' De Lorean blamed the price escalation on higher inflation in the United Kingdom than in the United States, and the unexpected strength of sterling (see Appendix A).

By the end of January it was plain that the De Lorean Motor Company (DMC) had a major cash crisis. Successive governments had already invested £70 million in the project, and now the firm wanted a guarantee of a £10 million bank loan to 'help resolve a short term **working capital** requirement'. The problem was that a series of production hitches had delayed the launch by six months. So continuing production expenditure, a wage bill of over £100,000 per week, plus steady stockbuilding were all draining cash at a time when none was coming in. In February the government provided the £10 million bank guarantee, but stated that no more public money would be made available to the project.

The crisis of confidence in DMC during January evaporated by May. Motoring journalists gushed over the 2.8 litre V6 engine, the gull-wing doors and the 15 year life span of the bodies. They referred to the 12,000 cars expected to be sold in the United States during 1981 at $25,000 each, and the resultant royalties of £2.4 million that the UK government could expect to receive (£185 on each of the first 90,000 cars, and £45 on each subsequent one). Throughout the media there was a feeling of admiration for DMC's achievement in creating a car factory from nothing; and a fervent wish that its success would boost Belfast. So when, on 22 May, the government announced a guarantee of a further £7 million, it received little criticism for changing its mind on increasing its financial commitment.

By August 1981 more than 2,000 people were employed at the Belfast plant. The firm claimed 50 to 60 cars were being built per day. Demand in the United States was said to be phenomenal. Yet in early 1982 DMC was put on a three day week and output was halved from 400 to 200 per week. It emerged that low demand had led to a stockpile of 2,500 unsold cars. De Lorean blamed this on the fierce recession in the US market for new cars; some of the dealers felt that the very poor standard of finish on the cars was the key factor.

The true market potential of the De Lorean car began to come under serious scrutiny. DMC's construction, production and cash flow difficulties had always been presented to the public in the context of an apparently guaranteed level of demand. It had been suggested that the firm's US dealers had placed firm orders for the first two years' production (40,000 cars). Also, the original government investment had been made after the McKinsey **management consultancy** had forecast demand for 30,000 units per year. What had not been revealed was that McKinsey had analysed the likely price elasticity of the car. At approximate price parity with the Corvette, demand should be for 30,000; but at $25,000 for a De Lorean against $20,000 for a Corvette the McKinsey formula forecast demand of just 15,000 units. Furthermore the forecasts were based on a healthy US car market, whereas 1981 proved the worst in 20 years. Sports car sales were hit especially hard as recession mentality took its grip on sales of luxury items. Of the 7,000 cars built by DMC in 1981, only 3,000 were actually registered to owners.

With DMC's problems becoming ever more public knowledge, rumours began to be reported in the press about De Lorean's 'Concorde lifestyle'. For the head of a publicly funded business in severe financial difficulties, his high profile in New York's social scene was disturbing. Especially as it became clear that De Lorean himself had never invested much capital in the project: a later Report by the Public Accounts Committee of the House of Commons showed that his total capital investment amounted to less than £1 million. On 28 January 1982 the Labour MP Bob Cryer said bitterly:

'**T**his particular venture appears to be a rip-off for the directors and a disaster for the workers.'

The following day 1,100 redundancies were announced at the plant, bringing the workforce down to 1,500. But this could not prevent the firm from insolvency. On 19 February 1982 the company went into voluntary receivership. It owed £31 million to its suppliers and had an unsold stock of 3,000 cars. The Receiver said he would keep the business going and look for a buyer. The hoped for upturn in US demand during the spring sales peak failed to materialise, however, and wave after wave of redundancies cut the workforce down to a few maintenance staff by the autumn. With no buyer for the firm and no customers for its products, virtually all the government's investment was lost. Attempts to retrieve some from John De Lorean (on grounds of fraudulent diversion of funds) faltered in the United States courts.

To Mrs Thatcher's government it was proof that governments should not get involved directly in business activity. The Labour opposition preferred to think of it as an example of how greedy and cynical entrepreneurs can be. Perhaps all it proves, however, is that the internal constraints upon the successful establishment of a new manufacturing firm are troublesome enough; the external factors make it a matter of luck as well.

Sources: Financial Times; The Guardian; The Times

Appendix A: UK & US exchange rates and inflation rates 1978–1982

	US $ per £	UK inflation %	US inflation %
1978	1.90	9.0	6.8
1979	2.10	13.0	11.4
1980	2.30	18.0	13.6
1981	2.05	12.0	10.4
1982	1.75	8.0	6.4

Sources: HMSO Annual Abstract of Statistics; U.N. Statistical Yearbook

Questions
(80 marks; 100 minutes)

1 Explain the meaning of the following terms (in bold print in the text):
'greenfield' site
restrictive practices
working capital
management consultancy **(12 marks)**

2 **a** Outline the risks involved in the De Lorean project that
could have been foreseen at the start. **(10 marks)**
b Given these, discuss whether there was any justification for
government financing. **(12 marks)**

3 During 1981, an average of 1,500 workers were employed at
DMC to produce 7,000 cars.
a How did this productivity level compare with that
anticipated in 1978? **(6 marks)**
b Why may this shortfall have occurred? **(10 marks)**

4 **a** According to McKinsey, what was the price elasticity of the
De Lorean car? **(5 marks)**
b Discuss the factors that may have influenced De Lorean's
decision to price the car at $25,000. **(10 marks)**

5 Examine the external constraints faced by DMC. To what
extent were they the cause of the project's downfall? **(15 marks)**

THE IRISH SAWMILL

A2
INTEGRATED
CASE

CONCEPTS NEEDED:

Balance sheets, Ratios, Pricing strategy, Value of the pound, Trade unions

The Rosscrae Sawmill had been established in the heart of Ireland for 60 years. The town of Rosscrae lay near to a range of mountains from which the wood was felled and transported by independent operators. The wood was then stripped of its bark and sawn into a range of lengths and widths by machine. The sawmill distributed its product to about 12 timber merchants in the region, and through its own factory gate wholesale depot.

The mill's layout and mechanisation had once seemed very advanced, but had come to look primitive. Much of the equipment was 20 years old and had long since been depreciated to zero in the company's accounts. So the balance sheet value of the business was very low, whereas the return on capital employed appeared huge (see Appendix A). Despite the appearance of success provided by the high rate of return represented by the €27,000 profit made last year, the firm faced severe problems.

When the Rosscrae Sawmill (RS) began, wood was a very cheap commodity. So the key to economic success was to maximise output with minimum labour or energy inputs. As a result, the mill's designer had thought nothing

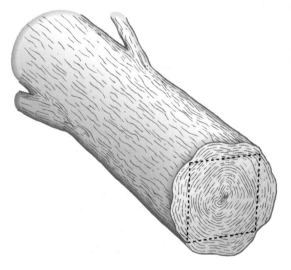

of installing cutting equipment that – on average – wasted 50% of the raw material.

With wood becoming a scarce and expensive raw material, this machinery was wasting too much to be economic. No less seriously, the rough finish to the wood left by the large-toothed mechanical saws meant that the firm's output was inferior to its competitors'. These included not only Irish sawmills but also, increasingly, imports of high quality timber from other European Union producers such as Norway and Germany. The firm's cost-plus pricing policy gave no flexibility to compete head-on with these rivals.

Counteracting these difficulties was the loyalty shown by the firm's 60 employees. Their average length of service was 22 years, and for the last three years they had accepted pay rises below the rate of inflation without complaint. This had much to do with the 12% unemployment rate that Rosscrae shared with much of the midlands of southern Ireland.

The Dooley family had always owned RS, but whereas the firm's founder John Dooley had been a bold and entrepreneurial man, the two grandchildren who now each held 50% of the shares took a short term, cautious view of the business. Both Frank and Jim enjoyed the large houses they had inherited, and aimed to generate enough profit from the business to keep themselves comfortably off, rather than risk investing in modernisation that, if unsuccessful, might threaten their lifestyle. Now the slide in the RS market share even threatened to send revenue below its low break-even point.

The Dooleys realised that investment in modern cutting machines along the same production line would improve quality, and therefore halt the erosion in market share. Yet the huge increase in depreciation and interest charges would increase fixed costs so much as to make the new, higher break-even level hard to achieve. So the only viable option was the much more expensive one of replacing the whole layout with a fully computerised modern system that would not only ensure quality, but would also make much better use of the raw material. By using 80% of the wood, these systems would cut variable costs per unit, and would therefore make it easier to operate profitably.

They had costed out the options, and found that the semi-modernisation would cost €700,000 and the complete job would cost €1,600,000. Given that the machinery they would be buying would have a low second hand value, they were not willing to borrow enough to fund such levels of investment. This left them with three options: to put the business into voluntary liquidation; to sell it; or to continue as they were, hoping that a local building boom or a slump in the value of the euro would boost sales to Britain or America.

Their accountant told them that liquidation would probably generate more than one might expect from looking at the balance sheet. The main reasons for this would be:

1 The property would fetch 40% more than its current book value.

2 The scrap value of the machines written down to zero in the books would be €7,000.

3 However, the stock might be sold for €4,000 less than the balance sheet valuation.

Armed with this information, the Dooleys put an advertisement in *The Irish Times*:

'**F**or Sale – Long Established Timber Mill And Wholesaler'

They received many inquiries, but only two firm offers: for €100,000 cash; and for €50,000 cash plus a 10% shareholding each in the new business.

To evaluate the latter bid, the Dooleys needed to look at the new owner's plans for the Rosscrae Sawmill. These proved to be in line with their own ideas for full implementation of new technology. Computerised scanning systems would calculate how to cut up each tree trunk in such a way as to maximise revenue (which would usually mean minimising wastage). Then the computer would instruct the automated saws to cut the timber up in that precise way. All the managers would have to do was ensure that the computer was storing correct information on the value and selling price of every possible cut of timber; and to monitor stock and demand levels to make sure that the system was not turning out thousands of 'economic' one metre lengths when the demand was for lengths of three metres.

As the bidder's break-even chart shows, the expensive machinery would cut manpower and material costs so much as to make the business look viable. With the prospective owner already having a chain of eight timber yards in the Dublin area, extra output could easily be absorbed. The Dooleys were not certain, however, that the bidder would find it easy to achieve its forecast of doubling unit sales from their current level of 200,000 per annum.

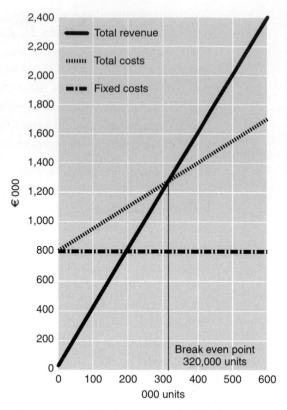

Rosscrae Sawmill – Forecast annual break-even chart after full modernisation

Appendix A: Rosscrae Sawmill – latest balance sheet

	€	€
Property	30,000	
Machinery	6,000	36,000
Stock	45,000	
Debtors	35,000	
Cash	4,000	
Creditors	26,000	
Overdraft	4,000	
Net current assets		54,000
Assets employed		90,000
Loans	8,000	8,000
Share capital	10,000	
Reserves	72,000	82,000
Capital employed		90,000

Questions
(80 marks; 90 minutes)

1 Calculate the rate of return on capital employed achieved by the Dooleys last year. Explain why it may be a misleading indicator of the company's financial efficiency. **(8 marks)**

2 The text shows the narrow production and financial orientation of the Dooleys' thinking. What pricing and distribution strategies might they have adopted to provide higher, long term demand levels? **(10 marks)**

3 If they put the business into voluntary liquidation, what payout could each of the Dooleys expect? **(10 marks)**

4 Discuss how the business might benefit from a slump in the value of the euro. **(15 marks)**

5 If the bidder offering a 10% stake achieves its sales forecast,
  a what income should each of the Dooleys receive (assuming full distribution of profits)? **(5 marks)**
  b how long will it be before the Dooleys receive more than they would from the other bidder? **(5 marks)**
  c what other factors should the Dooleys take into account before deciding between the options available to them? **(10 marks)**

6 **a** How might the workforce view the Dooleys' deliberations? **(8 marks)**
  b To what extent might they be helped by belonging to a trade union? **(9 marks)**

ROLLS ROYCE - THE GAMBLE THAT FAILED

CONCEPTS NEEDED:

Profits, Value of the pound, Product life cycle, Government intervention

Early in 1969, Rolls Royce shares traded at £2 10s (£2.50) each, so that 200 shares could be bought for £500. Two years later, those same 200 shares were worth just £14. In the meantime, one of the world's most famous companies had collapsed.

Although best known for its cars, over 90% of Rolls Royce turnover was from the manufacture of engines for civil or military aircraft. The aero-engine market had been a prosperous though unexciting one, but was just entering a new phase in the 1960s. With world wide passenger air travel trebling between 1960 and 1970, airlines were calling for much larger jet planes. Boeing responded by announcing the development of its 747 (Jumbo) jet, and Lockheed introduced the Tristar. Both aircraft would need engines capable of generating double the power of previous models.

The American Boeing and Lockheed companies worked on this development with

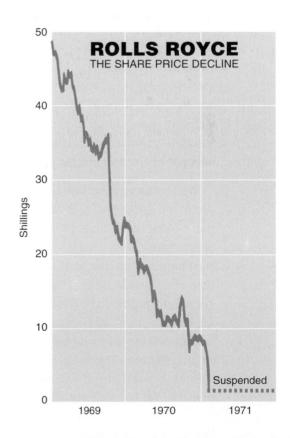

ROLLS ROYCE
THE SHARE PRICE DECLINE

Shillings

Suspended

1969　　1970　　1971

US aero-engine manufacturers. This threatened Rolls Royce with the prospect of missing out on a key market for the future, for the British firm had allowed its product range to become rather outdated. As its image lagged behind the US engine producers, Rolls realised that to break into this new market would require a technologically superior product.

In 1966, Rolls announced the RB211 engine, which would use an innovative new material called carbon fibre to provide a lighter yet more powerful engine than the new US ones. With the lightness would also come fuel efficiency, giving the vital customer benefit of longer flying range at lower cost per mile.

In September 1966, the Rolls selling drive got under way. From then until March 1968, there were always at least 20 Rolls Royce executives in America. Their airfares alone came to £80,000. By spring 1968, the airlines were ready to place their orders for the new, wide-bodied jets. The RB211 looked very attractive against its US rivals, for Rolls boasted that it was less noisy, more fuel efficient and – since the pound's **devaluation** in 1967 – priced at $55,000 below the $630,000 charged by General Electric of America.

While orders were being negotiated, Rolls discussed the financing of the next stage with the Labour government. For although five years had been spent on **Research & Development** for the RB211, Rolls estimated that a further £65 million would be needed to get it into production. Government approval for a grant of £47 million was clinched by the announcement of an order for 540 engines from Lockheed. The order (it later emerged) was at a fixed price and included severe penalties for late delivery. Rolls had to get the

first batch of RB211s from the drawing board to Lockheed by early 1971.

The government minister responsible, Tony Benn, was later to say:

*'**T**hey felt their survival as a company depended on a new engine. We backed them, but they set the prices and negotiated the contract. The government did not have the expertise to check the figures of the most experienced aero-engine company in Britain.'*

By early 1970, Rolls Royce management was aware of serious difficulties with RB211 development. Getting it from the R&D phase into volume production involved the company in its biggest ever organisational task, and this placed great strains on its financial and physical resources. Failures of coordination between designers and the production department meant costs escalated due to work having to be redone. This problem was compounded by the inability of the cost accounting team to cope with their workload – so no one was quite sure what costs were being incurred.

They also ran into a severe technical hitch. When completed engines were first tested, the engineers were especially interested in the performance of the carbon fibre used to make the fan blades – the heart of the jet. Tests on power output went well, but then came the shock. When planes take off or land, they often fly through flocks of birds. These can get sucked into the jet, so Rolls set up a test to simulate this. The carbon fibre blades shattered, causing the engine to fail. For some months the design engineers tried to get over this problem, but eventually they abandoned carbon fibre for a metal (titanium), which, despite being costlier and heavier, was well tried.

In November 1970, Rolls asked its bankers and the new Conservative government for extra help to finance a development cost that it now estimated at £135 million. The banks agreed to £18 million and the government to £42 million, on condition that independent accountants checked the accuracy of the estimate. In the following months Rolls made various confident statements such as this January 1971 announcement of R&D work on two new engines, the RB202 and the RB410:

'**A***t a time when the world's aerospace industries are passing through a recession, Rolls Royce feels it is vital to continue fundamental research in those areas that may produce big orders in the longer term future.*'

Within a fortnight, the *Financial Times* reported rumours that Rolls was in financial difficulties. The paper pointed to three pressures on Rolls' cash position:

1 Overspending on the RB211.

2 Rapid increases in development spending on its military aircraft engines.

3 The need for more working capital to fund aircraft manufacture.

The next day, 4 February 1971, the Chancellor of the Exchequer announced to the House of Commons that Rolls Royce had asked its **debenture** holders to appoint a Receiver to supervise the liquidation of the company. The reason for this was that the loss of resources already committed to the RB211 project plus the losses that would arise on fulfilment of its contract with Lockheed would exceed the company's **shareholders' funds**. The government, in a reversal of its previous policy of non-intervention in industry, was to take over the essential assets of the business. It soon became clear that this meant nationalising all the company apart from the profitable car division.

In a more detailed report to the House on 8 February, the Chancellor explained that the launch costs of the RB211 had reached £170 million. This was £35 million more than the estimate given four months previously. In addition, Rolls expected a production loss of £60 million on delivery of the 540 engines for which fixed prices had been contracted. Finally, £50 million would be lost under penalty clauses if Rolls Royce was six months late in its delivery times (which it regarded as an optimistic rather than a pessimistic timescale).

The government came under pressure from many directions. The American firms Lockheed and TWA warned that if the government let the RB211 contract fall through, it would cause a serious loss of confidence in Britain's aerospace industry. Rolls Royce creditors were left with £65 million of unpaid bills. Many of these creditors were small suppliers for whom Rolls Royce was their biggest customer. Trade unions and MPs were worried about the loss of jobs, thought by some to be as high as 40,000 if the government refused to honour the RB211 contract. Partly to deflect these pressures, Conservative backbenchers attacked Tony Benn for committing government funds in the first place.

Attention then switched to the Receiver, an accountant who was now in charge of Rolls Royce. His biggest short term problem was that suppliers stopped sending parts, threatening profitable production of cars and military engines. He assured people that all supplies received since his appointment on 4 February would be paid for in full, but some creditors still held out to try to obtain a promise that the earlier bills would be paid.

Slowly the Receiver's persuasive powers returned things to normal. He invited bids for the car division, and – crucially – managed to renegotiate the RB211 contract with Lockheed.

On 23 February, the government-owned Rolls Royce (1971) Limited was formed to take over the aerospace division, at a price to be agreed later when the Receiver had completed a valuation of its assets. Two months later Rolls Royce Motors was sold for £40 million.

Although the Rolls Royce share price had touched 1 penny on 9 February, the Receiver proved able to generate considerable sums from the liquidation. Eventually, spread over several years, shareholders received a total payout of over £1.40 per share.

More importantly, the longer term proved Rolls management correct in believing that the RB211 was crucial to the future of Britain's aerospace industry. The engine was to form the basis for most of Rolls Royce's civil aircraft sales during the 1970s, 1980s and 1990s. Since 1971, Rolls has taken care to base new engines for new aircraft on the proven technology of the RB211, and to ensure that they never slipped so far behind the competition that they needed a huge leap forward to keep up.

Sources: Financial Times; Rolls Royce and Bentley: sixty years at Crewe by M. Bobbitt, Sutton Publishing 1998; The Times

Airbus A300 powered by Rolls Royce RB211 engines

Questions
(80 marks; 100 minutes)

1 Explain the meaning of the following terms (in bold print in the text):
devaluation
research and development
debenture
shareholders' funds **(12 marks)**

2 Identify the major mistakes made by Rolls Royce, and suggest the problems it overlooked or underestimated in the decisions it took. **(15 marks)**

3 **a** If Rolls management had known in 1968 the cost details given to Parliament on 8 February 1971, and assuming its financial objective was to break even on the first 540 engine contract, what price (in sterling) should it have charged originally? **(9 marks)**
   b By how much did Rolls underprice the engine in dollars, given that the exchange rate in 1968 was $2.40 to the pound? **(9 marks)**

4 Use the test to help you explain the role of the Receiver in a company liquidation. **(8 marks)**

5 What light does this case shed on the cash flow, new product development, and extension strategy implications of Product Life Cycle theory? **(15 marks)**

6 Discuss the implications of the Rolls Royce case for the issue of whether or not governments should intervene directly in industry. **(12 marks)**

THE RISE AND FALL OF LAKER AIRWAYS

A2
INTEGRATED
CASE

CONCEPTS NEEDED:

Gearing, Marketing strategy, Cash flow, Government intervention, Deregulation

Freddie Laker started his freight airline in 1948 with £38,000 of borrowed money. It soon received a huge boost from the 1949 Berlin Airlift, for which his aircraft were hired round the clock to fly in food supplies. By the 1960s, it was a well enough established airline to be able to **diversify** by starting up a fleet of aircraft for the packaged holiday market – Laker Airways. The success of this move led Laker to announce in 1971 his intention to challenge the major transatlantic carriers by forming a no-frills, low price, London–New York 'Skytrain'.

At that time no passenger airline was allowed to operate on any route without government approval. The convention was that on major routes such as London–New York, each country was allowed to have two carriers. This was considered to be sufficient to provide competition, yet with enough control to ensure that competitive pressures did not force the companies to cut back on costly safety measures. So TWA and Pan-Am

battled with British Airways and British Caledonian for market share. Alone of the four, British Airways was state owned.

During the 1970s Freddie Laker became a well known figure as he struggled to get Skytrain accepted by the British and US governments. To do this, he had to take expensive court action to prove that the existing arrangement was a **cartel** that acted against the public interest. Only in 1977 did the first Skytrain fly from Gatwick, in a blaze of publicity in Britain and America. Prices were half those of the other carriers, and customers liked the fact that no reservations were possible; you just turned up on the day you wanted to fly, and bought a ticket as you would when travelling by train. Such was Laker's popularity that the Labour government that had fought him in the courts knighted him in the 1978 Honours List. Sir Freddie was born.

The demand for Skytrain was such that

travellers in the summer months found that they had to wait for days to get a seat. As Laker's base airport (Gatwick) was not yet fully developed, this could be uncomfortable. The cramped conditions did not seem to put people off, however, as the prices were so low.

By 1980, Sir Freddie had a 17% market share on the London–New York route, plus 23% and 30% respectively on his new London–Miami and London–Los Angeles flights. This success led him to order 10 Airbuses, with a view to using these European built planes to break open the highly regulated, high fare European airline market. The purchase was financed by a £130 million loan (in America, in dollars). The first Airbus was delivered in 1981, but no European government would agree to let him fly to their airports.

In the early 1980s, three factors affected the transatlantic airline business:

1 Whereas the initial impact of Skytrain had been to increase the number of people who wished to travel across the Atlantic, by 1980 an economic recession halted that growth in market size.

2 Having allowed Sir Freddie to break the cartel, the United States government then deregulated all air travel in 1978. This allowed many new, low fare US airlines to start a London–New York service.

3 Between 1978 and 1980 the cost of fuel oil doubled in the wake of the supply shortages that accompanied the Iranian Revolution.

As a consequence of these factors, all the original four transatlantic carriers were trading unprofitably. Pan-Am, which had plunged into heavy losses, decided to fight back in the summer of 1981 by offering a stand-by ticket priced at just one pound above Skytrain's. The other three followed, so now Laker had competition that offered better comfort and a Heathrow base, for only one pound more. Laker cut prices further to try to restore its advantage, but the rivals followed Laker's prices down in a classic price war situation. This would damage the profits of all

Major airlines – fare structure winter 1981/82

Single	London–NY	London–LA
First Class	£917	£1268
Business Class	£315	£684
Economy	£124	£169
Stand-by	£90	£131
Laker Skytrain	**£89**	**£130**

the carriers in the short term, but the major airlines knew that their revenue from First and Business Class would make it easier for them to survive than it would be for Laker.

Sir Freddie continued to make confident pronouncements about how loyal his customers were proving, but the increasing volume of traffic on the other airlines suggested differently. It was also significant that he introduced the option of booking reservations in advance, perhaps to assist cash flow. By the autumn of 1981, rumours spread in the financial markets that Laker Airways was unable to meet the interest payments on its loans. As these leaked out, passengers became more reluctant to book Laker flights. By January 1982 it was public knowledge that the banks that had lent Laker £220 million were desperately looking for a solution.

On 3 February, however, a beaming Sir Freddie announced that his cash crisis had been saved by £60 million of fresh loans. He said:

'**I** *couldn't be more confident about the future.*'

Within 36 hours, though, the banks had forced him to call in the Receiver to supervise the liquidation of the company's assets. Six thousand Laker passengers were stranded with worthless tickets as Laker aeroplanes from Gatwick were recalled in mid-flight. At Gatwick, the British Airports Authority impounded a DC10 aircraft to cover the company's unpaid bills for landing and parking fees.

Journalists rushing to Companies House to look up Laker Airways' company accounts were shocked to find that despite the legal requirement that up to date accounts should be filed there for all limited companies, the

most recent for Laker Airways were from March 1980. These showed just £23 million of shareholders' funds, and that the firm was 90% owned by Sir Freddie and 10% owned by his (former) wife.

They also revealed that on 31 March 1980, Laker forecast that it must make 41 million dollars of loan repayments and hire purchase instalments during the coming 12 months – a tall order for a firm that had never made an operating profit of more than £2.5 million (about $5 million) in a year. Appendix A shows a summary of Laker's five year financial record up to March 1980.

The Times reported that:

'**B**ankers said Laker's losses were running at £15 to £20 million a year. It owes banks £230 million, with a further £40 million owed to unsecured creditors. Assets were estimated at about £250 million* ... New figures showing worse than expected ticket sales, combined with disappointing forecasts for cash *flow in the months ahead were the final straw. No one could be confident that Laker would pay the bills ... By any standards the company was extraordinarily highly geared ... the banks showed a considerable lack of banking prudence.*

This proved a considerable over-estimate, as the second hand value of aircraft during a recession can fall sharply.

On the day the collapse was announced, there was an extraordinary outburst of popular support for Sir Freddie. However, his announcement, just one week later, of the formation of a new People's Airline was very poorly received by a public that had assumed that he had been ruined personally. Newspapers contrasted the losses of his ticket-holders with his 1,000 acre farm in Surrey and 85 ton yacht. Yet Sir Freddie's earlier successes ensured that he kept the respect of many people.

Two years later, his work in breaking the transatlantic cartel was to receive praise from Richard Branson when setting up Virgin Atlantic.

Sources: Companies House; *Financial Times*; *The Times*

Appendix A: Summary of the Laker Airways Balance Sheets (1976–1980)

	£000 (as at 31 March)				
	1976	**1977**	**1978**	**1979**	**1980**
Fixed assets	29,700	27,800	44,900	82,900	146,300
+ Net current assets	−1,100	−1,800	−1,800	−7,800	−11,700
= Assets employed	28,600	26,000	43,100	75,100	134,600
Shareholders' funds	3,500	4,300	5,800	13,900*	23,200*
+ Loans and HP debts	25,100	21,700	37,300	61,200	111,400
= Capital employed	28,600	26,000	43,100	75,100	134,600

*including £3.3 million of unrealised foreign currency gains in 1979; in 1980 this figure increased to £4.6 million (it proved an illusion as the value of the $ weakened in 1981)

Questions
(80 marks; 100 minutes)

1 Explain the business significance of the following terms (in bold print in the text):

diversify

cartel

prudence **(15 marks)**

2 When MPs discussed the liquidation in Parliament, some suggested that the blame lay primarily with state regulators and state subsidised airlines. What justification is there for this view? **(15 marks)**

3 Calculate Laker Airways' approximate gearing level in 1981. What was the significance of this in the events of 1981–82? **(12 marks)**

4 From a marketing point of view, how had Laker left his firm vulnerable to a price war by 1981? **(12 marks)**

5 As things became difficult, Sir Freddie was reduced to making bold but misleading statements about his sales and cash flow. This was to keep confidence high. How can loss of confidence make a difficult cash flow position impossible? **(10 marks)**

6 Western governments used to feel that passenger transport should be regulated by strict government controls and inspections. During the late 1970s and 1980s the mood shifted in favour of deregulation. Discuss the main issues raised by the freeing of passenger transport from state intervention. **(16 marks)**